Small Savings Mobilization and Asian Economic Development

Published in association with Keio University and in association with the United Nations.

Small Savings Mobilization and Asian Economic Development

The Role of Postal Financial Services

Mark J. Scher
Naoyuki Yoshino
Editors

An East Gate Book

M.E.Sharpe
Armonk, New York
London, England

An East Gate Book

Copyright © 2004 by Postal Financial Services Development

All rights reserved. No part of this book may be reproduced in any form without written permission from the publisher, M.E. Sharpe, Inc., 80 Business Park Drive, Armonk, New York 10504.

Library of Congress Cataloging-in-Publication Data

Small savings mobilization and Asian economic development : the role of postal financial services / edited by Mark J. Scher and Naoyuki Yoshino.
  p. cm.
An East Gate Book.
Includes bibliographical references and index.
  ISBN 0-7656-1483-9 (hardcover: alk. paper); ISBN 0-7656-1484-7 (pbk.: alk. paper)
1. Postal savings banks—Asia. 2. Postal savings banks—Asia—Case studies. 3. Asia—Economic policy. I. Scher, Mark J. II. Yoshino, Naoyuki, 1950–

HG1956.A78S63 2004
332.2'2'095—dc22   2004001192

Printed in the United States of America

The paper used in this publication meets the minimum requirements of
American National Standard for Information Sciences
Permanence of Paper for Printed Library Materials,
ANSI Z 39.48-1984.

BM (c) 10 9 8 7 6 5 4 3 2 1
BM (p) 10 9 8 7 6 5 4 3 2 1

Contents

List of Tables and Figures	ix
Foreword by Eiji Hosoda, Keio University	xi
Foreword by Ian Kinniburgh, United Nations–DESA	xiii
Preface by Mark J. Scher	xv
Acknowledgments	xix

Part 1: Postal Savings for Development

1. Introduction: Overview and Summary of Policy Proposals for Postal Savings in Developing Countries *Mark J. Scher with Naoyuki Yoshino*	3
2. Policy and Management Issues Confronting Postal Financial Services Today *Mark J. Scher*	21
The Evolution of Postal Savings	21
The Origins of a Global Postal Network	21
Creation of Postal Savings and Giro Remittance Services	21
Postal Savings for the People	23
The Public's Confidence in Postal Savings	24
International Giro: Safe and Cost-Effective Remittances	25
The Changing Economics of the Posts: Market Liberalization, Privatization, Cross-Border Entry and Acquisition	28
Market Liberalization: New Technologies and Privatization	29
The Charge of "Cross-Subsidization" as a Threat to Public Savings Institutions	32
Cross-Border Entry: The Express Package Delivery Wars	34
Financial Services through the Postal Infrastructure	36
Current Situation	36
Governance Structures of the Posts	36

Postal Systems and "Postbanks": Creation, Separation, Privatization, and Synergies of Reintegration	41
Postbank Creation and Separation from the Post	41
Loss of Postal Network and Savings Services after Privatization	42
Commercial Bank Strategies Replace Savings Linked to Development	43
Tackling the Problem of Financial Exclusion	46
Transition Economies and Privatization: Bailouts at Public Expense	49
The Private Sector Finds Opportunities in Postal Financial Services	50
Restoring Synergies: The Reintegration of Postbanks and Postal Services	52
3. Asian Experiences in Postal Savings Mark J. Scher	55
Introduction	55
The Legacy of Colonialism	55
Post-Independence: Mobilizing Savings	55
Management and Competition Issues in Asian Systems	57
The Organization of Postal Savings: Four Models	57
National Savings Organization: The Case of India	58
Postal Savings and Remittance Bureau: The Case of China	59
Linking Savings to Postal Payments: The Case of Kazakhstan	59
National Savings Banks: The Cases of Malaysia, Singapore, and Sri Lanka	60
Agency Problems: Disincentives to Mobilizing Savings	62
Are Postal Savings in Competition with Commercial Banks? The Case of Japan	64
Financial Technology: Choosing Appropriate Systems	66
Mobilizing Savings: Product Development and Market Analysis	69
Postal Savings in Rural Areas: Making a Link to Credit	69
Overseas Remittances via the Posts	71

The Intermediation and Investment of Mobilized Savings 73
Mobilized Postal Savings Funds and Economic Development 74
Is Financial Market Investment a Realistic Option for Placing Postal Savings? 75
Is Tax Exemption Necessary in Mobilizing Funds? 76

Part 2: Asian Country Case Studies

The Postal Savings Bureau Model

4. Developing Postal Savings in China
   Peng Min'an 79

5. Postal Savings as a Financial Intermediary in the Republic of Korea
   Chan Ki Nam 93

6. Postal Banking and the Financial Crisis in the Republic of Korea: Policy Strategy Proposals for the Postcrisis Era
   Jae Seog Park and Chan Ki Nam 109

7. Policy Challenges and the Reform of Postal Savings in Japan
   Mark J. Scher and Naoyuki Yoshino 121

National Savings Organization and the Post Office Savings Bank Model

8. The National Savings Organization and the Status of Small Savings in India
   Dhirendra Swarup and Anil Bhattacharya 147

   Appendix: National Savings Organization Plans Offered through the Post Office Savings Bank 163

9. The Post Office Savings Bank of India
   Ashok Pal Singh 167

National Savings Bank Model

10. Postal Savings in Sri Lanka
    Eastman Narangoda 183

New Postal Savings Start-Ups in Asian Transitional Economies

11. Report on the Postal Savings System in the Republic of Kazakhstan
    Serikzhan Mambetalin, with Arken Arystanov and Dauren Moldagaliyev 199

12. Vietnam's Postal Savings Service
   Cao Thi Hoai Duc 213

The Postbank Model

13. The Philippine Postal Savings Bank, A Thrift Bank
    Evangeline Felix-Racelis 227

Authors' Biographical Notes 251
Index 255

List of Tables and Figures

Tables

2.1	Data from the United Nations DESA Postal Savings for Development Survey	37
4.1	The Balance, Market Share, and Income of Postal System, October 2000	86
5.1	Income Statement	95
5.2	The Distribution of Post Offices	96
5.3	Deposits by Region	97
5.4	Number of Postal Savings Accounts	97
5.5	Postal Savings Products Summarized	99
5.6	Deposit Balances	100
5.7	Share of Major Types of Postal Savings Products	101
5.8	Percentage Share of Repurchase Agreements (RPs)	101
5.9	Percentage Investment of Postal Banking Funds	103
6.1	Non-Performing Loans at Financial Institutions	110
6.2	Status of Restructuring in Financial Institutions	112
6.3	Effects of Financial Sector Restructuring on Postal Savings	113
6.4	Public Funds and Their Major Sources	117
6.5	Mid- to Long-Term Business Strategy for Postal Banking	118
7.1	Comparison of Convenience: Postal Savings vs. Banks	134
9.1	Outstanding Deposit Balances with the POSB	170
9.2	Branches in the Indian Banking System, March 2000	171
9.3	Regional Distribution of POSB Deposits	172
10.1	NSB's Postal Savings Transactions and Agency Fee Payments	187
10.2	Bank Branch Network	190

x LIST OF TABLES AND FIGURES

10.3	Banking Density by Districts, 1998	192
11.1	Average Amount Invested in State Securities	207
12.1	Mobilized Savings Transferred to NDAF	220
12.2	Business Results of the VPSC	222
13.1	Philippine Bank Rate Structure	234
13.2	Schedule of Loan Portfolio	243
13.3	The Philippine Banking System	245
13.4	Regional Distribution of Banking System with Balance Sheet Accounts	246
13.5	Savings and Mortgage Banks' (SMB) Selected Indicators	249
13.6	Minimum Capital Requirements	250

Figures

4.1	Comparison of Market Share of China's Postal Savings System and Other Financial Institutions	81
4.2	Balance of China's Postal Savings: 1986–June 2002	82
4.3	Branches of China's Postal Savings System: 1986–2001	83
4.4	Market Share of China's Postal Savings: 1986–June 2002	83
4.5	The Balance of Postal Savings by Region	85
5.1	The Organizational Structure of the Postal Savings System in the Republic of Korea	94
6.1	Growth Rate of Deposits	115
6.2	Market Share of Postal Banking Deposits	116
6.3	The Role of Postal Banking	119
9.1	Number of Accounts at the POSB	169
9.2	Deposits in the Indian Banking System, 31 March 2000	170
9.3	Urban versus Rural Distribution of Branches, 2000	171
9.4	Percentage of Rural Deposits in POSB by States, 1998–99	172
10.1	Loans and Investments Portfolio	185
10.2	Total Deposits	185
12.1	Organizational Structure	218
13.1	Geographical Distribution of PPSB Branches, PPC Post Offices, and Rural Banks	232
13.2	PPSB IRS (International Remittance Service) Flowchart	238

Foreword

Keio University (The Center of Excellence Project funded by the Ministry of Education, Science and Culture) is delighted to have supported the research work of Professors Mark J. Scher and Naoyuki Yoshino, the authors of the present volume, *Small Savings Mobilization and Asian Economic Development: The Role of Postal Financial Services*. Dr. Scher, presently the Director of Postal Financial Services Development, was Visiting Professor of the COE Project. Dr. Yoshino, COE Project Leader, is a Professor of Economics at Keio University.

The chief objective of the Center of Excellence (COE) of Keio University is to deepen understanding of recent economic phenomena in Asia through specially promoted research. This book represents part of the COE Project mandate of funding independent research in the area of postal financial services as it relates to the Asian financial crisis and its macroeconomic policy responses. The reader will see that the authors, both experts on postal savings, analyze how postal savings can aid social and economic development, and the obstacles and trends that may undermine such systems. The Introduction, which lays out the broad themes common to developing countries and economies in transition, concludes with a set of policy proposals on postal savings in developing countries.

The contribution of Keio University's long-standing support to Dr. Scher's research over the years has enabled this imaginative collaborative effort between Professors Scher and Yoshino to cull from the senior postal and national savings bank officials from many Asian countries the narratives of their accomplishments and difficulties and enable them to share their experiences, not only in written reports, but also with their counterparts in practitioner workshops hosted by Keio University in Tokyo. This colloquy among the Asian countries began at international round-table workshops on small savings mobilization, organized by Professors Scher and Yoshino, which were hosted and funded by Keio University (COE) in 2000 and 2001, in coordination with the United Nations, and most recently, an international round-table workshop on Small Savings Mobilization and Overseas Worker Remittances, hosted and sponsored by Keio University together with Postal Financial Services Development, also co-chaired by Professors Scher and Yoshino, and held in Tokyo in 2004.

The result is a unique resource for policymakers and scholars, which lets each country's author speak in his or her authentic voice to describe in detail their own past experiences, current issues and expectations for the future.

Eiji Hosoda
Dean of the Faculty of Economics,
Keio University, Tokyo

Foreword

In its global survey of financial development in World Economic and Social Survey, 1999, the Department of Economic and Social Affairs (DESA) of the United Nations Secretariat drew attention to the role that postal savings could play in mobilizing domestic financial resources and in helping to extend financial services to under-served populations in developing countries, notably low-income people and particularly women and the rural populace. The Department continued this work by examining this potential role in more depth, beginning with a survey of the extent and characteristics of postal financial services around the world.

In January 2000 and 2001, the United Nations and Keio University in Tokyo co-sponsored two workshops to assess experiences in postal savings in Asian economies, thanks in particular to the efforts of Professor Naoyuki Yoshino, in collaboration with Dr. Mark J. Scher, who developed the United Nations Project on Postal Savings for Development. With support from Keio University, Dr. Scher visited a number of Asian developing countries to develop and research materials for this book, working with authors of what became the case studies in the book. With UN-DESA support additional information was also obtained concerning postal savings systems.

Professors Scher and Yoshino have written and edited a valuable resource and provocative analysis that policy makers and students of financial sector development should find a useful addition to the literature on mechanisms for mobilizing savings for development. The authors emphasize the contribution that postal savings can make to development, but they also recognize the difficulties that have arisen with such systems in many countries and make explicit recommendations to overcome such shortcomings.

In the Monterrey Consensus, adopted at the International Conference on Financing for Development in March 2002, Heads of State and Government highlighted the importance for development of national savings schemes. Policy makers need information and analysis on a broad range of institutional mechanisms and options for mobilizing domestic savings to assist them in deciding on arrangements that are suitable to their country's particular circumstances. We believe this book can help provide some of that information and analysis. The views expressed, however, are those of the authors and editors, and are not necessarily those of the United Nations.

Ian Kinniburgh, Director
Development Policy and Planning Office,
Department of Economic and Social Affairs,
United Nations

Preface

It can be said that some institutions take on a social value beyond their economic importance. Postal savings is one such institution. Today, postal savings systems, in countries where they exist, provide more access points for savers than all the world's bank branches combined. In this book we examine the experiences of fifteen Asian developing countries with postal financial services and the policy issues that have informed them. We also provide ten country case studies that examine in-depth postal savings and national savings institutions that utilize the postal infrastructure. These case studies focus on the institutions, the instruments, and policies used in meeting the needs of the public that they serve, especially those that are unserved by the commercial banking sector. The approach we take in this book is to follow actual practices and observe the maxim "one size does not fit all."

Postal savings has long served as an effective method to provide basic savings and other financial services, and remains in many countries the only safe means to accumulate small savings for households and individuals, especially those who are financially excluded, such as the economically disadvantaged, rural populations, the urban poor, and others who are socially discriminated against, particularly women, who often play an important role in local commerce, and all those who are unserved by other formal financial institutions.

This book is the result of more than a decade of work and field research on postal savings, shaped and informed by my first-hand observations of the experience of savers and those who serve them, whether in humble village post offices in developing countries in Asia and Africa, or in the urban automated operation centers of developed economies. Our goal in this book is to focus on the methods used in developing countries to mobilize domestic financial resources through individual and household savings, collectively a considerably large sum in many Asian countries, and the investment of those savings in meeting development objectives that will benefit the community of savers locally and nationally.

In July 1999, during my tenure in the United Nations Department of Economic and Social Affairs (UN-DESA) I initiated and authored the Postal Savings for Development Project Survey to assess the extent and characteristics of postal financial services around the world. The survey was distributed directly to the ministries and postal administrations of some eighty countries believed to have had postal savings. In the months following, as the Project Coordinator, I participated in the 23rd Congress of the Universal Postal Union held in Beijing August–September, and delivered a statement on "Postal Savings and Development" as part of the expanded debate on postal financial services. The purpose of the debate was to reconsider postal savings and financial services as a UPU-mandated activity which the UPU had dropped ten years earlier at its 1989 Congress in Washington D.C.

A basic observation in my address at the Congress was that developing a culture of thrift is the cornerstone for economic self-reliance and development and that the means for implementing those values was readily at hand, the ubiquitous postal network. It is puzzling that postal savings is rarely recognized as an institution for social and economic development by policymakers, on a national level, or even more rarely among the international development community. The reasons are manifold, but are chiefly centered on market liberalization and privatization policies advocated by proponents of globalization theories emanating from international institutions, and on the local level by entrenched private-sector interests. It is worth noting that no less an advocate of privatization of public services than Adam Smith praises the post office as both a necessary and successfully managed government-run mercantile project in his classic treatise, *The Wealth of Nations*.

Indeed the very existence of postal savings has now become a highly problematic proposition, not the least because for a decade and more, international lending institutions have tied development lending assistance with conditions for market liberalization and support to programs for the privatization of postal savings as well as privatization of many other public sector services. The consequences of market liberalization and privatization policies are points that are addressed in this book.

In Beijing I held meetings with some forty delegations from Asian, African, and Eastern European countries to discuss the Postal Savings for Development Survey and their participation in the project. It became clear that for these developing countries and transitional economies with postal savings systems, postal financial services was the core of their most profitable source of revenues and provided the fiscal underpinning necessary to sustain the overall operations of the postal network. These countries sorely needed assistance in developing their postal savings services, and many developing countries were being badly served by developed country programs that promoted financial technology and management practices that were discordant with the reality of developing country needs and experiences.

It thus became the primary aim of the Keio University workshops in Tokyo in 2000, 2001, and 2004, to develop a South-South dialogue between Asian developing countries. Many of the participants came from countries that had had a century or more of postal savings experience to exchange. The wealth of their experiences were shared with newcomers who had recently established postal savings.

In 2003, Postal Financial Services Development (www.postalsavings.org) was organized to advance the development of postal savings, payments systems and international remittance services via the postal network, to expand further the exchange of experiences, and to promote the best practices in postal financial services. It is hoped that the information in this book will be of assistance in helping government ministries and postal administrations, national savings institutions, policymakers and advocates, in government and in non-governmental organizations and international institutions, to build upon and expand the dialogue initiated here.

Mark J. Scher, Director
Postal Financial Services Development

Acknowledgments

I express my profound gratitude first of all to the postal savings and national savings institutions that generously gave their cooperation, hospitality and assistance to this research, and to the many postal savings officials and personnel who took the time and devoted the resources that made the field research for this book possible. I am privileged not only for the insights they provided, but for the warm friendship which made possible the many months of field research, and follow up visits over the past five years to the fifteen Asian countries participating in this study. Their cooperation, patience, and enthusiasm sometimes exceeded my own energies in seeing this study came to fruition.

My meetings in the participating countries with central bankers, officials from the ministry of finance and other government officials, as well as commercial and thrift banking institution officers, cross-validated my observations and provided additional insight into the problems facing developing and transitional economies.

The Keio University roundtable workshops in 2000, 2001, 2004 enabled postal savings professionals from the participating countries as well as the authors of the case studies to exchange information and enriched each others' knowledge with their reports while making note of what worked best and the limitations in comparative conditions among developing countries. I thank the Keio University Center on Excellence Project for its generous support that underwrote and hosted the Postal Savings Project Workshops, and Megumi Hamamura and the COE project staff for their help in all aspects of administration.

My interchanges with postal financial service professionals where I made presentations in meetings in Beijing, New York, Brussels, Bern, Amsterdam, Bangkok, Paris, and Tashkent, provided additional insights to worldwide conditions in developing countries in Asia, Africa, and the transitional economies in Eastern Europe, and I am very grateful to each and every one of them, even though they are too numerous to name here.

I must express thanks to Nina Garlo, Hans-Joerg Hess, Machiko Inoue, Asako Ishii, Mazhar Islam, Gloria Klein, Pei Lu, Johannes Majewski, Mai

Oldgard, Melek Oncu, Pirjo Onkalo, Silvia Pepino, Frank Rachor, and Stephanie Zeier. Although several years have passed since they assisted me in the research while interns at the UN, I am pleased that that they still continue to stay in touch with me about their own present endeavors and the progress of the study, forwarding any new information that they may have discovered on postal savings.

Thanks also to former colleagues at the United Nations: Béatrice Labonne, Alice Villarama, Patricia Dingcong, and Béatrice Frankard-Little, for their assistance and support for my work. Thanks also to Jozef Van Brabant and Sergei Gorbunov for their helpful comments.

My deep and sincere thanks to Keio University, where I was Visiting Professor and for its ongoing and generous support for my research, and to my colleague, dear friend and coauthor, Naoyuki Yoshino, leader of the COE Project, and my co-traveler on the journey to produce this book, who has been a continuing source of inspiration and support without which this work would have never been completed.

My special thanks to Avra Scher for her invaluable assistance in preparation of the many figures and tables that appear in this book, and to Ann Scher whose patience, support, and good advice sustained me throughout the many years that brought this book and project to fruition.

M.J.S.

Part 1

Postal Savings for Development

The authors Scher and Yoshino in front of a Japan Post truck at Keio University, Tokyo, September 2000.

1

Introduction

Overview and Summary of Policy Proposals for Postal Savings in Developing Countries

Mark J. Scher with Naoyuki Yoshino

One of the most pressing concerns for economies of the developing world is finding ways to mobilize their own domestic financial resources, thereby enabling them to reduce dependency on foreign capital, that is, borrowing the "savings" of other countries. Despite the variety of foreign assistance programs available to developing countries, all too few offer strategies to help them meet the financial service needs of poor and lower-income people, nor do they offer ways for these populations to harness their nation's resources for their own betterment and for the development of their country.

The human desire to save is instinctual, reflecting the basic need to conserve for the future and strive for self-sufficiency and independence. Savings are also necessary for a growing economy because savings permit investment. The mechanisms for savings are both monetary and in-kind (goods, such as gold or livestock, for example); in-kind savings tend to persist today only in cultures where there is an absence of a safe and secure monetary and financial system. Yet, all too frequently, economic policy has failed to sufficiently differentiate between the individual saver's primary need for the preservation of household resources and his or her potential ability to put any residual savings surplus at risk in profit-seeking investments. The failure to differentiate between these two goals, safety of savings versus risk investment, is the result of a reductionist approach that sees both as having the same economic utility, that is, to accumulate capital.

This book's research found that the foremost concern of individual savers is the safety of their deposits. The second most desirable feature in a financial institution is the ease of accessing funds when needed; third is convenience and design of the savings products offered; the fourth most popular feature is access to credit facilities, if needed; and the last consideration is the interest rate paid on funds deposited. As reported by participants at the first Keio University conference (January 2000, Tokyo), the demand for access to safe savings services was universal in developing and developed countries alike and, as such, was remarkably insensitive to interest rate incentives in all the participating countries.

As will be seen, postal savings systems as formal savings institutions have, since the mid-nineteenth century, provided a secure way for savers to save and for societies to mobilize savings for development. Historically a source of funds for economic and industrial growth in developed countries, most notably in Europe and Japan, today they remain the preeminent depositories by far of individual and household savings. This has also been true in a number of developing countries, particularly in Asia. The individual country case studies in this book examine the Asian experience in postal savings where, in most countries, postal savings have played a leading role in savings mobilization for a long time.

All too often, studies in small savings have focused on informal culture-bound savings mechanisms and the role of non-governmental organizations, often with a lopsided emphasis on initiatives based upon subsidized credit for the promotion of entrepreneurship. In fact, the demand for small savings services outstrips by five-to-one the demand for microcredit. Indeed, as will also be argued, microcredit is unsustainable without small savings, and yet on the other hand, the role of government-sponsored savings institutions has been almost entirely ignored.

As a collection system for small-scale savings of households and individuals, postal savings systems provide more access points for savings and other household financial services globally than all the world's bank branches combined. Understandably, these institutions have been the frequent targets of their perceived competitors, mainly the private commercial banking sector, which has often sought to restrict or eliminate, if not take over, publicly owned postal savings systems where and when it has been within their political power to do so. Indeed, the rivalry between the commercial banking sector and the posts has largely been one-sided in favor of the banks and, as we will show, with unhelpful results, since the commercial banking sector has shown little inclination or ability to service the financial needs of low-income populations, small farmers, and small businesses, particularly in rural areas.

Postal savings systems were begun as publicly owned institutions and in general continue to be so in almost all countries. In this book we will examine the experiences of postal savings institutions in a range of economic environments, including several countries that have attempted to address private sector concerns while continuing to meet the public's need for small-scale household savings. This chapter concludes with a brief summary of policy proposals to keep in mind as we discuss the reform and enhancement of postal financial services in developing countries. The proposals focus on:

the delivery of services to underserved populations including women, rural populations, and the urban poor; strengthening overall savings mobilization; creating facilities to collect overseas remittances; and social investment of funds for development.

The analytical chapters and case studies in this book review the experiences of a range of countries that have made use of the postal system to provide financial services to underserved population groups, highlighting in particular such services as postal savings, postal remittances, postal checking, and giro payment services (a credit-based payment system), all of which are collectively referred to as postal financial services. Other postal financial services may include pension and social benefit payments, tax and fee collection on behalf of government agencies, bill payments for utilities, foreign remittance services, and foreign exchange. In some countries, credit, pension, insurance, and investment products are also available, typically provided by private firms that have an agency relationship with the postal system.

The outstanding advantage in providing financial services through a postal system is the post's ubiquitous character. Postal financial services are usually available to most, if not all, of a country's population by virtue of the broad network of postal facilities. Such financial services are provided as a public service, as well as when the post acts merely as an agent on behalf of another institution or commercial bank, or when the postal system itself, as in a few cases, is privately owned—a relatively new phenomenon. The essential characteristic distinguishing postal financial services from private banking is the obligation and capacity of the postal system to serve the entire geographic and economic spectrum of the national population. This mandate is unlike the purpose of conventional commercial banks, which seek to service only the sectors of the population they deem profitable, namely, commercial and private banking accounts in urban areas. It is at this very point where the post's mandate and commercial bank strategy are often at odds, because in many developing countries, especially those with fragmented and dispersed populations, the post may represent the only significant service contact many people living in isolated areas have with their government. It may also well be the most visible government institution symbolizing national identity at the local level.

In some countries, funds collected by the postal savings system also play a significant role in financing public investment. In a number of countries the funds are intermediated through policy based financial institutions that invest the funds for the direct benefit of the community. In addition to financing public expenditure through purchase of government bonds and approved securities, in some countries postal savings resources are lent to national development funds, state governments, and municipalities for civil projects. In a number of countries the funds are used to provide mortgages for low-income housing and small enterprise loans, while in other countries the funds are intermediated by development banks and similar institutions for financing projects in agricultural, industrial, and infrastructure development.

The postal services' universal obligation and postal savings itself are founded upon a social mandate to serve the entire population. A key reason for the efficiency of postal savings is its ability to draw upon the strength of the postal network's widespread "brick and mortar" facilities, that is, post offices. Even when postal financial services are operated under agency agreements with separate savings banks or private financial institutions, it is the synergy between the postal and the financial operations that allows them to be uniquely efficient. Sharing expenses and common facilities across operations in high- and low-volume branches keeps down the overall costs of providing both postal and financial services universally to all segments of the population. Indeed, whether run as public enterprises or as regulated private monopolies, postal systems and their associated financial services should be able to operate without subsidy. However, as will be shown, difficulties can arise when the package of postal services is unbundled and the obligations of a once-public unified organization is newly broken into separate components that fail to sustain the network upon which socially mandated services rely.

Chapter 2 elaborates these points. It introduces the varieties of postal financial services and the factors that contribute to their success, even when operating under the most rudimentary conditions. The observations contained in this chapter reflect the author's work in this field over a number of years in a variety of countries on several continents. The field research for this book was conducted by Dr. Scher in fifteen Asian countries and Special Administrative Regions (SAR), meeting with personnel of national savings, postal savings, and remittance systems. There he observed postal financial services operations, training centers, and national savings institutions. He met with postal, national savings bank, central bank, and finance ministry officials in the following Asian countries in 2000: China, India, Indonesia, Japan, Kazakhstan, Republic of Korea, Malaysia, Philippines, Singapore, Sri Lanka, Thailand, Uzbekistan, and Vietnam. In the winter of 2003–4 he made follow-up visits to China, Hong Kong (S.A.R. China), India, Japan, Mongolia, Philippines, Sri Lanka, Thailand, and Vietnam. In addition, Dr. Scher visited Belgium, France, Germany, Morocco, the Netherlands, Switzerland, and the United Kingdom in 1999–2003 to observe postal financial services operations, consult with officials, and participate in international meetings on postal financial services.

Chapter 2 also examines major policy and management issues confronting postal financial services in both developed and developing countries. This chapter considers the role of public confidence in postal savings, which has been the strength underpinning the system, particularly in times of political anxiety and economic uncertainty when public distrust of the security of the banking system is high. Access to safe and cost-effective payment systems and remittance services through the postal network has proven to be one of its most vital elements, allowing households and small businesses to engage in financial transactions in familiar local settings. Another important element of the postal network is low-cost transmission of international remittances from overseas migrants and workers back to their families; international remittances are a significant source of foreign exchange for many developing countries. The importance of this service to overseas workers and to the postal financial system is discussed further in chapters 2 and 3 and is illustrated in several of the country case studies that follow.

Market liberalization and privatization of public services has had a significant impact upon the changing economics of the posts, another theme addressed in chapter 2. The posts typically come under the jurisdiction of ministries of communications. Yet, although its core business activity is the collection and delivery of letters and parcels, in a good number of countries a broad range of additional public services has become the main source of the posts' revenues. In the past, these services has included more than postal financial services; in most countries they also included telephone and telegraphic communications.

The posts in many countries, however, recently lost significant revenue through the split-off and privatization of their telecommunications branches and have had to find new revenue sources. A number of these posts are finding a solution in providing or reinvigorating postal financial services in order to increase revenues and restore profitability. Thus, the effects of market liberalization have become the prime impetus, albeit unintentionally, for establishing or reestablishing postal savings in China, the Republic of Korea, the Philippines, Kazakhstan, and Vietnam.

Postal financial services have become the chief source of the post's revenue in these and many other developing countries and a key source of profits. For example, in China, postal savings and remittance services accounted for 50 percent of China Post's revenues in 2003, up from 34 percent in 2000, and now represents 85 percent of its profits. The declining revenues from mail in China's case is due to the proliferation of new telephones. This same phenomenon was observed a century ago in Europe and North America after the introduction of the telephone, which immediately resulted in halving the volume of postcard mail. In addition, financial market liberalization in many countries has both harmed savers and left their deposits at risk, after a proliferation of private sector banks opened and then failed. This was especially true where governments had removed effective regulatory oversight or otherwise failed to protect the small-savings market. This in turn has given a boost to postal savings in Kazakhstan, the Republic of Korea, Vietnam, and the PostalBank of the Philippines, where local depositors have sought safety for their savings in their respective countries' postal savings systems.

Additionally, chapter 2 reviews how market liberalization has affected postal savings governance in developed and developing countries. It examines the different types of regimes the posts have been adopting as a result of market liberalization and deregulation. This chapter also contrasts the privatized sector's practice of "cherry-picking" only the profitable segments of the postal communications market against the post's social imperative to service the whole population. "Neoliberal" policies and their consequences, particularly in Europe, are reviewed. Although we find that cross-subsidization has been a recurring theme in the private sector's complaints about "unfair" competition from postal savings, at the same time private sector operators have expanded their cross-border acquisitions using revenues from protected monopolies in domestic markets. Several such cases are examined in chapter 2, including those economies in transition that have adopted market liberalization agendas. Creation of newly privatized postal banks and institutions has often been followed by failure and subsequent bailout at the public's expense. Nevertheless, the mantra of market liberalization has repetitiously called for the extinction of such government-owned institutions as a part of the new economic agenda for developing and transition economies.

Also discussed within the context of market liberalization is the loss of postal services that resulted in financial service exclusion for those with low and moderate incomes and those living in non-urban areas. These policies are examined together with the subsequent steps being taken in some countries to tackle the problem of financial service exclusion by restarting savings facilities through the postal network.

Chapter 3 examines the experiences of a number of Asian countries in postal savings. It addresses management and organizational issues, including savings product development, investment policy on funds collected, methods to increase availability and reduce costs in the transfer of overseas remittances, and issues relating to the introduction of appropriate financial technology.

It is interesting to note that, among those countries that have a shared colonial past and a shared postal savings model based on the British, French, and Japanese postal savings systems, various countries in their postindependence period took very different paths, including the socialist countries in the market economy era. This chapter organizes the Asian experiences in postal savings into four main types: (1) the national savings organization model found in India and Bangladesh; (2) the postal savings bureau model found in Japan, the Republic of Korea, and with socialist variations in China and Vietnam; (3) the linkage of postal remittance and benefit payments to postal savings account deposits in Kazakhstan and other Commonwealth of Independent States (CIS) countries; and (4) the national savings bank model found in Malaysia, Sri Lanka, and formerly in Singapore. The postbank model that has evolved in Europe so far is in limited use in Asia but can be found in the Philippines and Iran. In some countries, most notably Japan, private sector advocates are also promoting the conversion of postal savings from public ownership to several different proposed privatized models, all of which are in high political contention.

Asian experiences highlight a number of issues relevant to many developing countries worldwide. For example, management issues related to "agency" problems between the postal operator and separate ownership of the postal savings bank have manifested themselves as disincentives to mobilizing savings. This raises serious concerns about maintaining a fair balance in the agency relationship. Other issues include whether postal savings are in competition with commercial banks, and the policies designed to ameliorate conflicting interests that may arise. Further elaborated in chapter 3 are techniques the posts may use to mobilize savings through product development and market analysis, particularly as they relate to issues of credit and international remittances. This chapter asks whether additional incentives to savers, such as tax exemptions, are necessary and/or productive in promoting deposits.

The perils that developing economies entering the international marketplace face when purchasing financial technology for postal financial services are also briefly discussed, and difficulties in adopting the appropriate technology for financial transaction management are reviewed from the perspectives of countries in differing stages of economic development.

In Asia's developing countries, shallow financial markets prevail and postal savings funds are invested in economic development primarily through a variety of institutional mechanisms, such as domestic development banks. Chapter 3 examines the ways that postal savings funds have been intermediated for economic development in various Asian countries. This chapter looks critically at whether funds mobilized by postal savings should be placed in financial markets and whether or not the market approach is a realistic option.

The chapters that follow, chapters 4 through 13, present Asian experiences in individual country case studies based on updated reports initially presented by their respective authors at workshop meetings hosted and funded by Keio University, and co-sponsored by the United Nations, in January 2000 and 2001. The meetings were organized and co-chaired by the authors, Mark J. Scher and Naoyuki Yoshino. These country reports are grouped into the five basic models identified in chapter 3: the postal savings bureau model, the national savings organization and post office savings bank model, the national savings bank model, new start-ups in Asian transitional economies, and the postbank model.

The Postal Savings Bureau Model

The postal savings bureau model is represented in the individual case studies of China, the Republic of Korea, and Japan together with an additional essay on Korea's financial crisis and its postal banking system.

Chapter 4 describes China's Postal Savings and Remittance Bureau that was reestablished in 1986 after a thirty-four-year hiatus. Significant progress has been made in establishing a nationwide network that now has a market share of savings exceeded only by China's "Big Four" state-owned banks. More important, these savings represent for the most part new savings from both urban and rural markets previously unserved and therefore a previously untapped resource for financial investment.

Also discussed is the institutional development of China's postal savings bureau that was responsible for the tremendous growth in new savings mobilized, particularly within the past ten years. This chapter reviews the development of remittance services, payment systems, and the utilization of technology in establishing a nationwide network. The author describes the transformation of the postal savings services from an agency of the central bank to a full-fledged bureau of the China State Posts that operates within the investment policies laid down by the central government.

Chapters 5 and 6 describe Korea's postal savings system. Established in 1905 after the Japanese takeover of the Korean postal system, it has had a long and varied history reflecting both its colonial legacy and more recently its increased importance following the 1997 Asian financial crisis. Chapter 5 details the role of postal savings since its reestablishment in 1983, following the government's market liberalization program that shut down postal savings in 1977. Detailed in the chapter are some unique savings products offered and the reasons for their special appeal. Also outlined are how mobilized savings are invested through Treasury Loans and Investment Special Accounts and other government programs by being intermediated through specialized policy-based development banks.

Chapter 6 details the important role the Korean postal savings system played in restoring stability to the financial sector following the 1997 financial crisis. It also offers a number of lessons and recommendations drawn from that experience and proposes a strategy for postal savings to accommodate the competing interests of private sector financial institutions over the long term.

From the very beginning Japan has harnessed postal savings for state development goals, including the national goals of industry building, improving transportation and the military infrastructure, and carrying out anti-inflationary and economic stimulus policies. Chapter 7 discusses the current challenges to the existence of Japan's postal savings system, the longest operating postal savings system in Asia. As the world's largest financial institution and the main repository for Japan's household savings, some critics have argued that the Japanese postal savings system is too successful. All too frequently, critics and policymakers have erroneously conflated the investment of mobilized funds that occurred under the government's Fiscal Investment and Loan Program (FILP, a section of the Ministry of Finance) with the collection mechanism managed separately by the Ministry of Posts. Chapter 7 examines the Ministry of Finance's fund management through FILP and the more recent introduction of market risk against the context of the public's continued fears about and lack of confidence in the private financial sector due to the ongoing banking crisis. Both the utility and prudence of the search for market-oriented investment policies is questioned in view of the public's fears over the safety of their savings.

Also critically reviewed are Japanese policymakers' current proposals to liberalize, if not privatize, not only the postal savings system but also the post delivery system itself. The potential consequences of such changes are examined not only in the context of the economics of the posts, but also in terms of the potential loss of other essential services to rural populations.

National Savings Organizations and the Post Office Savings Bank Model

National Savings Organizations (NSO) play a unique role in promoting small savings, and work in tandem with the Post Office Savings Banks (POSBs) in several South Asian countries. Chapter 8 describes India's NSO, a division of the Ministry of Finance, which devises, develops, and tests the savings products sold through the POSB. The social and cultural factors that enter into the design of these products are noteworthy. Savings and pension products are designed with special features that are targeted to appeal to specific segments of the population, such as farmers and rural workers, housewives, urban salaried workers, industrial workers, civil servants, and professionals. Commissioned sales agents are trained by the NSO to promote each type of product. Each product is described in an annex to the chapter. Particularly noteworthy are the outreach efforts made by the NSO to educate and bring in both women and other disadvantaged groups as depositors by using specially trained female agents and offering savings products and services designed both for housewives and for outreach to rural populations.

Chapter 8 describes India's investment policy with respect to the funds mobilized by the NSO and lent to the States in which the funds are raised, including the role of State governments and their small-savers organizations.

Policy issues relating to interest rates and the efficacy of tax-free incentives on certain savings products are discussed.

Chapter 9 analyzes how India's Post Office Savings Bank provides agency services for the NSO's savings products and the steps the POSB has taken to modernize its operations. India Post, with 154,000 post offices, has the world's largest postal savings system. Each post office serves as a collection and withdrawal point, and some 89 percent of its branches are located in rural areas. It has 110 million account-holders and a 21 percent market share of all bank deposits in India. The number of POSB account-holders has consistently doubled every decade over the past thirty years, and the POSB has experienced a 3.6–fold increase in its volume of deposits over the last ten years.

National Savings Bank Model

Outside India, several post office savings banks in Asian countries have been transformed into National Savings Banks (NSB) and are no longer owned by national post offices. Such NSBs have established their own branch networks in urban markets while still utilizing the postal branch network mainly in rural areas. Mutual dissatisfaction has arisen out of the agency agreements between some NSBs and their respective national postal systems. Chapter 10 examines some of the issues in contention in the ongoing agency relationship between the National Savings Bank of Sri Lanka and the Sri Lanka Postal Department, focusing on the post's efforts at small-savings mobilization. The NSB has been dissatisfied with the relatively low volume of the post's savings collection compared with the NSB's own urban branch network, even though the post's efforts for increasing postal savings collections have yielded mixed results. Analysis and observations presented in the chapter are from the NSB's perspective, with some significant comments from an independent research report prepared by the Sri Lanka Centre for Development Studies (Marga Institute).

New Postal Savings Start-Ups in Asian Transition Economies

Postal savings operations have recently been started in several nations that have transition economies, including Kazakhstan and Vietnam in 1999. Both of these countries, without any prior experience in postal savings, have made rapid advances in only a few years' time. Also, economic liberalization measures opened their respective markets to private sector banking, and this resulted in losses to the postal system of their traditional telecommunications revenues.

As in most countries in Europe, Asia, and Africa, telecommunications, that is, telephone and telegraph services, were owned by the post office, hence the post was known as the PT&T. In Kazakhstan's case, detailed in chapter 11, telecommunications services were the post service's main source of revenue and received a disproportionate share of the posts' development budget during the Soviet era. In the 1990s, telecommunications was detached from the posts. Since then, in order to maintain the viability of the postal delivery network, the primary task for the newly reorganized and corporatized postal system known as Kazpost was to replace the lost telecom income by developing postal financial services as a new source of revenue. To form the basis for developing postal savings, Kazpost turned to its inherited role of providing the payment system for pension benefits, which is common to all the CIS countries. By transforming the existing cash payout of social benefits into individual saving accounts, Kazpost created new postal financial services, including salary transfer services, overseas remittances, foreign currency accounts and foreign exchange facilities, and securities brokerage and dealer activities, agency services for utilities, and insurance and pension fund payments. These services are particularly important in rural areas that have gone without access to savings facilities since the former National Savings Bank closed its rural branches and was reorganized as a privatized commercial bank.

Chapter 12 discusses Vietnam, which established its postal savings system in 1999. In Vietnam, many newly established private sector banks failed following the financial market liberalization in the 1990s, weakening the public's confidence in the banking system. Although overall economic reforms have generated large amounts of cash, much of it has not been deposited or invested with any financial institution. The objective of Vietnam's postal savings system has been to mobilize these funds in order to build infrastructure and key economic facilities through the National Development Assistance Fund. This is an area in which Vietnam and many other developing countries have typically been unable to attract foreign investment. This chapter describes Vietnam's plans to expand its postal savings network through the development of "cultural post offices," which is expected to triple the number of customers served, primarily in the countryside. Vietnam's postal savings system expects to double its deposit base from 5 percent of the savings market in 2002 to 10 percent by 2005.

The Postbank Model

The Philippines first introduced postal savings in 1906, and it was a profitable as well as popular institution throughout its seventy years of existence.

During the financial liberalization period of the 1970s, low capitalization policies were set for banks. This permitted the formation of many new banks that were owned by politically influential families in rural areas, putting them in direct competition with the postal savings system. Postal savings was then abolished by the Marcos regime in 1976.

In 1992 the Philippines postal system was reorganized as a public corporation, and in 1994 the Philippine PostalBank was reestablished but with the proviso that it not "unduly compete with rural, commercial, or universal banks." This has severely limited the PostalBank's scope of operations by denying it its main competitive advantage, the use of post offices to service banking clients.

The postbank model is a relatively new phenomenon in Asia. In the case of the Philippines, the PostalBank is organized as a credit-granting and deposit-taking thrift bank. As one of four Authorized Depositories for municipal and provincial governments and publicly owned organizations, PostalBank's extensive governance procedures and high reserve requirements give depositors confidence in its stability. This is especially important at a time when Philippine commercial banks have declared 19 percent of their loans as non-performing, second highest among Asian countries in 2001. Furthermore, undeclared non-performing loans are said to be in the 30 percent range, although still less than in Indonesia and Thailand, which have also undergone a similar financial market liberalization.

Detailed in chapter 13 are the Philippines' Postalbank's products and services, including its remittance services catering to Overseas Filipino Workers (OFWs), its policies in granting loans in the countryside, and its extensive governance procedures on credit and the investment of funds.

Conclusions and Policy Proposals on Postal Savings in Developing Countries

The ultimate premise of this study is that postal savings and giro payments systems can be important mechanisms for mobilizing indigenous financial resources, which can then be applied to domestic development. The discussions in this book point to a number of areas in which new policies might enhance existing advantages of postal financial services and meet the challenges to savings mobilization through the wider provision of financial services through the postal infrastructure. Also analyzed in the chapters that follow are the conspicuous market liberalization and privatization problems that have confronted posts in both developed and developing countries. What follows below are some considerations for policy reforms drawn from the experiences detailed in this book:

1. When a government is deciding whether to ensure that a specified set of communications and financial services to be made available nationwide at moderate cost to all users, it must be made aware of the consequences of any policies made in this crucial economic sector. Once a government has decided in favor of such services, the question is to select the best way to provide them. A national network of posts has been able to provide a set of related communications and financial services in the form of a fiscally viable network that is effective in serving the poor, women, and rural populations as well as small- and medium-size business interests.

On the other hand, as countries now experience the general withdrawal of the state from heretofore public services, particularly as specific services are deemed to be less warranting of protection, the financial viability of the postal system itself comes into question. This could affect the range of services offered, such as the provision of postal savings and other financial services to the underserved and unserved. If that happens, the only choices are to close down major portions of the postal network or subsidize it in order to cover its operating costs. Alternatively, as they currently exist, postal financial services have been shown to provide essential services as well as allow the postal network to remain financially viable.

2. Many countries' postal administrations have changed from government departments to state-owned corporations, responsible for the profits and losses of their operations. There are strong incentives for management, under a corporatized model of postal governance, to seek to add new profit-making services and create more efficiency in all areas of operations. The need to move toward this model is particularly critical for those countries in which government institutional bureaucracies have been cited for inefficiency and as outlets for political patronage.

3. Postal management and policymakers must obtain the hard data needed to make informed decisions. A regular diagnostic accounting analysis that tracks and assesses the costs versus benefits of the postal savings system's separate operations and products is required. Systemwide analysis would develop an information base, expediting management decision-making, and assist in the ordering of government priorities, including either possible termination or upgrading of specific services and a more realistic assessment of proposals for purchases of new technology and equipment. Many postal financial systems have not yet undertaken such an analysis at all.

4. In addition to the aforementioned analysis, knowledge of the operating costs for each of the system's services would allow determination of the cost at which postal services are meeting their mandate relative to revenues earned.

Therefore, such knowledge and analysis could enable or fortify political support for achieving social, economic, civil, and cultural development goals through the posts. The following are some areas upon which a cost/benefit analysis could focus: meeting rural communications needs, providing financial services to low-income and rural populations, small business development, educational/library class post rates, non-governmental organization rates, and public service and government's free-franking privileges. At the same time, postal service rates that result in subsidies to private interests should also be examined. An example is the subsidized rate given to forms of mail that are used for primarily commercial purposes, such as bulk rate advertising postcards and underpriced parcel delivery.

5. It is equally important that governments contemplating privatization proposals understand the social value of the assets they are offering for sale. All too frequently governments have undervalued the postal savings network as a socioeconomic asset. This is illustrated in chapter 2 in the merging of postal savings and government-owned postbanks with commercial institutions in order to avoid the political ramifications of a direct government bailout of a failing private bank. Instead, the failing bank is provided with the postbank's stable deposit base to prevent the failing private bank's collapse. In other cases, publicly owned services are privatized out of the ideological convictions of domestic policymakers or to satisfy conditions set by international donors of economic assistance programs. More generally, as will be seen in the European cases in chapter 2, institutions that privatized then followed a commercial strategy that deprived rural areas and the poor of continued access to financial services. For emerging economies, this resulted in the loss of an important development resource, the means to mobilize domestic small savings. The expectations of the outcomes of privatization policies need to be reexamined by both governments and international development institutions.

6. In Europe and in some developing countries, government restrictions led the posts to consider separating the posts and establishing a separate "postbank." One attraction from the postal management perspective was that its postbank could then obtain licenses to broaden the range of financial services offered and expand the investment and commercial lending possibilities of mobilized funds. However, the creation of the "postbank" often came in tandem or was soon followed by the post's loss of its ownership stake in the postbank. When this occurred in Scandinavia, the posts lost revenue that would have been brought in by the shared facilities. This in turn undermined the economic viability of the postal infrastructure network and forced the closure of many branch post offices upon which postal savings and many

other community services depended. In assessing the pros and cons of separating postal savings ownership from the posts and establishing a postbank, or the consequences of privatizing, consideration should be given to providing continuing incentives to the posts and the postbank so they actively cooperate in continuing the operations of postal financial services. Such incentives can include some form of the posts' ownership stake in the bank, or an annual franchise fee paid by the bank to the post based upon the total value of deposits plus fees on a per-transaction basis.

7. In most developed countries, even before the advent of the postbank concept, postal savings offered credit services to their clients, recognizing the important role consumer credit and home mortgage lending plays in building a savings institution's base of depositors. However, a survey written by Mark J. Scher for the UN Postal Savings for Development project (see chapter 2) shows that 80 percent of the developing countries' postal savings systems offer no credit facilities. All too frequently this is the result of overly restrictive policies. In some cases these policies are based upon historical legacies from the colonial period, or in other cases the posts are denied licenses on the rationale that they would unduly compete with private sector financial institutions.

There are a number of ways to provide these services in a less competitive way than postbank creation. In many countries the posts have agency agreements with independent financial institutions, allowing them to provide financial products that the posts are not normally permitted to provide under existing financial regulatory regimes. This has the added benefit of allowing the posts to offer new services in which they have no experience, skill, or managerial infrastructure. In particular, this approach permits the marketing of credit and investment products without the posts themselves incurring the high risks associated with credit evaluation and debt collection or the investment of funds in inherently risky markets. Other alternatives include having the postal savings system enter into joint agreements with savings and policy-based development institutions in order to perform some of these functions, with appropriate incentives to each party, or having the posts acquire outright a financial institution that has credit evaluation capabilities and debt collection experience.

8. Using the postal infrastructure, postal savings has been the main vehicle for mobilizing rural savings and providing financial services to low-income populations and women in many countries. This has been accomplished through general savings promotion campaigns undertaken by the postal system. While postal management may see these campaigns simply as marketing, they also help inculcate the values of thrift while having a

broader development function. A related area requiring attention is the development not only of savings products suitable for rural and urban markets, but also the development of products for specially targeted groups within those markets that have been traditionally underserved.

Successful microcredit operations need a microsavings component such as postal savings in order to be self-sustaining. Without access to low-cost small-savings deposits, microcredit organizations in developing countries have had to rely upon far-higher-rate interbank loans from major banks to fund their credit operations. As a result, it is common to see microcredit institutions charge their clients monthly interest rates of 6 percent, an effective annual rate of 72 percent, even though among microcredit clients in developing countries the default rates average a minuscule 2 percent. While a 2 percent default rate would be unusually low in developed countries, it is rather typical among microcredit clients in developing countries, for example, in Mexico's Finca microfinance organization (*New York Times,* 19 March 2003; 24 March 2003).

Some institutions, such as national savings organizations, may address the need to create and promote savings products as part of a coherent national plan to mobilize savings. Other institutions, such as national savings banks, may provide a link between the collection of funds and their intermediation back into the community. Examples of this are providing mortgages for low-income housing, and funding development banks that can assess sustainable projects for agricultural, industrial, and infrastructure development. Other strategies that can successfully be employed include creating alliances with microcredit organizations, for which the posts can provide deposit-taking functions.

9. Domestic development would also be assisted by placing a portion of postal savings resources with qualified microfinance institutions whose job would be to promote small business enterprises and grant small-scale agricultural credits (a program of this type was undertaken in Morocco). This policy would have the twofold effect of providing credit to the poor, who are often women, as well as giving encouragement to rural savers by returning investment funds to their communities through local microcredit institutions. An expected benefit for the posts would be greater use of postal financial services through the opening of small business accounts and remittance services.

10. An opportunity currently exists to adapt the postal payment systems to include savings facilities, particularly in CIS countries and other transition economies, as well as in developing countries where postal payment systems already are extensive. By allowing direct deposit of payments into

personal savings accounts, large amounts of financial resources that would otherwise move upon receipt into the cash economy could instead be mobilized in the financial system. In addition, savers would have a safe place for funds that earns interest for them. From a managerial standpoint, there are also many synergies achieved by joining the operations of postal savings and postal payments services and the use of the same counter service windows and equipment.

It is crucial, however, that clients be able to easily withdraw funds from their savings accounts. This has already been achieved in the usually crowded city post offices in China and in the Republic of Korea with the introduction of "cash cards" that are speeding up service through the posts' automatic cash withdrawal machines (ACMs). The benefit of ACMs depends, however, on a variety of factors, including the volume of customers, the cost of providing additional counter service, and the existing competitive market conditions vis-à-vis other financial institutions, as discussed in chapter 3 on the appropriate use of technology in developing economies. In a further application of this idea, some commercial banks have ATMs that are linked to the postal savings system. This convenience can result in a higher retention rate of savings by minimizing unnecessarily large early withdrawals.

11. For many developing countries in Asia and elsewhere, a significant amount of foreign exchange comes in the form of remittances from overseas workers. Yet, for the most part, only expensive or inadequate and unsafe systems of remittance are available. The availability of lower-cost and safe remittance services would encourage more remittances from abroad and perhaps increase the total inflow to the home country. International postal giro remittances to postal savings and giro accounts with direct deposit features are an established transfer mechanism between many developed countries. Steps should be taken to extend this service to developing countries in Asia as well as Africa and include the international giro systems of Europe, Japan, and the Republic of Korea. A comprehensive solution would be enactment of an international treaty that provides for universal giro services through the posts, similar to the provisions for the universal exchange of mail between member countries of the Universal Postal Union (UPU).

In Conclusion

Postal savings and giro services have long played a vital economic and social role in many countries by providing financial services to those who have the least access to the banking sector. However, the vector of forces of financial sector development, market liberalization, domestic and foreign entry and acquisition, privatization, and technological change have dramatically reshaped the financial sector in many countries. This has challenged the continued provision of public services and diminished the opportunities to expand, or in some cases even to continue, to deliver postal financial services to low-income populations, women, and discriminated minorities, especially in rural areas. Yet, a review of Asian developing countries' experiences suggests numerous ways for developing countries, relying on their own efforts, to help themselves mobilize domestic savings and provide domestic financial services through postal savings and remittances, thereby providing financial services to those most likely to be excluded.

Finally, this study is the product of both research and discussion in many countries in Asia. These nations' experiences reflect the often-significant differences in their economic, social, and cultural development compared to the developed countries, primarily those in Europe. These differences along with other relevant issues underscore the importance of South-South colloquies on shared concerns, such as postal financial services and economic development. This book is a product of such a colloquy and focuses on the policies and practices used to increase the institutional efficiency and effectiveness of postal financial services in developing country environments so that they may build their capacity to mobilize savings and to serve the people.

2

Policy and Management Issues Confronting Postal Financial Services Today

Mark J. Scher

The Evolution of Postal Savings

The Origins of a Global Postal Network

The posts first came into existence to serve commerce and privilege. Organized to meet the needs of royal courts in Asia and Europe, formal postal operations were intended for royalty and their use was reserved for the needs of the state. The Mongol Empire's postal service stretched from Korea to the Ukraine by the thirteenth century. In the fifteenth century, European royal franchises were given to private postal carriers and local courier services to serve merchants, bankers, and others privileged enough to afford their high fees. With the rise of the modern nation-state in the late eighteenth and nineteenth centuries, vested private carrier operations were consolidated into national postal systems whose services were inexpensive, profitable, and therefore self-sustainable. The benefits of affordable communication to both commerce and civil culture were readily apparent, and universal postal service for the delivery of letters and parcels at uniform rates soon became the norm. To this day the posts remain unrivaled in their worldwide scope of operations, with over six hundred thousand post offices providing universal service to virtually all communities (Data of Universal Postal Union, *Postal Statistics, 1980–1999* [Bern, 2000]).

Creation of Postal Savings and Giro Remittance Services

The combination of financial services with the posts predates the modern era. Merchant bankers from medieval times in Europe and Asia carried correspondence for fees along with letters of credit, payment guarantees, and other financial instruments for their clients. After the institution of municipal mail delivery systems, local merchants came to expect that their local post offices would be utilized for commercial payment settlements, thus leading to the establishment of municipal postal giro systems in which payments were remitted through the postal system in many cities. As an alternative to the giro systems, some postal systems offer postal checking services, similar to those found at banks in the United States, the United Kingdom, and elsewhere, which employ paper checks debited against an account. These two payments systems were culturally informed by two distinct traditions, the ancient Egyptian system based on credits (giro) and the ancient Babylonian debit system that employed cuneiform clay tablets as debit instruments (checks).

In the nineteenth century, postal financial services were instituted nationally from two distinct but complementary services, postal savings, based initially on the British model, and the postal giro system. The word "giro" comes from the Greek word γυρος (gyros), meaning revolving, a reference to its ability to maintain the circulation of funds through the postal payment system. The giro payments idea was first introduced on a national scale in 1883 in Austria and was instituted throughout the Hapsburg empire, which also encompassed present-day Hungary and the various Balkan and Central European countries under its rule. The giro system enabled migrant workers to remit their wages safely and easily to their families in their home villages. It also aided the Austro-Hungarian State by reducing the amount of coinage it had to mint and by providing the treasury with the use of these funds while they resided in postal giro accounts. In developing countries the giro payments system is found extensively among the former French colonies, especially in Africa and in the former Dutch colonies such as Indonesia. It was not adopted by the United Kingdom, however, until 1968 and therefore is generally not found among former British colonies that had already achieved independence. Today the postal giro system is a retail payment system widely used in Europe, Japan, and some developing countries. It is based on written transfer orders submitted through the posts and/or standing payment orders. In recent years many developed and some developing countries have added electronic payment giro cards used at the point of sale that directly credit the account of the vendor and debit that of the payee.

Furthermore, today the benefits of the giro system to overseas workers apply more than ever, and the posts continue to be an integral part of many countries' payments systems. Especially in countries in which there are weak and unreliable banking institutions or where bank service fees are high, postal financial services offer a secure alternative and are the preferred payment system. Postal giro systems also give postal patrons an easy and affordable way to pay bills (such as for utilities, license fees, and taxes) and receive pension, social insurance, and welfare benefits.

As one example, Swiss Post reports that giro payments comprise over 50 percent of Switzerland's financial transactions. In fact, postal financial services are by far the Swiss Post's most profitable activity, since it suffers heavy losses from its parcel delivery service and makes only marginal profits from letter delivery operations. Swiss Post's efforts to establish not only postal savings operations but also a full range of banking services have met strong opposition from the banking industry (Swiss Post *Annual Report*, 2000).

Postal Savings for the People

The introduction of savings accounts at post offices followed the rise of the savings bank movement in Scotland and thrift movements elsewhere in the beginning of the nineteenth century. In 1861 the United Kingdom organized the first national system of postal savings through post office savings accounts, which were seen as a safer alternative to some of the earlier thrift movement failures. The institution of national postal savings systems followed in many other European countries, in British North America and its Pacific territories, and Japan. Soon thereafter the United Kingdom, France, Austro-Hungary, and later Japan went on to introduce postal savings into their colonies. Most present-day postal savings systems in developing countries were introduced or first patterned after colonial systems. However, in many countries these institutions were not well supported in the postindependence period and in a number of cases fell into disuse.

In the 1990s, postal savings was restored in many of today's transition economies. In particular, the countries in Central Europe and the Balkans that had once belonged to the Hapsburg empire reintroduced the Austrian *Postsparkasse* model during this period. There has also been a revival of interest in a number of developing countries. Several countries in Africa have also restored postal savings, and in Latin America, Brazil has introduced postal savings and giro services.

The existence of postal financial services in some countries and not in others reflects historical circumstance. In some countries, savings bank institutions came about independently from postal savings yet significantly paralleled the development of postal savings. Notably, the German *Sparkassen* in the nineteenth century influenced the development of the Russian *sberbank* system, which in 1841 became the first national state-owned savings bank system. This was later centralized under the State Bank of the Soviet Union and is now prevalent throughout the countries of the Commonwealth of Independent States. Although institutionally separate from the posts, since 1889 the *Sberbank* has utilized the postal infrastructure, sharing counter space within post office buildings, mainly in remote areas where it is too costly for the bank to maintain its own branches.

The Public's Confidence in Postal Savings

Not only do postal savings systems thrive in many countries, history demonstrates time and again that the use of postal savings systems dramatically increases when the public's distrust of banks rises or when there is an unusual amount of political anxiety or economic insecurity. During the Great Depression of the 1930s, postal savings account deposits in the United States rose to $1.2 billion, a nearly eightfold increase over the $153 million on deposit in 1929 (*In Business*, July 1999). Japan's ongoing banking crisis, which began in the early 1990s, still continues to stimulate increased growth in postal savings deposits. Political and economic uncertainty in Niger and Togo in the 1980s may have been the reason for a dramatic increase in postal savings deposits in those countries. In Niger from 1985 to 1990, there was a 329 percent increase in deposits; similarly in Togo, from 1984 to 1986, a 45 percent increase was experienced (*Postal Statistics*, 1980–97, UPU). Postal savings deposits in the Republic of Korea have jumped since Korea's financial crisis began at the end of 1997. Postal savings officials in China and India reported that fears of economic contagion also influenced their depositors, even though they were not directly affected by the crisis, and deposits jumped as well at Philpostbank, a thrift bank owned by the postal administration, during political unrest in the Philippines (see country case studies that follow).

Depositor confidence in postal savings is directly related to an implicit, if not explicit, guarantee by the government regarding the safety of deposits, which is the primary concern of all savers. In Malaysia the National Savings Bank (NSB), which utilizes the postal infrastructure, prominently displays a sign printed in four languages (Malay, English, Chinese, and Tamil) that states: "Your savings are guaranteed by the Government." Even in the Netherlands, which has fully privatized its postal savings system, survey data show the widespread persistence of the mistaken belief that postal savings are still secured by the government.

In fact, so strong is the postbank's brand name that some banks that had been created out of postal savings systems and that ceased to use postal facilities as service points continued to call themselves "postbanks." In Hungary and other countries that had postbanks in the pre-socialist era, "Postbank" entities continued into the socialist period as commercial banks without a postal savings function. In 1999, Singapore's DBS Bank, a commercial bank that had acquired POSBank and immediately began to shed the POSBank branches, found in public relations surveys that the original POSBank brand name exceeded DBS's own name in familiarity and consumer confidence. In 2001 it reversed its decision to drop the POSBank name (author's interviews).

The security of the postal savings system is generally not hard for the government to guarantee, as the investment of postal savings funds is usually restricted to government-guaranteed or approved bonds and equities. The safety backing their savings encourages depositors to leave their funds in the system. Hence, postal savings institutions typically have a broad base of depositors, many with small accounts, who tend to maintain their accounts on a long-term basis. The cost of servicing a higher percentage of small deposits is offset by the smaller number of withdrawals per account, compared to current accounts at commercial banks.

Depositors tend to have confidence in the postal savings system, even when the system operates under the most rudimentary conditions using simple procedures without special equipment and even when, in some places, the customers may have to wait a long time for service. Critics of postal savings systems point to bureaucratic inefficiencies and/or corruption in national postal services that may be challenged to deliver a letter in a timely fashion. Not surprisingly, however, such countries typically do not have a postal savings system. In those countries where private sector institutions are strong, usually there exists a strong and dedicated public sector as well; in those countries where the public sector is weak, the private sector institutions are typically also weak and inefficient. Indeed, as a case in point, banking industry critics of Japan's postal savings system complain that the postal savings system is too successful.

It must also be kept in mind, moreover, that usually very few, if any, alternatives to postal savings are available for the poorest depositors in developing countries. In most cases, people must resort to burying or hiding their money in unsafe places. In some African countries, such as Benin and Mali, in rural areas, and among the poor, people are accustomed to paying fees to obtain even a low level of security against loss. Savings may be deposited with so-called "money-keepers," unlicensed, informal deposit-takers who charge a fee for holding a client's savings. That people pay the fee indicates the value placed on the safekeeping function ("Role and Impact of Savings in West Africa: A Case Study of Benin and Mali," B. Kalala, UNDP, 2001).

International Giro: Safe and Cost-Effective Remittances

For many developing countries, a significant amount of foreign exchange comes from the remittances of nationals working overseas. Emigrant workers from the Middle East, and North and West Africa are employed in the European Union countries and within Africa itself; workers from South Asian countries are employed in the Persian Gulf states. Similarly, contract workers travel between economies in transition and industrial countries, and between Central America, the Caribbean, and North America, to name just a few of the regional patterns of worker migration.

Overseas remittances are the leading foreign exchange resource of many developing countries. For example, Mexico, Latin America's largest economy, received $13.8 billion in 2003, up from some $10 billion in workers' remittances from the United States in 2002. After petroleum exports, these remittances are Mexico's second-largest earner of foreign exchange, exceeding even tourism. Mexico accounts for some 36 percent of the $38 billion in emigrant workers' remittances sent from the United States to Latin America and the Caribbean in 2003.

For overseas workers, a safe and convenient way to remit income to their families in their home villages is an important concern. Although international money orders via the posts have existed for many years, their use has been limited because the receipt of funds is slow, and not all countries provide this service. On the other hand, the cost of electronic bank transfers, typically between $35 and $45, is extremely high when compared to the modest sums typically being remitted. Extremely disparate remittance fees and currency exchange rates exist for bank transfers to developing countries in comparison to developed countries. In 2002, Sweden's Nordea Bank was found to be charging emigrants from developing countries fees that were twice the rate of remittances to developed countries. The exposure of Nordea's practices in the Stockholm press brought about an immediate reversal of their discriminatory remittance fee policy. As discussed later in this chapter, Nordea Bank figured prominently in the closure of Sweden's postal savings system in 2001. In response to such factors, many migrant workers frequently resort to informal couriers or unregulated funds transfer services that charge lower fees but subject the funds to greater risk.

In some countries the regulatory regime has prevented the posts from providing giro remittance services that compete with banks and private money-transfer firms. Companies like Western Union and Moneygram, the two largest non-bank global operators that offer rapid cash remittances, have agency agreements with many banks, the postal system, and others. Generally the success of these companies derives from their cost-effective use of the postal system's extensive network. For example, a majority of Western Union's more than one hundred thousand worldwide agency locations are post offices. In addition, the recipients are mostly in countries where the posts do not offer reasonably prompt transfer payment options. Nevertheless, despite their use of the postal infrastructure, Western Union's and Moneygram's fees to customers are disproportionately high in relation to the amounts remitted, and an extremely disadvantageous exchange rate may be charged in markets that lack competing services. In those countries that lack alternative remittance services, the result can be $25 to $30 in fees for remittance and exchange of a $100 transfer of funds, typically only $3 to $5 of which goes to the post office (author's interviews; *International Herald Tribune,* 16 August 1999).

Mexico's huge remittance market has not escaped the notice of international banks. A number of them have acquired Mexico's largest banks in hopes of capturing a portion of the nearly $1.1 billion in fees this market generates. Bank of America recently acquired a 24.9 percent stake in the Mexican subsidiary of Spain's Banco Santander, in order to capture its share of fees generated by workers sending remittances from Bank of America's western U.S. branches to Mexico. Other large international banks in the Mexican remittance market are Bancomer, the largest Mexican retail bank, which is owned by Spain's BBVA and allied with California-based Wells Fargo Bank, and Citigroup, which bought Banamex, Mexico's second largest bank in 2001. HSBC of the U.K., which bought Grupo Financiero Bital, plans to use Household Finance International, a consumer credit lender which it also owns with branches throughout the U.S., as its remittance agency (*Financial Times,* 12 December 2002; 17 December 2002; 29 March 2004; *New York Times,* 25 March 2002).

Although it is expected that the use of bank debit cards will reduce fees to 10 percent, a fundamental limitation of Mexico's banks in providing debit card service is that their ATM networks do not extend to the small, impoverished villages where many of the poorest emigrant workers come from. Lack of access to banking facilities is a problem typical throughout the developing world, where bank branches, let alone bank ATMs, are not found outside of major cities.

Peculiarly, Mexico's 9,875 post offices that handle registered mail and postal money orders, by far the institutional network with the largest and broadest coverage in the country, does not service the remittance market. A distant second is the government-owned telegraph agency, Telecomunicaciones de México, with eighteen hundred offices, which until 2002 processed only Western Union's remittances. Getting even a small portion of this remittance market would erase the Mexican postal administration's chronic deficit. More important, it would enable the country's poorest to receive their remittances at reasonable fees. A pilot program of the U.S. Postal Service to provide remittances to Mexico, Dinero Seguro (Safe Money), has been placed instead with Bancomer, with the result that the client is charged a 10 percent commission per transaction.

Postal checking and giro accounts, where they exist, are strikingly popular. They are cheaper for households and small businesses to maintain than commercial bank accounts and provide a secure, affordable way to transfer money. The "informal economy" in many developing and transition-economy countries often relies on giro accounts to make transfers. As evidence of the utility and economy of the giro accounts system, the use of giro accounts extends beyond national borders. West African and North African countries as well as many European countries, Japan, the Republic of Korea, and recently Brazil and China have entered into bilateral giro agreements and utilize the private sector Eurogiro platform for international giro payments. Cross-border payments from European countries into accounts in North Africa, for example, enable overseas workers to make inexpensive and safe remittances to their home countries. To date, however, there is no universal multilateral giro remittance agreement to which all countries may subscribe. For many European countries, the Eurogiro system, a private-sector venture, makes inter-European payments and remittances as easy as domestic giro payments. Recently some North and West African, and Asian countries, including Japan, Republic of Korea, and China, have joined Eurogiro as well. The Eurogiro platform, however, is not multilateral and each member country is still required to conclude separate bilateral agreements to begin service. Furthermore, Eurogiro membership is restricted to countries that allow outbound, as well as inbound remittances, a problem for developing countries that have foreign exchange controls.

The Changing Economics of the Posts: Market Liberalization, Privatization, Cross-Border Entry and Acquisition

In recent decades, public-sector universal postal networks faced the severest threat ever to their existence due to the private sector's desire to provide services formerly handled exclusively by the posts, and due to the concomitant separation of different components of public services from the posts according to their susceptibility to private competition. The legislative process in this regard is not always inevitably toward full market competition. For example, originally scheduled to terminate at the end of 2002, the German Parliament in July 2001 extended Deutsche Post's monopoly of domestic letter delivery for an additional five years, until the end of 2007 (*Financial Times*, 18 July 2001). Private or privatized public operators have come to dominate markets, sometimes through questionable strategies, including predatory pricing, the illegal subsidization of cross-border acquisitions with protected monopoly profits, or other anticompetitive activities, often resulting in a net reduction of postal services and the capacity of the post's network. Most affected are rural and low-income areas where post office closures have resulted in the loss of postal savings and other financial services to communities previously served as well as the loss of postal services.

In a particularly egregious case the European Commission (EC) ruled that the newly privatized Deutsche Post was guilty of abusing its officially sanctioned monopoly in letter mail delivery in Germany to subsidize the losses of its private express parcel-delivery service and to undercut competing delivery providers (*Financial Times,* 21 March 2001). Acting on a complaint by the U.S. parcel delivery service UPS, the European Union Competition Commission's three-year probe criticized Deutsche Post, whose domestic letter rate is among the highest in Europe, for using its protected mail monopoly profits to finance its cross-border acquisitions, which we discuss in a later section, and for deliberately slowing the incoming mail delivery of overseas rival firms (*The Economist,* 18 November 2000). Deutsche Post was required to pay 570 million euros (US$537 million), the largest penalty ever ordered, in restitution to the German government for violation of E.U. state-aid rules and as a warning to postal operators in France and the Netherlands who had been accused of similar offenses (*Financial Times,* 14 June 2002).

In addition, several postal systems themselves have been privatized, in whole or in part—in the Netherlands, New Zealand, Singapore, and in Germany. This shifting of assets from public-sector control to private ownership in these cases appears to have been based upon at least three basic presumptions. First, private ownership is inherently more efficient than public ownership. Second, large sums of money would thereby be raised for state coffers. Third, for many transition and developing economies, privatization would bring development assistance from international lending institutions and favorable consideration for entry into the European Union and its regional associations. The outcome of a number of cases that are relevant to communications and savings sectors are detailed below and in several of the country case studies that follow.

Market Liberalization: New Technologies and Privatization

The market liberalization wave of the last decades of the twentieth century presented serious challenges to postal systems by placing disabling trade restrictions upon the posts in their capacity to respond to new technology. Postal systems had continually faced changes in technology over the past 175 years by putting these developments into service for the posts. Advances in communications arose out of the creation of highways for stagecoaches, the building of railroads, and the advent of the airplane. In each instance the post rapidly incorporated the benefits of an expanding communications infrastructure, granting valuable service contracts to the new transportation operators to reduce costs and enhance mail delivery. In many countries the posts provided direct subsidies or took over early private telephone and telegraph companies that went into bankruptcy, or provided the initial capital to build the telegraph and telephone infrastructure. In many countries the Ministry of Posts became the triad of Posts, Telegraph, and Telephone (PTT), with the expanding telecommunications business the chief source of profits.

At issue today for policymakers, the post, and its customers is the reordering of the regulatory and competitive framework in which telecommunications and other profitable communications technologies operate. Under reprioritized regimes, domestic and foreign private competitors are allowed entry in the market while the post is restricted or eliminated from competing in markets in which it has been a longtime stakeholder. Although in many cases the government through the posts had heavily invested public funds in industries such as national posts and telephone systems, in the market liberalization process the posts lost these important assets without compensation or opportunities for creating new revenues. The effect of liberalization and privatization trends in market structure has been to undermine the foundation of universal service. Once-viable postal institutions are being threatened with extinction while new, highly competitive private operators have been allowed to capture the most profitable segments of the postal communications network that employs new technologies, most notably parts of the telecommunications sector and express parcel delivery.

Today in most countries the telecommunications branch of the posts has been detached and subsequently privatized. Government privatization of telecoms, frequently cited as a model for privatizing the posts, started in the 1980s and gained strength in the 1990s, particularly after the 1997 WTO Telecommunications Agreement and the 1998 European Union Agreement on cross-border telecom acquisitions and market liberalization. Initial expectations for these policies have been shattered. The basic services, that is, telephone, mobile phone, and so forth, are profitable. Telecom stock prices collapsed in 2002, however, due to aggressive expansion in cross-border acquisitions and unrealistic bidding for new generation mobile telephone technology licenses by the privatized telecoms, which in turn took on massive debt to finance their speculative adventures. Deutsche Telecom posted the largest loss in Europe's history, 24.6 billion euros ($27.1 billion) in 2002. France Telecom had a 9-billion-euro loss ($9.3 billion). Government guarantees on debt refinancing were implemented in 2002 after a 20.7-billion-euro loss ($23 billion), the largest corporate loss in France's history. France Telecom stood with $70 billion in debt and a share price loss of 90 percent off its peak in 2000. Similarly, collapses in the share prices of the Dutch KPN, Finland's Sonera, Spain's Telefonica, and others telecoms, which have burnt pension fund buyers and other investors, have made consideration of further share offerings unrealistic. Likewise, as mentioned earlier, in the case of Deutsche Post AG, its unprofitable acquisition program and subsequent share price loss have made the German government's sale of its remaining 69 percent stake particularly unrewarding at this time.

The loss of departed telecom revenues by the postal administrations in Kazakhstan, the Republic of Korea, Thailand, Vietnam, and other Asian countries in this study has been the main reason for their seeking to create a new profit center in postal financial services (author's interviews).

The market liberalization and privatization policies adopted by many developed countries, especially in the European Union, have also been made requirements of the development assistance programs of the multilateral banks. Privatization conditionalities are attached to some three-quarters of the World Bank's loans or credits (*World Economic and Social Survey,* United Nations, 2002). In particular, the World Bank's prescription for privatizing public services includes the privatization of telecommunications, water supply utilities and sanitation, and electricity (World Bank *Annual Report,* 2000). Similar programs also exist for the privatization of postal services and postal savings systems. The World Bank's Private Sector Development Department addresses postal sector reform in *Redirecting the Mail* (K. Ranganathan, 1996). It is worth noting that no less an advocate of privatization of public services than Adam Smith praises the post office as both a necessary and successfully managed government-run mercantile project in his classic treatise, *The Wealth of Nations.*

Later in this section and below we will take a closer look at several case studies of countries whose posts have experienced the consequences of market liberalization and privatization, the issues upon which the World Bank's initiatives have focused. The antipathy of the World Bank and other international lending institutions to postal savings begins with their core belief that private-sector financial institutions are sufficiently equipped and motivated to meet the savings needs of the public and hence that publicly owned financial institutions, such as postal savings, compete needlessly with the private sector. The reality of and logic behind these suppositions are also discussed below and in the following chapters within the context of the case studies on privatization, commercial bank strategies, and financial exclusion.

In recent years in several CIS republics, postbanks have been created as private entities. For example, in Uzbekistan the Aloqabank competes with the People's Bank, a public sector savings institution that has efficiently utilized post office facilities for many decades. Aloqa, a commercial bank owned by several former state-owned communications enterprises, had hoped to qualify for loans from the European Bank for Reconstruction and Development (EBRD), whose policies prohibit it from lending to the public sector, as well as loans from other international lending institutions, such as the World Bank. This strategy of establishing a private bank to qualify for loans from official international financial institutions that lend to the private sector has been advocated by private sector consultancies to transitional economies. It has raised concerns on the part of the finance ministries in these countries about the potential for abuse in bank lending practices. In China, another example, the creation of a credit-granting postbank was put on hold after objections were raised to China Post being allowed to create its own "money-pot" (author's interviews).

The Charge of "Cross-Subsidization" as a Threat to Public Savings Institutions

The charge of cross-subsidization—using profits on one market or line of business activity to cover losses in another market or business activity—has become the main complaint of private financial institutions that are seeking to capture the markets served by public institutions. This is perhaps most clearly illustrated in a number of legal actions brought against German public sector financial institutions at the European Commission. Germany has a well-developed network of 564 *Sparkassen* (municipal savings banks). (The *Sparkassen* system originated in the early nineteenth century and thus predates the founding of the German state.) With a 55 percent savings market share and a highly loyal depositor base of 36 million clients, the *Sparkassen*'s S logo is recognized by 98 percent of the German population, second only to the crucifix, according to market researchers. Postal savings, in contrast, was not introduced until Germany's takeover of Austria during the Nazi period when Austria's *Postsparkasse* was incorporated into the German postal system. Deutsche Postbank, now a commercial bank, was thus a relative latecomer owing to the strong incumbent position of the *Sparkassen* (author's interviews; *Euromoney*, March 2001).

The *Sparkassen* network for small-scale savers feeds funds into the twelve State-owned *Landesbanks* (regionally-based development and wholesale credit banks). Challenges to the continued existence of the *Landesbanks* have come before the European Commission premised on the *Landesbanks'* having lower-cost funding than private sector banks. The complaint, first lodged by the European Banking Federation (a private-sector lobbying group), attacks both the *Landesbanks'* public ownership status (*Anstaltslast*) and the State's supporting guarantee (*Gewährträgerhaftung*) to supply additional capital against any unmet obligations of the *Landesbanks*. In fact, these recapitalization guarantees are formally no different than those requiring shareholders of private banks to meet their bank's minimum capital requirements. The difference is that a private shareholder may be unable or unwilling to do so, so that the bank goes bankrupt. On the other hand, the "too big to fail" policy provides an implicit government guarantee for large private banks that the government will serve as the "lender of last resort." The complaint claims that the *Landesbanks* and the *Sparkassen* are able to function at lower costs than Germany's private sector commercial banks; they have traditionally been the most profitable banks in Germany, reporting returns of 18 to 20 percent in the mid-1990s.

The complaint was widely seen as part of the strategy of Germany's commercial banks to force privatization by changing the legal structures of the *Landesbanks* and *Sparkassen* to joint-stock companies, allowing them to be bought and sold and then taken over by commercial banks. The demutualization of savings institutions had already destroyed thrift banking in Italy and the United Kingdom. Even though the *Sparkassen* are not involved in cross-border activities—67 percent of their balance sheets are retail deposits (which is the actual source of their funding advantage), and their lending is primarily to local small- and medium-sized enterprises—the EC agreed to consider the case that the recapitalization guarantees by the State governments to the *Landesbanks* and the *Sparkassen* represented a "cross-subsidization" that might disadvantage foreign entrants into Germany's retail banking market. The German Federal government, for its part, has agreed to phase out State guarantees for the *Landesbanks* by 2005 (*Euromoney,* March 2001; *Financial Times,* 17 July 2001, 12 June 2002, 3 January 2003). On the other hand, the government-owned development bank Kreditanstalt fur Wiederaufbau (KfW) is the proposed lead vehicle for the sale of KfW-backed, triple-A-rated bonds that will pool the loans of troubled private commercial banks, offloading up to 50 billion euros (US$55 billion) in commercial bank loans by securitizing them as collateral for the KfW bonds. The purpose of the tax-free transfers to KfW is to enable Germany's five largest commercial banks to free up capital by taking the loans off their balance sheets, thus providing private commercial banks the type of subsidized, government-backed capital guarantees that are now denied the *Landesbanks* (*Financial Times,* 23 April 2003).

The cross-subsidization issue has been a recurring theme in other countries in which private financial institutions have sought to take over the market of publicly owned savings institutions. In particular, Japan's commercial banking sector has for the past decade repeatedly called for the breakup and privatization of the postal savings system, also charging "cross-subsidization." Meanwhile, it may be noted, some ¥8.4 trillion (US$80 billion) in public funds has been injected into the recapitalization of sixteen major commercial banks and eleven regional banks, mostly in March 1999, and the Bank of Japan has lost the credits it extended in its fruitless attempts to stave off the bankruptcies of Long-Term Credit Bank, Nippon Credit Bank, Hokkaido Takushoku Bank, and a host of regional banks. We will discuss this question in more detail in the cases in the section, "Transition Economies and Privatization: Bailouts at Public Expense," and further on in the section in chapter 3, "Are Postal Savings in Competition with Commercial Banks?"

The implication of the "cross-subsidization" charge for the future of postal financial services and similar government-sponsored national savings, insurance, and pension programs is that if it succeeds in Germany and Japan, it may provide a means in other countries as well for cross-border and domestic private capture of postal savings' markets. However, both the German *Landesbanks* and *Sparkassen* and the Japanese postal savings system enjoy a large amount of regional and local political support. In the face of difficult economic times, the German government is also looking to these State-owned institutions to help fund small- and medium-size companies (*Financial Times*, 1 November 2001). In addition, the Japanese postal savings agency purchases a large part of government bond and public agency issues, an important consideration for Japanese policymakers. Both Germany and Japan are bank-centered financing regimes, so their governments' policy responses to the "cross-subsidization" issue are of some interest to many developing countries where bank intermediation is also the chief source of corporate finance, particularly for small- and medium-size firms. In the next chapter, we discuss the intermediation and investment of mobilized savings within the context of Asian developing countries.

Cross-Border Entry: The Express Package Delivery Wars

The policy of the European Union to create a single internal market has allowed cross-border entry into services that were once a national postal monopoly. A number of EU regional association agreements, such as the European Union Mediterranean Partnership Agreement (the European Commission MEDA II Program, November 2000), as well as EU technical assistance programs such as Phare (Eastern Europe) and Tacis (CIS and Mongolia) are also aimed at market-opening policies in preaccession and other non-member countries. This has led to the unfettered entry into various national markets of express package-delivery companies, including some owned by the major privatized postal operators. Germany's privatized national postal operator, Deutsche Post, spent $8.6 billion acquiring DHL and thirty other express delivery and logistics firms and financial institutions. The French and Italian state-owned postal operators jointly formed Geopost, a parcel delivery company that is now competing with the document and parcel delivery firms owned by the privatized postal operators of Germany and the Netherlands, namely DHL and TNT, as well as with independent operators such as Federal Express and United Parcel Service (UPS), which have sought to exclude competitors from their own U.S. home market. After UPS's takeover of Mail Boxes Etc, Inc., independent store franchise owners are being forced to rebrand as UPS and exclude Federal Express from their service locations.

Each operator has been aggressively challenging the others as well as the Express Mail Service (EMS) courier service of postal operators in targeted countries. While severely destabilizing the financial underpinnings of domestic postal operators in the markets they have entered, these new "international logistics operations" have so far proven to be rather unprofitable investments, not even meeting the cost of capital. For example, despite accounting for 42 percent of revenues, express and logistics services contributed only 7 percent to Deutsche Post's profits, a distant third compared to its domestic mail monopoly, which contributed 34.5 percent of revenues and 74.3 percent of profits, and the postal financial services franchise, which contributes 23.5 percent of revenues and 18.7 percent of profits (Deutsche Post *Annual Report,* 2000; *Financial Times,* 20 November 2000).

The strategy of these new entrants is to "cherry-pick" the market, that is, target the most profitable market segments. In some cases, governments do not accept this. For example, Deutsche Post withdrew from bidding for a stake in Hellenic Post after the Greek government attached a condition that the German group would be required to deliver packages anywhere in Greece (*Financial Times,* 26 June 2001). In other countries, newcomers have been allowed to skim profits from urban markets while leaving unprofitable areas to the nation's postal service. In those countries the post must compete with well-capitalized private operators in the urban, higher-volume commercial areas while also fulfilling its mandate to provide delivery services to widely dispersed, low-volume and therefore unprofitable regions. One consequence has been a drastic reduction in the scope of the post's network in a number of countries owing to cost reduction measures.

The loss of the posts' telecommunications and express mail delivery services in commercial urban areas that was seen in Europe has been repeated in developing countries as well, where the challenge posed has been greater. For developing countries, non-letter revenues are crucial to maintaining the fiscal viability of their postal network since mail volume is generally quite low, especially outside large urban, commercial areas. For example, while the average annual mail volume in the European Union is 275 letters per capita and in the United States 734, among the developing countries it typically ranges between five to ten letters per capita per year, and less in the least developed countries (Universal Postal Union, *Postal Statistics* [Bern, 2000]). It is estimated that 91 percent of the cost of postal operations is expended in the logistics of sorting, moving, and delivering letters and parcels (J. Lohmeyer, World Bank, 2001). The economic difficulties of postal administrations are often further compounded by politically mandated low postal rates. It is therefore no surprise that letter delivery, the core business of the posts, generates losses and often requires revenues from the post's other activities in order to maintain its network. One solution for them is to create and/or expand the role of postal financial services as new centers of profit.

Financial Services through the Postal Infrastructure

Current Situation

In order to develop a picture of the extent and character of postal savings operations around the world, the United Nations Department of Economic and Social Affairs undertook a survey in 1999 of postal savings authorities. Fifty of the countries on which data was collected had postal savings facilities, as listed in Table 2.1: Data from United Nations DESA Postal Savings for Development Survey. Based on other information, it is believed that an additional 27 countries and territories currently have postal savings systems (see notes to table). In addition, 33 of the 64 countries that responded to the survey had postal checking or giro payments operations.

The list of countries in Table 2.1 indicates widespread usage of the postal savings system in a variety of countries, both developed and developing. A number of Asian countries are particularly highly ranked in the number of accounts per capita, which reflects the high rate of individual savings found in many Asian countries but also the effectiveness of the systems in those countries, which we discuss later in chapter 3. Two Asian transition economies, Kazakhstan and Vietnam, had just begun their postal savings operations at the time of the survey in August 1999. Most striking, however, is the absence of the postal savings systems in certain developed countries that only a decade earlier had headed the list. In particular, Norway and New Zealand, which after a 13-year break, resumed postal savings in 2002. In addition, since the data were compiled, Finland and Sweden ceased postal savings; the reasons for their closing are addressed below in the discussion of privatization and the loss of postal savings services.

Governance Structures of the Posts

Generally, postal systems are operated under one of three governance structures: first, a traditional model centered on a department of government; second, corporatization of the posts to a business model operating under public

Table 2.1

Data from the United Nations DESA Postal Savings for Development Survey

Country	Year	Number of Savings Accounts	Number of Accounts in Country per Person
Japan	1998	113,690,000	0.899
Korea, Republic of	1999	18,164,000	0.822
Sri Lanka *	2000	9,007,530	0.476
Greece	1998	4,500,000	0.426
Slovenia	2000	160,000	0.358
France	1997	20,000,000	0.341
Austria	1998	2,300,000	0.284
Italy	1998	15,000,000	0.261
Sweden	1999	2,226,000	0.252
Germany	1998	19,670,000	0.240
Tunisia	1998	1,871,500	0.202
Mauritius	1999	210,296	0.183
Gabon	1998	159,884	0.137
India	1999	116,000,000	0.117
Egypt	1999	7,500,000	0.112
Trinidad and Tobago	1999	143,000	0.111
Finland	1998	2,392,913	0.097
China	1999	104,000,000	0.082
Czech Republic	1999	830,000	0.081
Bahamas	1993	17,178	0.063
Aruba	1999	6,028	0.062
Benin	1999	330,000	0.054
Côte d'Ivoire	1998	708,000	0.046
South Africa	1999	1,700,000	0.040
Syrian Arab Republic	1999	565,550	0.036
Morocco	1998	1,029,905	0.036
Belgium	1998	310,639	0.030
United Republic of Tanzania	2000	1,003,224	0.029
Burkina Faso	2000	323,924	0.028
Croatia	1999	126,502	0.027
Central African Republic	1997	68,099	0.019
Comoros	1998	12,629	0.019
Niger	1992	115,000	0.014
Macao, China	1998	500	0.011
Jordan	2000	54,000	0.011
Mauritania	1999	22,300	0.009
Pakistan	1999	1,000,000	0.007
Vietnam	1999	204,816	0.003
Yemen Republic	1998	53,721	0.003
Mongolia	2000	6,000	0.002
Sierra Leone	1999	6,700	0.002
Iran, Islamic Republic of	1999	71,380	0.001
Congo, Democratic Republic	1997	17,402	0.000
Kyrgyzstan	2000	1,280	0.000

(continued)

Table 2.1 *(continued)*

Country	Year	Number of Savings Accounts	Number of Accounts in Country per Person
Kazakhstan	1999	482	0.000
Bangladesh	NA	NA	NA
Malawi	NA	NA	NA
Hungary	NA	NA	NA
Slovakia	NA	NA	NA

Source: Mark J. Scher, "Postal savings and the provision of financial services: policy issues and Asian experiences in the use of the postal infrastructure for savings mobilization," DESA Discussion Paper No. 22 (December 2001), United Nations Department of Economic and Social Affairs, p. 9.

Notes: Questionnaires were sent to the ministries and postal administrations of approximately 80 countries on August 4, 1999 and were further distributed by Mark J. Scher at the Universal Postal Union Congress in Beijing in late August–September 1999, and with the further assistance of the Congress Secretariat to all the attendees. As of April 2001, information has been collected directly from 64 countries, either as survey responses or as parts of reports contributed as case studies. A significant problem affecting data collection is that many privatized postbanks and national savings banks that utilize the postal infrastructure do not report statistical information to the postal authorities, which supply information to the UPU for its statistical publications. In addition, in some countries the postal savings bank also had stand-alone facilities, whose accounts were not disaggregated from the accounts mainly transacted at the postal branch offices. Moreover, in some countries many of the reported accounts were dormant. Thus, data on postal savings as reported in this table and as published by the UPU should be used with caution.

*Denotes national savings bank, which also utilizes the postal infrastructure.

Postal savings operations are believed to currently exist in the following countries and territories, which did not supply DESA with information: Algeria, Brazil, Cameroon, Cape Verde, Iraq, Ireland, Israel, Kenya, Democratic People's Republic of Korea, Libyan Arab Jamahiriya, Madagascar,* Malaysia, Mali, Namibia, Nepal, Netherlands, Norway, Portugal, Samoa, Senegal, Sudan, Taiwan Province of China, the Former Yugoslav Republic of Macedonia,* Togo, United Kingdom, Yugoslavia, and Zimbabwe (*denotes national savings bank that also utilizes the postal infrastructure and has additional stand-alone facilities).

The following countries' postal savings systems are privatized: Aruba, Austria, Belgium, Cape Verde, Côte d'Ivoire, Czech Republic, Germany, Hungary, Kyrgyzstan, Netherlands, Norway, Slovakia, and Trinidad and Tobago.

The following countries provide postal counter facilities under agency agreements with private sector banks: Australia, Denmark, Indonesia.

The following countries had postal savings that were subsequently suspended or abolished: Bosnia, Bulgaria, Canada, Chad, Finland, Guyana, Mozambique, New Zealand (resumed in 2002), Nigeria, Romania, Singapore, Sweden, United States of America.

The following countries reported to DESA their having postal giro and/or postal checking services: Austria, Belgium, Burkina Faso, Central African Republic, Chad, China, Côte d'Ivoire, Croatia, Czech Republic, Democratic Republic of Congo, Denmark, Dominican Republic, Egypt, Finland, France, Germany, Indonesia, Italy, Japan, Republic of Korea, Latvia, Mauritania, Morocco, Mongolia, Niger, Pakistan, Slovakia, Slovenia, Spain, Sweden, Syrian Arab Republic, and Tunisia.

In addition, the following countries, which did not respond, are also believed to have postal giro systems: Algeria, Benin, Burundi, Cameroon, Gabon, Iceland, Israel, Liechtenstein, Luxembourg, Madagascar, Malta, Netherlands, Norway, Poland, Rwanda, Senegal, South Africa, Switzerland, the Former Yugoslav Republic of Macedonia, Togo, Turkey, United Kingdom.

ownership; or third, a fully privatized postal operator. With liberalization as a general economic strategy, many countries have moved from a traditional model to a government-owned corporation, and several to privatized systems. Europe has had the most occurrences of privatization of postal operations, with both the Netherlands' and Germany's systems having been privatized. Netherlands Post is 50 percent owned by ING Barings Bank and is also the owner of the Postbank. In the case of Germany, 69 percent of Deutsche Post AG is still held by the government, another 10 percent by KfW, the government-owned development bank but operates as a privatized entity. The remaining 21 percent of DPAG shares are traded in the market and are mostly in pension fund portfolios. Additional government-owned shares are slated to be sold in the market using KfW as an interim holding vehicle.

The Traditional Model of Postal Governance

Here the posts are run by a department of the government under a ministry of communications or similar government body. It operates within a budget determined by the government, and all revenues from its operations are returned to the treasury. Under this regime the postal administrator's managerial imperative is to operate within the budget, although competing budget priorities in developing countries seldom result in the posts being adequately funded. Typically, income derived from postal savings or postal financial services as well as from all other services is reported on the basis of gross revenues collected, most often without any analysis of actual transaction costs to determine net profits, or more likely in the case of most mail delivery operations, net losses. Furthermore, with government-mandated postal rates often set below actual costs, the government and the post's fiscal problems are compounded. Clearly this governance structure provides no incentive to progress beyond the predetermined targets set by the government.

The Corporatized Model of Postal Governance

The need to rationalize operating costs under a traditional mode of operation has motivated many governments to corporatize their postal system. Such postal systems are no longer departments within the government but are government-owned companies. Such entities are responsible for the profits and losses of their own operations and, like private corporations, must maintain overall profitability or at least not run at a loss. This governance regime contains incentives to raise the efficiency of postal operations. Being government-owned and thus supervised by a board of official appointees, such entities could also continue to be directed to fulfill public policy objectives. In addition, there are strong incentives for management under this model to try to add new profit-making services to its operations and to create more efficiency in all areas of operations.

In such an environment, management is compelled to analyze the cost of providing different services and the fees needed to cover costs. Rates are still likely to be set by policy and will perhaps not cover all costs for all services. This means earnings from more profitable services would "cross-subsidize" the deficits of others. Private sector financial institutions, for example, when engaging in similar unprofitable practices typically refer to them as "cross-selling opportunities." The deregulation of financial markets in recent years has led the banking and insurance sectors, along with others, to market each other's services and products or to acquire and merge operations. The cross-selling of each other's products has yielded little or no profit in many cases but is seen as essential to retain clients and sustain their respective institution's market share (author's interviews).

In postal operations, overall subsidies are not necessarily anticompetitive practices but rather may serve otherwise unmet public needs. Without denying that inappropriate policies have been applied in some cases, subsidies remain legitimate instrumentalities by which government mandates to the postal administration to provide services at "socially determined" prices may be carried out in the interests of national policy. Subsidized postal rates for books, newspapers, and the like generally reflect a policy to promote a democratic civil culture, and other subsidies are similarly intended to promote other public welfare objectives. What is essential is that postal management has a clear analysis of transaction costs and is able to articulate the nature and extent of such underwriting so that the domestic political process can better assess the cost within the context of its social benefit.

The Privatized Postal Model

The most complete break with the traditional model of operation is the fully privatized postal operator. In this case the government gives up direct oversight of management of the postal system and the role of the state is limited to that of a regulatory authority over a private operator. Supervision is usually by a governmental agency or commission. The postal operator is required to conform to government standards and practices so as not to conflict with the public good and to fulfill its mandate as a regulated public utility. Placing national postal systems in the hands of privatized postal operators in the 1990s was a relatively new occurrence in modern times, although its historical antecedents date back to the feudal days of Thurn und Taxis and the Holy Roman Empire. (The Counts of Thurn und Taxis held the hereditary postal franchise from 1460 to 1867 for the Holy Roman Empire and its successor German States.) The current privatization phenomenon has largely occurred within the framework of market liberalization of public services.

Postal Systems and "Postbanks": Creation, Separation, Privatization, and Synergies of Reintegration

Postbank Creation and Separation from the Post

It is not unusual for postal savings operations to be restricted in the range of financial services they may offer. They are often denied licenses for issuing consumer credit and small business and agricultural loans by the financial regulatory authorities, and, as a practical matter, often lack the institutional capacity to undertake the intermediation and investment of mobilized funds on a large scale. This combination of factors has led to the creation of an entity known as the "postbank."

Postbanks have existed in Europe, originally as state-owned institutions, since the early part of the twentieth century. Postal savings banks frequently provided services for the small-scale consumer, agricultural credits, and housing mortgage facilities (the primary reason for their conversion to postbanks was to provide for a greater range of investment options beyond small-scale retail loans and the purchase of government securities). Postbank proponents were especially interested in providing large-scale commercial credits.

In the UN-DESA Postal Savings for Development Survey, 80 percent of the developed countries reported offering credit facilities to their clients while only 20 percent of the developing countries' postal savings systems reported this function. The British postal savings model, unlike its continental European counterparts, did not offer credit facilities to its clients. This historical circumstance may explain why the credit function is seldom found in the postal savings systems of former British colonies. In the following chapter the importance of credit services, especially in rural areas, and its link to savings mobilization in developing countries, will be discussed.

Fully licensed postbanks are regulated by the ministry of finance or the central bank or a similar government agency and operate through use of the postal infrastructure, especially for deposit collection and withdrawal, although they may also have freestanding branches. The more commercially oriented operation of the postbanks in developed countries in recent decades has exhibited two tendencies that should be of concern to developing economies. First is the demise of postal savings functions and the loss of this method for mobilizing funds for developmental purposes when postbanks adopt commercial banking strategies. Second is the fiscal weakening of the postal network's infrastructure, which provides a wide range of civil and social services besides mail services, including postal financial services.

It will be seen in the cases that follow that once ownership of the postbank is separated from the posts, the goals of the postbank's management come into significant conflict with those of the post. An important issue is thus whether the posts should retain an ownership stake in the postbank irrespective of whether the postal system itself is government-owned or under private ownership. Holding an ownership interest provides the posts with the means to resolve what could otherwise be a difficult problem of loss of incentive to promote savings. Otherwise, after the postbank is separated from the post's ownership, the mutually sustaining synergy between the posts and postal savings typically disappears.

Loss of Postal Network and Savings Services after Privatization

Although postbanks were wholly owned by the postal system when first organized, many were subsequently privatized. Governments all too often have sought to maximize their immediate gains from the sale of a postbank at the expense of long-term benefits to postal savings operations and the posts. For example, before the auction sale of the Austrian postal savings bank to BAWAG Bank in 2000, Austria Post sought to purchase a 25 percent ownership stake. The government rejected the request on the basis that it would dilute the ultimate purchase price of the *Postsparkasse* to potential private buyers (*Der Standard*, 5 May 2001).

An increasing volume of evidence in European cases attests to the losses of synergy that result when the government sells the postbank to private sector banks. As will be seen in the cases below, in a common scenario the privatized postbank begins by using the postal service as its agent. It also often inherits having to pay only a nominal transaction fee for its use of post office services and infrastructure, well below what it might be charged for similar transactions as an unrelated private financial institution. When the postal system owned the postbank, earnings from its ownership stake offset the low transaction fee. With privatization, the post's revenues from financial services are reduced to these nominal fees alone without the benefit of dividends from postbank shares. As a result, overall postal revenues decline to such low levels that many marginalized post office locations are shut down. At the end of this scenario, the private takeover of the postbank has compelled a series of negative consequences, including the closing of many post offices that previously provided both mail and postal financial services to local communities. Isolated communities and low-income areas that are not typically included in a private bank's marketing strategy are especially hard hit.

Commercial Bank Strategies Replace Savings Linked to Development

The scenario described above was most clearly played out in the Scandinavian countries, which were early movers toward the separation of financial services from ownership by the postal system. Their subsequent experiences with privatization led to the eventual elimination of postal savings and other postal services. For example, the Finnish Postal Savings Bank (PSP) was founded in 1887. The PSP first invested in state bonds and in the 1920s and 1930s increasingly channeled loans into the Cooperative Credit Societies for agricultural credits under terms negotiated by the Ministry of Finance. In 1939 the PSP's ownership was separated from the Department of Posts and Telecommunications, but the PSP continued its development bank functions, funding state-owned hydroelectric power and electrification plants and providing credits to forestry and wood-processing industries and housing before turning to industrial credits in the 1950s.

As of 1987, 90 percent of the cashier transactions of Postipankki (Postbank), the former PSP, took place in Finland's 3,200 post offices (*Postipankki: The First 100 Years*, 1987). Postipankki, however, was also increasing its independent branch network. In 1987, in addition to the many post offices, it had 50 branch offices in 33 cities and towns, 13 of them in the Helsinki area alone. Following Finland's commercial banking crisis in the early 1990s, Postipankki rapidly increased its stand-alone branches by acquiring failing private banks in the high-volume commercial areas of Finland's larger cities. With its new base of urban commercial clients, Postipankki adopted a new corporate strategy that deemphasized the postal network clients. It negotiated a reduction of its annual franchise fee to the posts and at the same time expanded its independent branch network, which by 1999 stood at 83 retail branches, 55 commercial branches, and 18 devoted to private banking clients. This in turn led to a hastening downward spiral of loss of revenues to the posts, which forced the closing of 65 percent of Finland's post offices between 1990 and 1995, following the first large-scale negotiated fee reduction in 1990. The number of postal branches that handled savings fell from 2,700 to 927. Following a second large-scale fee reduction in 1995, the total number of postal savings points was further reduced to 477 by 1998, which also marked a dramatic loss in the availability of all postal services in rural regions and among lower-income populations. Not surprisingly, the reduction in the number of post office branches was accompanied by a drop in the number of savings accounts; from between 3.2 and 3.4 million accounts at the end of each year in the first half of the 1980s, the number of accounts fell to an average of 2.5 million in 1994–98. At the same time, the average size of accounts rose from 2,673 markkas (Fmk) to over Fmk14,250 in these two periods, indicating that the composition of the clientele had become more heavily weighted toward higher-income people, suggesting that Postipankki was following a strategy to shed its least profitable clients by its closing down post office–based savings accounts, upon which rural and lower-income populations were largely dependent for financial services.

Following these reductions in the postal network, Postipankki was renamed Leonia Bank (April 1998) and became fully commercialized. At the outset of privatization negotiations, Leonia Bank demanded further reductions in its annual fee payments to the posts, citing the decreasing utility of the postal infrastructure to its corporate strategy. Leonia Bank asserted that the volume of financial services at the least busy post offices (i.e., in rural areas) had declined, owing to "the increased use of ATMs, bank cards, the telephone services, online banking" (Leonia Bank *Annual Report,* 1998).

Claims relating to the use of home Internet and telephone banking services in place of postal counter services in Finland and other countries invite further scrutiny. Although Internet usage in Finland is 50.7 percent (2004), a wide gap exists between electronic banking usage by younger and more affluent clients and elderly pensioners to low-income populations that do not have access to personal computers. In Deutsche Postbank's case, three-quarters of all bank transactions are still handled at postal counters, even though it has a highly regarded Internet-banking website and also offers telephone banking for its wide range of brokerage, funds management, currency, and derivatives trading services for its commercial and retail clients.

Later in this section we will discuss in more detail the issues of financial exclusion and the "unbanked" in the United Kingdom and see how personal Internet banking has not provided a solution. Although Internet usage is relatively high in developed countries (especially in Scandinavia), in sub-Saharan Africa, for example, less than 1 percent of the population (2004) has Internet access, with relatively advanced South Africa accounting for .41 percent of this usage. In the next chapter the use of financial technology based on telecommunications within the context of developing countries will be discussed.

Such claims notwithstanding, Finland Post reported that 50 percent of post office staff activities were still being conducted on behalf of Leonia Bank (*Helsingin Sonomat,* 28 October 1999). When fully privatized and part of the Sampo Insurance Group, Leonia Bank ultimately refused to renew its agreement with the posts. By the end of December 2000, Finland, which once had among the highest per capita usage of postal savings in the world, was completely without a postal savings system and in many areas without post offices as well (Finland Post Ltd. *Annual Reports,* 1999, 2000; *Postal Statistics,* UPU; *Financial Times,* 10 July 2000).

In Sweden, another early convert to privatization of postal banking, similar reductions in postal banking services have been reported. After a ninety-year history of providing both savings and loan services, the Swedish Postal Savings Bank was separated by the government from the post's ownership in 1974 and merged with the Swedish Kreditbanken to form the government-owned Post and Kreditbanken (PK Banken). In the aftermath of the Swedish banking crisis in 1994, the Swedish cabinet attempted to rescue the failing private Nordbanken by merging it with PK Banken. Since then Nordbanken has undergone repeated mergers and several changes of ownership, first merging with the Finnish private bank Merita. Merita-Nordbanken then became part of Baltic Holding Ltd., now called the Nordea Group, a pan-Scandinavian international financial consortium. From the privatization through the Nordbanken takeover in 1994 to June 1999, 85 percent of Sweden's 14.8 million postal savings accounts were closed (UN-DESA Postal Savings for Development Survey; *Postal Statistics,* UPU), the bank having changed its corporate strategy to market its services to a wealthier clientele, in effect abandoning the nation's postal savings franchise. The result of all these mergers was a decline in post office revenues from financial services, a leading factor in the closing of over 1,000 post offices in Sweden between 1989 and 1998. Seven hundred fifty post offices were replaced by partial postal service operations at gas station and shop counter locations. Thus all postal services were drastically reduced. Postal savings were terminated in April 2001 (author's interview; Sweden Post AB *Annual Reports,* 1996–2000; Merita-Nordbanken *Annual Report,* 1998; Nordic Baltic Holdings *Annual Report,* 1999).

At issue in the cases of Finland and Sweden are the changing character and priorities of the postbank institution. Its initial mission was as a public sector institution providing financial services to the whole population, including rural, disadvantaged, and small savers, local commerce, and small enterprises, and providing the intermediation of savings for development. As a private commercial bank, its purpose changed to the maximization of private shareholder value, and its investment strategy changed to the wholesale intermediation of funds. In 1999 the Finnish Bankers Association (FBA), headed by the president of Merita Bank (Merita-Nordbanken Group), sought state subsidies for servicing lower-income clients. The chairman of OKOBank, a major cooperative savings bank group, in opposition to the FBA, declared "that his banks' doors will remain open to all, without recourse to state subsidies" (*Helsingin Sonomat,* 4 November 1999). Indeed, these differences in objectives and outcomes between public and private sectors are a matter for policymakers to consider when privatization is contemplated, which is not to say that banks have no interest in the utility of the postal infrastructure. For example, in 2001, OKOBank sought unsuccessfully to acquire the Finnish postal system. Banks-as-posts and posts-as-banks are interesting propositions since postal financial services are a valuable revenue source and a fiscal mainstay for many postal administrations. Later in this chapter we discuss private sector interest in finding opportunities in postal financial services.

Tackling the Problem of Financial Exclusion

The loss of access to financial services for low-income and rural populations has been a matter of great concern in the United Kingdom, where the postal savings concept first originated. Founded in 1861 as the Post Office Savings Bank, its chief purposes were to give people a convenient, government-secured way to save, and to provide the government with a source of funds for borrowing, including the sale of savings certificates and government bonds. In 1969 ownership of postal savings operations was separated from the posts, renamed National Savings, and transferred to the treasury, with the post office subsequently playing an agency role. The National Savings system then fell rapidly into disuse and, although 20.4 million accounts still exist, many of them have been long dormant with only nominal amounts on deposit. The sharp decline in use has largely been due to cumbersome, outmoded account posting procedures that require the account owner to send his passbook along with the deposit or withdrawal request to the National Savings Agency postal counter service. Otherwise, withdrawals are limited to £50. In many developed and developing countries, passbook savings have been superseded by statement savings accounts. In the U.K. in 2004 National Savings announced the ending of Ordinary Deposit Accounts, replacing passbook use as of August 2004 with the new Easy Access Savings Accounts that is based on cash cards, telephone withdrawals, and mailed quarterly statements. The use of outmoded procedures such as passbook savings are a problem in many developing countries and are addressed in the next chapter and in the country case studies.

Among other postal financial services, in 1990 the U.K. postal giro system was sold to a private institution, Alliance & Leicester, although it too continues its services through the posts. In 1986 the Post Office had been reorganized into three separate businesses: Royal Mail Letters, Parcelforce, and Post Office Counters, all under a state-owned Post Office group (briefly known as Consignia). In June 1994 the Conservative government published a green paper calling for the Post Office's privatization. Excluding the giro system and non-giro bill payments, such as taxes and so forth, the remaining main activity of postal financial services in the United Kingdom is the disbursement of pensions and benefits. Some £50 billion a year is delivered in cash to post offices to be disbursed monthly to 15 million recipients. Some 61 percent of the post's income is derived from providing financial services, primarily pension and benefits payments, but also bill payments, banking, and national savings, while the mails account for only 23 percent of revenues (Post Office Report and Accounts, 1998/1999).

Who You Are and Where You Are: The Unbanked in the United Kingdom

Banks in the United Kingdom have reduced their branches over the past decade from 17,000 to just over 12,000 in 2000, with more closures expected, leaving many small towns without financial services. The British Financial Services Authority (FSA) has reviewed the social impact of these changes and found that over 20 percent of the adult population lacks current accounts, and upward of 37 percent of households do not own savings accounts or investment products. Despite obvious safety and security concerns, these funds largely remained in the cash economy. In addition to belonging to low-income populations and members of some minority ethnic groups, the likelihood of households being excluded was also higher in Scotland, Wales, and certain sections of Greater London ("Understanding and Combating 'Financial Exclusion,'" Rowntree Foundation, March 1999). Consistent with the reports of other countries, the FSA attributes this largely to the closing of commercial bank branches over the last decade and the banks' failure to extend government-mandated banking services to the poor through low-fee accounts. The banks' strategic goals over the past decade have been the cross-selling of financial services such as investment brokerage accounts and insurance products to wealthier clientele, ignoring the low-income, rural, and aged populations that have traditionally relied on the post for their financial services and often harbor an antipathy toward, if not mistrust of, banks, where they feel socially as well as economically excluded (author's interviews; *In or Out? Financial Exclusion*, FSA, July 2000).

Restoring the Network

In an attempt to address the issue of the "unbanked," the U.K. government decided to direct all pension and benefit payments into formal sector bank accounts by 2003. This change resulted in a loss to the Post Office of £400 million in fees that are derived from pension and benefits payments. These fees accounted for 40 percent of postal operation profits, and their loss would have resulted in the closing of many of the post office branches that provide financial services. Concern over these outcomes led the U.K. government to reinvigorate the postal infrastructure's more than nineteen thousand post office branches, some 50 percent of which are in rural areas—typically a section of a village shop and a focal point of community activity. Recognizing the important social role the post office branches play in their communities, it thus became a policy priority of the government to provide both financial services to those excluded and to restore a sound fiscal base for maintaining the postal infrastructure to prevent future rural post office closures (*Counter Revolution: Modernizing the Post Office Network*, Cabinet Office, June 2000).

A new Post Office–based Universal Bank was launched in April 2003, jointly owned by the Post Office, the High Street (the main retail/commercial) banks, and other financial institutions. The mission of the Universal Bank is to tackle the issue of financial exclusion by providing a wide range of financial services in rural and disadvantaged urban areas as a non-competitive neutral agent for private sector financial institutions. Private institutions were reluctant to contribute the £180 million they were assessed for the plan. However, the U.K. government maintained that, since these private sector institutions were being gifted with the government's direct deposit of pension and social benefit payments, their contribution to the Universal Bank plan was obligatory. (This Universal Bank should not be confused with the multisector financial institutions also known as universal banks that are found in Germany, Switzerland, and increasingly in other countries as a result of financial deregulation.)

Envisioned in the U.K. government's plan is the outlay of £1.1 billion for the creation of a PC-based online "banking engine" that will implement computerized counter service in all U.K. post office and branch network locations as well as the use of debit cards allowing access to the LINK network's twenty-eight thousand cash machines. With respect to Internet banking in the United Kingdom, it should be noted that those financially excluded are more likely not to have a telephone (40 percent) and even more so a computer (over 90 percent). Internet usage in the United Kingdom is 60 percent of the population (2004), but highly skewed to younger adults. Critics point out that, not only do many banking clients have a distinct preference for managing their financial affairs on a cash basis at the post office, any arrangement that gifts the government's direct deposit of pension and benefit payments provides a significant cross-subsidy by government to the big four High Street banks. These are the very banks that have failed to provide adequate access to the financially excluded through their own diminished branch networks despite their dominance of retail banking services. The implementation and outcome of the plan should invite further study as it progresses (author's interviews; *Competition in UK Banking: Report to the Chancellor of Exchequer,* D. Cruikshank, March 2000; "Access to Financial Services," O. Pilley, 2000).

Transition Economies and Privatization:
Bailouts at Public Expense

Another issue of importance in the privatization of postbanks, particularly in transition economies, is how poorly the privatization process and subsequent government oversight have been carried out. Almost as soon as postal savings services were reintroduced in the transition economies of Central Europe and the Balkans, they were targeted to be sold under privatization programs, often at bargain prices, along with other state-owned institutions. In some cases, governments offered up hasty sales of state-owned property to foreign corporate investors that were not fully aware of the weak financial condition of their acquisition, ultimately forcing these governments into large-scale bailouts at public expense.

For example, the Czech Government merged the Postbank with the financially troubled Investment Bank in 1994 and then privatized the merged institution for 200 million koruna (CzK) ($6.1 million). In the process, the newly formed Ivestční a Postovní Banka (Investment and Post Bank—IPB) gained access to the Czech Republic's 3,400 post offices and the CzK75 billion ($2.3 billion) deposits of the post's 2 million savings account holders. From the perspective of the posts the deal represented a serious loss inasmuch as the posts retained only a 6 percent ownership interest in the new bank. In 1998, Japan's Nomura Investment Bank purchased the Czech government's 46 percent stake in IPB. IPB, however, had failed to disclose $7.5 billion in outstanding loans to client firms in which it owned shares. Ultimately IPB collapsed amid charges by the Czech government of asset-stripping by Nomura and countercharges by Nomura of cronyism between IPB's managers and their clients and unfair subsidies by the government to rival banks. IPB was seized and resold by the government to Československa Obchodní Banka (ČSOB, the former state foreign trade bank, owned since 1998 by KBC Bank of Belgium). The reported size of the Czech government's bailout of IPB as part of the merger deal with ČSOB was CzK95 billion ($2.5 billion) in government guarantees against all prior loan losses. The IPB bailout, the most expensive so far among the European transition economies, cost Czech taxpayers some 5 percent of GDP. The International Monetary Fund (IMF) estimates the total cost of the government's rescue of the privatized banking sector at 21 percent of GDP (*Financial Times*, 10 August 2001; 21 November 2002; *New York Times*, 6 December 2002).

Hungary's Postbank, privatized in 1988, went into bankruptcy in 1998 as a result of non-performing commercial loans and dubious investments, necessitating a 152-billion-forint (Ft.) ($750 million) rescue. Taken over again by the government, the Postbank, representing 9.3 million accounts accessible in 3,250 post offices, by far Hungary's largest savings account network, is once again making a profit under the state post's administration. However, this was only temporary, as the Ministry of Finance privatized the Postbank once again, selling it in 2003 to Austria's Erste Bank for $457 million (*Financial Times*, 7 March 2001, 20 November 2001, 21 October 2003; *The Economist*, 27 July 2002).

The relentless push to privatize state-owned postal savings institutions that are both functional and profitable, and the issues raised here, are not exclusively European nor the sole province of developed and transitional economies. For example, Indonesia's Posbank was merged during the market deregulation of the 1990s with a commercial bank owned by the family of former Indonesian president Suharto. The Suharto commercial bank had concealed a massive bad loan portfolio that quickly forced the Posbank into bankruptcy with the resultant loss of postal savings operations. Some four hundred private Indonesian banks were also created during the market liberalization era. This phenomenon of private bank creation followed by failure and consolidation has been repeated in a number of the transition and developing economies, including the Asian cases in chapter 3 on Kazakhstan, the Republic of Korea, Vietnam, and the Philippines, and in the country case study chapters that follow. In these countries, savers seeking safety and stability have turned to postal savings.

The Private Sector Finds Opportunities in Postal Financial Services

Market liberalization and privatization of postal savings functions have been going on for more than a decade. Other financial institutions with alternative retail strategies have sought to enter into agency agreements or even purchase entire postal systems. There have been two major categories of buyers. First, commercial banks and insurance companies have vied for the franchise opportunities represented by the large and stable deposit base of postal savings and for the opportunity to sell other financial products such as insurance, pension plans, and investment funds to postal savings customers. In this context, financial conglomerates have expanded beyond their national boundaries to acquire postal financial services in other countries. Large financial firms such as Citibank and Belgium's Generale Bank (now part of the Fortis insurance and financial group), and the Dutch firm ING Barings (insurance and financial), which owns Netherlands Post with TNT Post Grope, have sought to expand through foreign direct investment in postal financial operations and the retail payments systems in other countries. Fortis, which owns Belgium's postal savings franchise until 2010, is also seeking the postal life insurance franchise, which was recently in the hands of its rival, AXA Insurance. The combined franchise would provide a significant cross-selling opportunity for the insurance component of the Fortis group. With 1.5 million accounts, postal financial services comprise 30 percent of the Belgian post's revenues (author's interviews). For the most part, however, private franchise holders have not adopted proactive plans to further develop the postal savings deposit base but tend to see their franchise ownership from a strategic management perspective, as an important asset to be prevented from falling into the hands of potential competitors or as a source of fresh capital. Deutsche Post AG (DPAG) made an initial public offering (IPO) in June 2004 of a 49.9 percent share in its successful Postbank, hoping to raise 3 billion euros to expand Deutsche Post's European mail and parcel delivery operations before the liberalization of Europe's postal sector in 2009. The IPO, however, resulted in the sale of only 33 percent of Postbank shares—22 percent off the target price. Furthermore, Deutsche Post's own share price had fallen some 20 percent in the months preceding the IPO debacle, reflecting the market's questioning of the wisdom of DPAG's management in selling off a substantial portion of one of its only proven cash-cows (author's interviews; *Financial Times,* 25 March 2004, 17 June 2004, 24 June 2004).

The second major category of buyers of postal financial services systems is privatized postal systems themselves. When Deutsche Post reacquired at a discounted price Deutsche Postbank in 1999, from which it had been separated by the German government nine years earlier, it also acquired a commercial credit institution. Deutsche Post's financial services account for almost a quarter of its revenues and rank second in profitability after its protected monopoly in domestic mail services (Deutsche Post *Annual Report,* 2000). In addition, the Dutch postal system under ING Barings–TNT Post Grope is also offering a wide range of financial business services, including factoring and equipment leasing.

Also interesting in this regard is the fact that privatized posts-cum-banks, such as Deutsche Post, as well as the banks mentioned above, have sought to invest in postal financial services internationally. Foreign-investing private operators, whether banks or postal systems, expect substantial earnings from their investment in postal and financial services business in other countries. Particularly attractive to foreign banking interests is the central role that postal remittance services play in individual and household payments in CIS and Eastern European countries, especially the delivery of pension payments, social welfare benefits, and payment of bills for utilities, taxes, and the like. This is unlike the commercial banking sector, which plays only a minor role in personal retail payments in these countries. It has been estimated that postal financial services account for a significant amount of postal revenues, upward of 80 percent in these countries ("Harmonization of postal money orders [including Giro systems]," a report of the ING Postbank Consultancy for the European Union Phare Program, 20 June 2000).

The benefits of strengthening postal financial services are also not lost on developed countries where the post remains a state-owned enterprise. For example, the French government, over the banking sector's opposition, has given the state-owned La Poste permission to offer housing mortgages in 2005. The government's intention is to expand La Poste's postal banking operations to offset the loss of revenues due to the structural decline in mail delivery business. La Poste is preparing a 3.4 billion euro investment to modernize its mail sorting and delivery systems and to increase its competitive position in preparation for the forthcoming liberalization of the European postal delivery market (*Financial Times,* 25 March 2004).

Restoring Synergies: The Reintegration of Postbanks and Postal Services

We referred earlier to the German experience in which the postbank was separated from its postal system, privatized, and later reacquired by the now-privatized postal service. As with Deutsche Post, the Netherlands' postal system underwent a similar transformation. Both have sought to make full use of the synergies of the postal network, which has increasingly drawn them further into postal financial services.

Like Deutsche Post today, ING Postbank functions not as a stand-alone institution but as a part of a multifunction service strategy utilizing post office counters. The Dutch postal savings system and postbank were efficient operations when they were publicly owned. However, as a result of a decision of the Dutch cabinet to attempt to rescue the failing Netherlands Middenstandsbank (NMB), a private commercial bank, the Postbank was merged into NMB to provide it with a stable base of depositors. NMB-Postbank, unable to overcome the NMB's problems, was ultimately acquired by the ING Insurance conglomerate, now known as ING Barings. The Postbank has functioned more successfully under its latest owner, most likely because ING Barings is also the 50 percent owner of the Netherlands Post and operates the postal giro payments system as well, an important profit center. With the Postbank and the Netherlands Post under the same ownership, the two institutions can again tap the synergies possible in agency relationships based on mutual interests (author's interviews; "Best Practices in Postal Banking: Case Study 'the Netherlands,'" ING Barings Postbank). The same would be true of cross-owned institutions.

By contrast, in Germany, division of the post and the postbank led initially to severe operational discord. When ownership of the Deutsche Postbank was separated from the posts by the German government, the result was a nine-year period from 1990 to 1999 marked by constant disagreements at all levels and areas of operations between the Postbank and the posts, accompanied by the Postbank's yearly demands for further reduction of franchise fees to be paid the posts. Only after Deutsche Post reacquired the Postbank and common ownership was reinstated in 1999 was managerial harmony restored (author's interviews). After rejoining Deutsche Post, the Postbank strategically shed three hundred thousand of its least profitable accounts, mostly pensioners. This might not be too troublesome for these depositors since Germany has a well-developed network of 564 *Sparkassen* (municipal savings banks) for small-scale savers.

In sum, the cases we have discussed illustrate some of the major hazards of the privatization process. Chief among them, as was seen in Finland, Sweden, and the United Kingdom, is the potential destruction of the important symbiosis between postal financial services and the posts whereby postal financial services significantly support the cost of maintaining the postal network upon which both are dependent. The separation of the postbank from the posts effectively destroyed synergies that made providing financial and postal services to lower-income and rural populations financially feasible. The cases of the transition economies also make a point that should be underscored here. As was seen, many governments have undervalued their postal savings institutions both as financial and social economic assets. This in turn led to opportunistic mergers and sales, subsequent liabilities requiring intervention and bailouts and, worst, the reduction or elimination of services. On the other hand, some private sector operators, such as Netherlands Post and Deutsche Post AG, have realized opportunities afforded by the postal network and restored profitable synergies with postal financial services.

In other words, in the policy debate over separation and privatization of postal savings operations, analysts seem to have missed a crucial point. Postal financial services make possible more intensive use of the postal network, reducing costs through economies of scale in transactions through the postal infrastructure. This synergistic relationship produces opportunities to provide low-cost services such as postal savings, postal checking and giro, postal life insurance and pension plans, money orders, overseas remittances, and so on, as well as mail delivery. However, after policymakers split apart postal and financial services, it seems that at least some privatized operators rediscovered these synergies after recombining them. As policymakers in developing and transition economies contemplate the separation and privatization of their own financial and mail delivery components of their postal systems, these experiences might be fruitfully kept in mind.

3

Asian Experiences in Postal Savings

Mark J. Scher

Introduction

The Legacy of Colonialism

The countries that have had the most extensive experience with postal savings outside of Europe have been in Asia. The origins of the Asian systems trace back to the merchant and military operations of the European imperial powers. Spain and Portugal, then Holland, Great Britain, and France gave an international scope to postal operations as their merchant fleets carried mail as well as cargo to and from ports in Asia, Africa, and the Middle East. With the advance of colonial conquest into the interior, a system of colonial posts routinely supplanted the native merchant post infrastructure. Many colonial postal savings programs were established toward the end of the nineteenth century, but catered primarily to serving the savings and remittance needs of colonial civil service employees. At that time no thought was given to the mobilizing of those savings to improve conditions in the colonies or to make any effort to meet the financial service needs of the indigenous populations.

Post-Independence: Mobilizing Savings

It was after national independence from British colonial rule in Asia that the Post Office Savings Bank (POSB), a nineteenth-century British institution, began to evolve in different directions in different countries. Some resulting types include POSBs in Bangladesh and India that operate not as banks but as agencies of their respective countries' National Savings Organizations (NSOs). In Malaysia and Sri Lanka the POSBs have been transformed into National Savings Banks that have independent branch networks with full banking functions. They still utilize the postal infrastructure, but with severe limitations on the services and products that may be offered through them.

The savings system has evolved as well in several CIS countries. As noted earlier, the *Sberbank,* a national savings institution, had been the only savings institution under the Soviet system. In the Russian Federation it remains under the ownership of the State Bank (central bank) and is by far the largest and safest of all financial institutions. In many other CIS countries, such as Kazakhstan, the chief savings institution (formerly *Sberbank*), now renamed Narodni Bank (People's Bank, Halyk Savings Bank in Kazakh), has sought earnings opportunities by transforming itself into a commercial bank and relinquishing its original mission of offering savings and financial services to serve the broadest possible population. At the same time, market liberalization forces have also given the impetus for the implementation of new postal savings systems in Kazakhstan and Vietnam, as the posts have sought to create new profit centers to replace the loss of former telecom earnings.

In China, all personal savings accounts, including postal savings, were transferred from their home institutions and subsumed under the People's Bank of China, the central bank, in 1952. In 1986 postal savings was reintroduced at the initiative of the central bank in an effort to mobilize savings. Postal savings then demonstrated remarkable growth in the 1990s as a repository of rapidly rising personal savings resulting from the opening and development of the private sector economy. A similar rapid growth in postal savings resulting from private sector activity began in Vietnam after it established postal savings in 1999.

In Japan the postal savings system has long been an important collector of savings and a provider of financial services for middle- and low-income and rural people, and it has played an important role in the financing of public capital investment. The Japanese postal savings system was established in 1874, a time when Japan had just left behind centuries of feudalism and isolation. Its leaders took note of the foreign indebtedness of the Chinese and Ottoman Empires and, using its new postal savings system as a foundation, the Japanese state was able to avoid all foreign borrowing for twenty years, from 1885 until the Russo-Japanese War. The Japanese model has also had an impact on the Republic of Korea, Taiwan Province of China, and many other areas in Asia that came under Japanese colonial and military occupation ("Postal Savings System," M.J. Scher, in *Encyclopedia of Japanese Business and Management,* ed. A. Bird; London: Routledge, 2002).

Other models have had some influence on the development of postal savings and postal checking in Asia. These include the Dutch postal system in Indonesia; the Austrian model of postal savings and giro system during the time of the Ottoman empire, which was followed in Turkey,

Iraq, Lebanon, and Syria; and the Philippines' system, which first established postal savings in 1906 under a U.S. administration, its success contributing to the introduction of postal savings in the United States itself in 1910. The American-appointed Civil Governor William Howard Taft first proposed postal savings in 1904 in the Philippines. Taft was later elected U.S. president, and it was during his presidency that postal savings was first instituted in the United States.

Although many of the Asian postal savings systems in this study were founded during the colonial era and have been informed by a colonial past, all have evolved in their own right, adapting to their respective countries' social, economic, and political environments. All offer valuable lessons to developing countries in the differences and similarities of their experiences.

In what follows, we examine institutions that are being successfully used in a variety of economic and institutional environments in Asia. The focus is on issues that lie at the heart of the concerns of developing countries relating to the mobilization of postal savings: private sector competition, financial product development and promotion, postal savings in rural areas, the credit function and the building of partnerships with other institutions, the investment and intermediation of funds for development, management operations, and the utilization of technology. It is also within this context that the issues of market liberalization, foreign entry and acquisition, and postbank creation, separation, and privatization discussed in the previous chapter are analyzed in terms of how they may affect savings institutions in developing countries and transition economies. We also discuss issues bearing on postal payment systems, particularly international transfers. This discussion is based on the author's observations and interviews in the countries concerned, and the experiences discussed at the workshops held at Keio University in Tokyo in 2000, 2001, and 2004.

Management and Competition Issues in Asian Systems

The Organization of Postal Savings: Four Models

One may distinguish four types of organizations that provide savings services through the postal infrastructure in Asia: (1) the national savings organization, as in Bangladesh and India; (2) the postal savings bureau, as in China, Japan, the Republic of Korea, and Vietnam; (3) the linkage of savings to a postal payments system, as in Kazakhstan and other CIS countries; and (4) the national savings bank's use of the postal infrastructure, as in Malaysia, Sri Lanka, and formerly in Singapore. The postbank model described in the previous chapter has been proposed in several Asian countries, and as credit-giving thrift institutions, variations of the postbank exist in Iran and the Philippines. Individual country cases serve to describe the different types.

National Savings Organization: The Case of India

India has by far the world's most extensive postal savings network and the oldest one among developing countries. Some 154,000 post offices all offer postal financial services, even in small and remote villages, 90 percent are in rural areas; overall it is estimated that they service some 116 million account-holders with some 1,875 billion rupees (Rs.) on deposit (approximately US$42 billion in 2000). Originally organized during British rule in 1883, since India's independence in 1947 the Post Office Savings Bank (POSB) has offered an extensive array of postal savings schemes and other financial products, albeit acting as an agent of the National Savings Organization (NSO), a division of the Ministry of Finance. Currently the POSB offers some eight different savings instruments, each crafted to meet the savings requirements of different markets (see appendix to chapter 8, "National Savings Organization Plans Offered through the Post Office Savings Bank").

The NSO designs the various savings products and markets them through a trained sales force of five hundred thousand licensed agents, one-third of whom are women. These agents are assigned to sell specific savings plans to targeted markets, such as rural women, industrial workers, and the like, and they receive a 1 percent commission on the deposits they collect and deposit in the POSB. Since 1947 the NSO has introduced, revised, and/or withdrawn some 230 plans in response to market conditions and mobilization objectives. Although many of the same NSO products are also offered by government-owned commercial banks, those sold by the post office account for some 85 percent of all household savings in financial institutions in India.

One hundred percent of the funds mobilized go to the States (as of April 2002), and each Indian State Government has a Small Savings Organization that vigorously promotes postal savings. For example, some States operate lotteries with cash prizes tied to savings deposits, or encourage small businesses to deposit funds in postal savings rather than in commercial bank accounts in consideration for additional and/or future government business or other inducements, such as the speedy approval of business licenses.

In 2003 the NSO was reorganized and renamed the National Savings Institute (NSI), with the administration, supervision, and training of the sales force transferred to the State Small Savings Organizations. In its redefined mission the NSI will continue to design the savings products offered and will focus on research and development of the savings market.

Postal Savings and Remittance Bureau: The Case of China

Following the reestablishment of China's postal savings system in 1986 after a thirty-three-year hiatus, both postal savings and remittances have shown dramatic growth, particularly in urban areas, and have an increasingly large market share in the collection of individual household savings. Initiated with the assistance of the People's Bank of China (PBC, the central bank), with all funds transferred to the PBC, the Postal Savings and Remittance Bureau has served as a vital link in mobilizing the income and profits derived from the private sector activities that have been encouraged by the government's economic reform program.

In its first years of operation, from 1986 to 1989, the Postal Savings and Remittance Bureau functioned merely as an agency of the PBC, receiving a fixed commission of 2.2 percent of the funds on deposit. In the subsequent decade, market principles were introduced and the post was able to profit on the difference between the PBC's wholesale rate and the retail rate. Until 2004 all funds were deposited with the PBC. Most recently the Postal Savings and Remittance Bureau has become a separate corporation under the State Post Bureau and has been given permission to intermediate new deposits to other financial institutions through the interbank market.

At the end of June 2002, 663 billion yuan were on deposit in the postal savings system in some 104 million postal savings accounts. Postal savings services are provided by 34,540 of China's post offices, of which 80 percent are located in rural areas. However, only 30 percent of all deposits are from these rural branches, as incomes are lower in the countryside and there is strong competition from rural credit cooperatives (author's interviews). Postal savings deposits exhibited an extraordinary annual growth rate of over 50 percent per annum in the first half of the 1990s and over 24 percent per annum in the second half of the decade. Its market share in savings rose to 8.11 percent in 2002 (from 6.99 percent in 2000); this 16 percent growth in market share was largely due to new savers, reducing the market share of three of China's big four state-owned commercial banks. The Postal Savings and Remittance Bureau now ranks fifth in savings deposits after China's big four banks.

Linking Savings to Postal Payments: The Case of Kazakhstan

Kazpost is the name of the Republic of Kazakhstan's State Enterprise of Postal Services. With a relatively small and declining population (14,952,000 in 1999), Kazakhstan had 2,390 post offices in 2002, spread over a territory almost the size of India (2,724,900 sq. km.). In August 1999, Kazpost established the first postal savings system among the CIS republics. Savings mobilization has been an outgrowth of the main financial service of Kazpost, which is to operate an extensive payments system for individuals and households on behalf of the government, as is the case in most of the other CIS economies in transition. Kazpost has the primary responsibility for distributing pensions and other social-benefit payments as well as salaries, including those paid by some private enterprises. Twice a month, pensioners and other recipients line up at their village post office on an appointed day to receive their pensions in cash, which is delivered to the post offices by armored vehicles. If the funds are not claimed within three days, they are returned to the central accounting office. Government regulations had required that personal delivery be effected and prohibit the direct transfer of these funds into customer savings accounts handicapping postal savings' growth. This regulation was changed to permit the signing of direct deposit agreements with individual pensioners.

In 2000, after a year's operations, less than one-fourth of Kazpost branches were offering postal savings accounts. However, in the same year Kazpost initiated eight different types of savings products. Savings can be held in domestic tenge or in U.S. dollars. In 2001, postal savings offered a 10 percent interest rate guaranteed by the government on tenge accounts to its depositors. The minimum account size is 500 tenge ($3.52), and $10 for U.S. dollar accounts. Kazpost is restricted from offering a greater variety of products or higher interest rates than its commercial bank competitors are allowed to offer. The National Bank (central bank) requires that all postal savings funds collected be invested in government securities (tenge- and U.S. dollar–denominated).

Halyk Bank, the national savings bank, had been the bank where household savings were mainly held. The majority of depositors of both Halyk Bank and Kazpost are pensioners and salaried workers. In 1999 the two institutions reached an agreement by which Halyk Bank would transfer its rural operations to Kazpost and retain its strong urban franchise through its own independent branch network. Halyk Bank, pursuing its own goal of privatization, has been transformed into a commercial bank. By October 2002 the number of Kazpost offices providing postal savings services had increased to 72 percent, 2,444 out of 3,387 post offices, and the volume of savings on deposit had more than doubled since 2000 to 728 million tenge. Halyk's share of the individual savings market had declined to one-third.

National Savings Banks: The Cases of Malaysia, Singapore, and Sri Lanka

In some cases, postal savings regimes have been converted from post office savings banks (POSBs), a division of the post office, to national savings banks (NSBs). This was the case in Malaysia, Singapore, and Sri Lanka, where the POSBs were newly chartered as publicly owned savings institutions in the early 1970s. New NSBs began to open banking branches in urban markets that were separate from the postal branch offices while continuing to rely on the postal infrastructure in an agency relationship, especially in rural areas. Sri Lanka's NSB has continued to use all of the nation's 4,012 post offices and postal substations. Malaysia's NSB, by contrast, set about creating an extensive independent branch network, relying on the postal network only in remote regions where independent branches were not economically feasible. In recent years Malaysia's NSB has had to scale back the number of its bank branches in favor of again using post offices, finding that it had overreached in its original plan in some areas where it was too costly to maintain separate branches.

With the intention of building their own independent branch networks, the NSBs in all three countries, to a greater or lesser extent, have adopted urban service strategies aimed at competing with commercial banks for the more affluent, upscale market of young professionals. In adopting such strategies, however, they have departed from their primary, or at least initial, mission of providing financial services to all segments of the population. This shift in focus has been accompanied by a deemphasis on rural savers and the urban poor, who have only post office branches (and not NSB branches) geographically near them. Under this regime, postal branches offer only a limited number of financial products with restrictions on services, particularly savings withdrawals, compared to the much more extensive range of products and services offered by stand-alone NSB branches, thus creating a two-tier savings system. Nevertheless, many customers say that they feel more comfortable patronizing the post office branches.

The development of a two-tier system has been reflected in the widely differing physical conditions of the servicing facilities. Aging, deteriorated conditions in the post office branches contrast sharply with the air-conditioned urban minibranch savings-bank offices. This was especially true when NSBs first came into existence in the 1970s. In Malaysia and Singapore the posts have since been modernized so that their counter facilities run as smoothly and efficiently as in any commercial bank, and in Sri Lanka some post offices have been modernized as well.

Singapore's POSBank provides an extreme example of a two-tier system. It first embarked upon an independent branch network strategy in the 1970s based on a two-tier infrastructure like the one described above. By the 1980s the Singapore POSBank abandoned the use of the post office's branch network and separated completely from the postal infrastructure. In 1999 the government merged the POSBank with DBS Bank, the former government-owned Development Bank of Singapore, to provide a deposit base for what would be a new, private commercial bank. DBS Bank, which did not have the social obligations of POSBank, immediately adopted an upscale marketing strategy targeting affluent young professionals and entrepreneurs. More than half of POSBank's 133 branch operations were soon closed; all of them were in poorer residential areas. It also raised the no-fee minimum for passbook savings from one Singapore dollar to S$500 (US$287). Consistent with this overall strategy, the latest figures indicate that 80 percent of the POSBank's branches were closed as of 2000.

In 2001 the Singapore government became concerned about the nation's unbanked population. Echoing the worries regarding social banking issues discussed in the United Kingdom case in chapter 2, it is seeking to mandate limited low-fee accounts at all domestically owned banks as a solution. In 2003, DBS's new management team was considering revising its policies to better accommodate small savers (author's interview).

Agency Problems: Disincentives to Mobilizing Savings

Issues bearing on the nature of agency relationships and disincentives to mobilizing savings arise when management of savings operations in the posts is separate from ownership of the savings operations, as earlier discussed in the European context in chapter 2, in the subsection on the loss of savings services after privatization of postal savings. This has been the case in Asia as well, whether the savings facility takes the form of a national savings organization (NSO), as in Bangladesh and India, or national savings bank (NSB), as in Malaysia and Sri Lanka. Principal-agent relationships, both managerial and economic, require contractually defined incentives for the posts as agents to align their interests with the owner-principals, such as the NSO, NSB, or postbank. If no such incentives exist, then disincentives govern the relationship. The latter has been the case even when both sides are publicly owned, as were the posts and the NSOs and NSBs in the Asian case studies, or as was seen in the examples discussed in chapter 2, when the publicly owned posts in Finland and Sweden were separated from their postbanks, which were then privatized, or in the case of Deutsche Post and Deutsche Postbank, when both were corporatized separately.

Sri Lanka provides an example of incentive problems that can arise in an agency relationship between the posts and an independent NSB. The separation of the Post Office Savings Bank (POSB) and its reconstitution as the National Savings Bank in 1972 led to a dual system of savings networks: an independent system of NSB branches in the major cities and a separate network covering the whole of the country that utilizes the postal infrastructure with postal employees as its agents. Despite increases in the gross value of postal deposits, the NSB has complained that the posts are not doing their best to promote savings, since postal deposits have steadily declined in terms of their percentage of the overall value of NSB deposits. The value of postal deposits decreased from 66.9 percent of NSB deposits in 1972 to 22.7 percent in 1982, to 12.4 percent in 1992, and to 8 percent in 2001, suggesting that the NSB might be doing a more effective job in mobilizing funds through its own branch network in the major cities than through the post office network. On the other hand, these figures may also reflect the different growth rates of income and savings in rural and urban areas. Moreover, many Sri Lankans find it necessary to hold two accounts, one at the post office, since only the post office savings accounts allow them to make deposits and withdrawals at all post offices throughout the country, and another account at an NSB branch, which is limited only to that district but offers more savings products and services. Recent figures show improvement in the volume of post office-based deposits, which have grown annually at an average rate of 17.6 percent per year from 2001 through 2003 in both ordinary savings and fixed-term deposits. The greatest growth has been in ordinary savings, with an average increase of 18.4 percent, while the number of post office-based accounts also grew by 2.3 percent.

Nevertheless, the Sri Lanka Post cites a number of reasons for the comparative decline in funds deposited with the NSB branch-based accounts, chief among them, increased competition from the savings bank sector. Between 2000 and 2002 the number of licensed branches has increased threefold to 972 branches, including the expansion of the NSB branches near post offices. Other reasons cited by the post office include the easy terms and conditions for loans from thrift societies that are not available to postal savings customers; that the NSB business is not a core business of the post office and that there are no personal benefit incentive schemes for the postal employees that are tied to their performance in selling NSB products; that NSB savings products offered through the post offices are limited and that there is less marketing and publicity for these products by the NSB at the rural level, the postal network's key area of competitive strength.

The postal system, from its perspective, views its relationship with the NSB as underrewarded, especially since the NSB puts more of its resources per depositor into its own branches and targets the more affluent savers. In 2000 the Sri Lankan posts raised the possibility of obtaining new revenues by replacing their relationship with the NSB with other agency relationships with rival financial institutions. Such a change occurred in Malaysia, when the posts broadened their agency relationships after the NSB eliminated its use of post offices in urban areas in favor of its own branch network. In India, postal officials have voiced dissatisfaction that their compensation is based solely on an annual franchise fee without the commission fees that other agents and financial institutions receive for similar services. As a result, India Post has begun to market the investment products of private financial institutions.

For the posts, getting appropriate recompense for their services requires both testing the market for its agency services and assessing the costs of providing the services. Sometimes, despite the immediate availability of information, neither the post nor the NSB does the requisite cost analysis, and opportunities are neither seen nor seized. In the case of Sri Lanka, monthly reports have been generated for years from all of the country's over four-thousand post offices. These reports, which give a daily accounting of the number and size of transactions, are not analyzed for transaction costs. This may reflect a lack of incentive owing to the NSB's long-standing agency agreement with the posts, by which the posts' compensation, except for an inflation adjustment clause, has not changed since the early 1980s. The agreement provides no incentives to the posts to promote savings deposits or to go beyond fulfilling only the minimal contractual obligations. In the case of India, the POSB does not provide client data below the State level that would be useful to the NSO in devising savings products nor to the State Small Savings Organizations data that would aid in targeting appropriate locations for its savings campaigns. The disfunctionality of the relationship between the posts and the savings institution or organization of which they are the agent is a core problem hindering the promotion of postal savings.

The Sri Lankan and Indian experience is illustrative of a phenomenon that commonly arises when the posts contract to act as an agent for an institution in which they are not a stakeholder, typically a separately chartered postbank or savings bank, either privately or publicly owned. Often the contracts provide that the post act as agent, but with little or no incentive added to promote postal savings. Most agency agreements that this author has examined were based on a flat annual franchise fee to the post, calculated on some historically based estimate of the number of annual transactions. In some cases, however, compensation to the post was on a per-transaction basis; in others the post rented its counter space to an assortment of financial firms that were not necessarily savings institutions. Supervisory government authorities therefore have an interest to ensure that appropriate incentives are built into any agency relationship established for the providing of postal savings services.

Are Postal Savings in Competition with Commercial Banks? The Case of Japan

In Asia and elsewhere, postal savings has been sharply criticized as "unfair" competition for commercial banks. As a case in point, for many years the Japanese banking industry has clamored for the breakup and privatization, if not the abolishment, of the postal savings system, commonly referred to as *yu-cho*. Postal savings deposits in 1995 exceeded the combined savings deposits of Japan's six largest banks (Dai-Ichi Kangyo, Sumitomo, Sanwa, Tokyo-Mitsubishi, Fuji, and Sakura Banks), amounting to some 34 percent of all household savings deposits in all financial institutions nationwide. By 1997 this figure was some 42 percent and on the rise as Japanese public confidence in its banking system continued to fall due to the non-performing loan problem plaguing the banking industry that is well covered in the Japanese press. In 2002, postal savings deposits exceeded the total of household and individual savings deposits in all of Japan's commercial banks combined.

Critics from the banking industry have complained that numerous exemptions, including exemptions from all national and local taxes, payments to the Deposit Insurance Corporation, Bank of Japan reserve requirements, and the requirement that private banks pay dividends to their shareholders give unwarranted advantages to the postal savings system. The sad irony of this argument is that the banks' chronic losses over the last decade have also resulted in their paying no taxes and issuing minimal or no dividend payments. Bank critics further argue that postal revenues subsidize the entire infrastructure of the postal savings system. The post, in turn, has refuted these charges, with its own analysis of the costs allocated to labor and its apportioned use of space. In addition, postal officials counter criticisms by pointing to the costs they bear in providing postal, savings, and life insurance services in rural areas. It is likely that without postal financial service revenues, many small and rural post offices in Japan would have to be closed, as was the case in Finland and Sweden (discussed in chapter 2).

Putting these charges and counter-charges aside, the success of the Japanese postal savings system in attracting deposits is much more likely attributable to the confidence factor and to the fact that the more than 24,000 post offices in Japan function as collection points for its savings system, far outstripping the 16,000 branches of all commercial banks. Japanese people are on average within 1.1 kilometer from a post office, the offices of which are uniformly distributed in rural, urban, and suburban populations, while bank branches are typically found clustered in business districts. Of the 3,235 cities and municipalities that have post offices, 567, some 18 percent, are without banks.

The existence of the postal savings system has also helped raise the quality of private banking services available to the general public and keep the private sector competitive in the services offered. The consumer-oriented Japanese postal savings system offers products such as life insurance as well as a nationwide network of 25,184 automatic teller machines that can be used to make deposits or withdrawals, make credit card payments, pay utility bills, or transfer payments to anywhere in the country at lower fees than those charged by banks. As a result, banks have begun to respond to the competitive pressures of the postal savings system.

One of the commercial banks' major complaints about the postal savings system is that the commercial banking sector relies heavily on individual and household savings, chiefly from the accounts of employees of the client firms of a bank. These accounts have historically formed the mainstay of a bank's deposit base under Japan's so-called "main bank system" whereby corporate finance in Japan has been largely mediated by the banking sector, especially within groupings of affiliated companies. (See Mark J. Scher, *Japanese Interfirm Networks and Their Main Banks;* London and New York: Macmillan/St. Martin's [USA and Canada], 1997.) The shift of household deposits out of these employee accounts into postal savings has been quite a significant loss to the commercial banks and thus a factor in the declining efficacy of the corporate lending system.

Although cost efficiency explains part of the competitive edge of the Japanese postal savings system, the ongoing banking crises and the instability of Japanese banks due to their huge portfolio of non-performing loans, together with the Tokyo Stock Exchange's poor performance since its collapse in 1989, have left the public with few safer, convenient alternatives to the security of the postal savings system.

Financial Technology: Choosing Appropriate Systems

Whatever the organizational form of postal savings, important management decisions have to be made regarding the technological upgrading of savings services. Long before the advent of computers or even electronic data processing, simple and effective means were developed to service savings accounts through post offices. For example, small savers were able to purchase low-denomination savings stamps, which they affixed to postal savings deposit cards. When the card's numbered spaces were filled, the total value of the stamps were credited to the saver's interest-bearing account or the saver was issued a savings bond. This system continues to be used in some developing countries and by children's savings programs in several others. Comparably simple low-tech methods developed over time by the posts to mobilize small savings often still provide efficient and economical service for many developing economies without the need to invest in high-technology equipment. For example, in Sri Lanka, account verification procedures are conducted by fax when clients need to make rapid withdrawals, and elsewhere low-tech microfiche readers are used for signature verification for withdrawals throughout the system. The similar use of fax machines in Morocco and the United Republic of Tanzania points to the value of establishing mechanisms for the exchange of practical experience in the use of suitable technology between developing countries in a field otherwise dominated by developed countries' vendors selling costly high-tech systems. The sufficiency of many low-tech methods notwithstanding, consultants and equipment salespeople typically urge the posts to upgrade to the technological level of private sector banks, resulting in a needless and wasteful diversion of scarce financial resources. These expenditures often ignore the fact that many high-tech systems and services are not designed to meet the needs of the typical constituency of postal financial services in developing countries. The outcome can even be that the NSB or postbank, needing to rationalize its investment in these systems, reorients its marketing strategy to compete with commercial banks in serving the needs of an upscale urban clientele.

The lack of fit between the objectives of many consultants/salespeople and those of developing countries is evident from the consultants' recommendations that were reported by various postal administrations in Asia (author's interviews). For example, the capability to perform online interactive processing of transactions is generally presented by consultants as a necessity, even when private sector financial institutions are not using such systems, or only in limited geographic areas, such as in the capital city and perhaps some other major city. Typically, to acquire an online transactional processing capability requires investing in a telecommunications infrastructure as well as new hardware and software computer equipment to handle the task. Private sector banks typically employ overnight batch processing, which requires only the limited use of one phone line at non-peak hours rather than interactive online processing that would require a more complex communications network. Overnight batch processing is the norm in the regional operations of many banks in developed countries as well.

Also, technological advances in hardware, software, and communications networking continue to expand quite rapidly as prices for such systems fall steadily. Developing countries can reap benefits from not adopting such systems before they are necessary. Such benefits include declines in acquisition costs, the development of entirely new technological platforms, or other Internet developments. In addition, inexpensive, modularized, off-the-shelf systems, well tested by banks in different market environments, are available and may be customized to fit both the specific financial products and the technical requirements of developing countries. These systems dwarf the capabilities of old-technology systems still in place in the postal savings systems of some developed countries. Unfortunately, these old systems are being promoted to developing countries despite that fact that they are many times the cost of new off-the-shelf systems. Moreover, such "legacy systems" are based upon financial products designed for the clientele of developed countries and may lack the capabilities to process the financial products suitable for clients in developing country markets.

Some of the developing countries in Asia, such as India and Kazakhstan, have or are developing their own dedicated computer systems, although issues of compatibility with other financial systems in their own countries and abroad have not yet been addressed. Compatibility with other systems is a prerequisite for the electronic transfer of overseas remittances (international giro), and acquiring open architecture–based financial technology systems would help the posts create agency relationships with other institutions in the future. While establishing compatible platforms remain an issue to be resolved, there have also been significant problems created by vendor-country consultants' selling of high-tech online systems. Such mismatches have led to the elimination of essential financial services in developing countries still using the existing paper-based international money order (IMO) remittances, long a mainstay for recipient beneficiaries in developing countries.

For example, the IFS (International Financial Systems) electronic money order system being promoted by certain developed countries requires investment in hardware and the initial as well as annual software franchise fees that cannot by justified by the debt burden in financing the purchase of required hardware or by the lower labor costs in most developing economies. In Sri Lanka's case, some twelve countries with which it had agreements on paper-based international money orders now have been reduced to only six countries (author's interviews). The reduced options for remitting funds have provided great opportunities to private international remittance services, such as Western Union and Moneygram. Despite their high transaction fees for remittances to developing countries, they have been able to dramatically increase their market share as alternative remittance options such as paper-based postal money orders to developing countries have disappeared. For example, Western Union's and Moneygram's "instant" transfers necessitate that the remitter be able to independently notify the recipient of the transaction number and code so that when the beneficiary goes to claim their remittance, the receiving agent, typically a post office, is able to confirm the transaction information with the transfer company by telephone and/or fax.

Postmasters in Asian developing countries complain of the small compensation their institutions receive from these transfer companies despite the post's bearing most of the administrative burden of the company's remittance business. Reliance on local agents, ususally in sub-post offices, who have only low-tech methods at their disposal, such as the telephone and sometimes a fax machine, places a burden on the remitters who must independently notify their beneficiaries by telephone, if possible, in order to achieve the self-styled "instant" remittance service for which the remitter is paying exorbitant fees to the transfer company. Cost-effective alternatives options need to be both restored and enhanced in ways that do not become yet another burden on countries that can ill-afford the costly high-tech solutions proposed by developed country vendors and consultants.

Mobilizing Savings: Product Development and Market Analysis

Developing countries that have policies to promote postal savings typically offer a wide range of postal savings products appropriate to their economies, with features designed to appeal to specific segments of the population. Some in use in Asia today include: products designed for women in households or those engaged in entrepreneurial activities; products aimed at the needs of small-scale enterprises, including small-scale farmers and agricultural businesses; and products for industrial workers, salaried workers, civil servants, professionals, overseas workers, youths, and students. There are also specially designed products that adhere to religious laws (such as *Shari'a*), and special services and products for those who traditionally save in kind, such as in gold, livestock, or land. The following section examines issues that have arisen in Asian countries with respect to the socially important area of product development and marketing.

Postal Savings in Rural Areas: Making a Link to Credit

The social mandate of postal savings is to offer access to financial services to all population groups. To do so effectively requires offering products to rural farmers, for example, that are different than products designed to attract salaried civil servants. In many countries, postal savings products are tax-exempt in order to appeal to urban salaried workers whose income is taxed. This kind of product has little appeal in rural areas where farmers are either exempt from taxation or are taxed in-kind on their production of grain.

Chief among the concerns of rural savers, after safety and accessibility to savings, is access to credit, particularly where in-kind savings predominate and are not easily liquidated to meet short-term emergency cash needs. The postal savings systems of most developing countries do not offer credit. Rather, agricultural credit cooperatives often have an established position in the countryside as a result of the credit they offer to farmers. These cooperatives may also take deposits. Despite the apparent competitive positions between the postal savings system and the credit cooperative, a symbiotic relationship may be forged. For example, in rural areas of India, long-term savings are usually held in the postal savings system and short-term savings in credit cooperatives. Following a harvest there is generally a rise in the number of time certificate deposits at the postal system as farmers deposit a portion of their earnings in longer-term savings plans. Farmers transact short-term deposits and withdrawals year-round at credit cooperatives. In addition, farmers and others are allowed to use postal savings deposit certificates as collateral for loans from credit institutions to cover additional credit needs.

In China the Postal Savings and Remittance Bureau has a less symbiotic relationship with rural credit cooperatives and thus has a smaller rural presence than postal savings in India. This reflects in part the decentralized character of China's posts and also the fact that these posts lack a national program as well as specific strategies to meet the differing needs of the rural areas of China's thirty-two provinces and special administrative areas. Even more important, however, is that rural credit cooperatives already collect deposits and extend credit in the countryside. Moreover, postal services themselves are subcontracted in rural areas by the posts to the respective local People's Committees, which have close political ties to the credit cooperatives, resulting in a reduced "corporate" presence for the posts.

A similar situation exists in the Republic of Korea, where the chief competitor of postal savings in the countryside is the Bank of Agricultural Credit (BAC). In 1977 the Ministry of Information and Communications, which supervises the Korean Postal Service (KPS), decided to concentrate its resources on the development of a telecommunications division within the KPS. The functions of the postal savings system were transferred to the BAC. Later, the KPS was stripped of its telecommunications division and it resumed postal savings operations once again, but now with a formidable competitor of its own making in the countryside. Nevertheless, the introduction by KPS of competition in banking in the rural areas has been seen as a benefit to the local population. Today, 30 percent of KPS deposits are from rural areas due to an extensive branch network that is 70 percent rural, even though the Republic of Korea is rapidly becoming urbanized. On the same principle, the Bank of Mongolia licensed the Mongolian State Posts to introduce postal savings in rural areas to counter the market dominance of the agricultural credit cooperatives.

The foregoing examples are not intended to suggest that postal savings institutions should themselves extend credit. Postal staffs are generally untrained in assessing client creditworthiness, whereas agricultural credit association staffs are trained for this function, as are staffs in microcredit institutions where they exist. In Thailand and Vietnam, for example, senior planners and managers in their respective departments of posts expressed the feeling that they were hampered in their ability to compete with the banking sector by a lack of knowledge of financial service industry practices, as their training was in postal matters and not in financial services. Not only does the staff have to be able to identify promising credit prospects, they also need to work with customers in providing ancillary services, such as advice to small-business owners. Given their respective strengths and shortcomings, postal savings systems and credit cooperatives as well as non-governmental organizations involved in microcredit schemes can form alliances to provide together the complementary operations of small savings and credit.

Postal financial systems, for example, as in Indonesia, can complement the operations of credit institutions by acting as an agent for them in the disbursements of prearranged loans as well as in the receipt of installment repayments of the loans. The postal service network can provide essential agency services for local agricultural credit cooperatives, microcredit, as well as financial institutions that lack a rural network infrastructure. However, as mentioned earlier, in any agency relationship entered into by the posts, it is essential that the agency agreement be drawn appropriately to be mutually beneficial.

In many countries, agricultural credit cooperatives come under the jurisdiction of the ministry of agriculture, small-business credit institutions under the ministries of commerce or industry, while mortgage-lending institutions may come under the ministry of housing or some related government entity. In such situations, fostering interministry cooperation is a necessity for the posts in promoting its financial services.

Similar concerns arise regarding banks and their regulators. Thus China, with the active support of its central bank, and the Republic of Korea have been able to come to a modus vivendi with their respective private sector financial institutions and regulatory ministries. In other countries, such as Japan, Kazakhstan, the Philippines, Thailand, and Vietnam, the posts have been at loggerheads with private financial sector interests as well as with their respective central banks and finance ministries on a number of issues, such as limiting the size and scope of operations, investment policy, allowing the full use of the postal network's infrastructure, limitations on the range of savings products offered, and competition with existing commercial and savings institutions. In a number of countries, despite the potential for expanding the natural complementarities of postal savings and remittances with credit institutions and other financial service institutions, bureaucratic obstruction and institutional rivalries often prevent this from taking place.

Overseas Remittances via the Posts

For many developing countries in Asia and elsewhere, a significant amount of foreign exchange comes from the remittances of nationals working overseas. Examples include Philippine nationals working in the Hong Kong Special Administrative Region of China, Singapore, and the Middle East, and workers from Bangladesh, India, Pakistan, and Sri Lanka employed in the Persian Gulf states. Some 6 to 7 million South Asians work abroad, earning more than $20 billion, their remittances exceeding all Western donor country aid. Remittances account for more than half of Bangladesh's development budget, 40 percent of India's trade deficit, and most of Pakistan's foreign exchange sources. The Philippines is the world's second-largest exporter of labor, after Mexico. Constituting the Philippines' second-largest source of foreign exchange, some 5 to 7 million overseas Filipino workers (OFWs) remitted some $7.6 billion in 2003 through the banking system and upwards of another $7 billion sent through non-bank channels. Women make up around 50 percent of Asia's international migrant workers.

In China, overseas remittances to family members by emigrants also provide a substantial flow of income to certain regions of the country and are reflected in the relatively higher amounts of postal savings deposits in provinces such as Fujian, Guangdong, Hainan, and other regions with high overseas investment activity. In Vietnam, high levels of overseas remittances are reported in the southern half of the country, mainly from the Vietnamese immigrant community in the United States.

Bank remittance services and private money-transfer firm fees are quite costly, as noted in the previous chapter, and are not available in the impoverished home villages where most emigrant workers come from. However, in a number of countries there are alternative methods of long standing by which foreign exchange remittances may be handled on a more affordable basis, namely, postal giro payment facilities, postal checking, and savings accounts with direct deposit features. Where they have been introduced, international giro payments have low fees. The transaction fees for remittances among the European countries, Japan, and the Republic of Korea are equivalent to only a few dollars each.

Foreign currency exchange into local currency is another aspect of international remittance operations that can be brought in-house by the posts to the benefit of both the client and the post. Kazpost, Kazakhstan's postal operator, obtained a license for dealing in foreign exchange, thereby avoiding the foreign exchange commissions charged by the commercial banks to process overseas funds transfers. This is especially important since many Kazakh nationals have emigrated to other CIS and European countries with which Kazpost has postal remittance agreements and can send money to their relatives in Kazakhstan. It is important as well to the high volume of Kazakh "shuttle-traders," who buy goods in other Asian countries, such as China, India, Republic of Korea, and Thailand.

Kazakhstan's post has established—and China and the Philippines plan to introduce—U.S. dollar–denominated postal savings accounts, in part to encourage overseas remittances. Kazpost's service helps its clients retain more of their savings through a simplified transaction that eliminates fees to third parties. In addition, these money-changing activities provide Kazpost with an important source of revenue. As the Kazakh tenge is freely convertible with the U.S. dollar and with the euro, this service also aids in important cross-border trade between Kazakhstan and several of its CIS neighbors.

Another important issue is the design of savings products that will enhance the volume of overseas remittances. These include special savings vehicles relating to family housing, farmsteads, investment in small businesses, and the education of family members. Savings funds that benefit their local home community's public works, such as hospitals and schools, can also attract the special interests of overseas workers, as has been the recent experience in the Philippines.

The Intermediation and Investment of Mobilized Savings

Government policy on the investment of postal savings funds has been historically predicated on maintaining the public's confidence in the safety of postal savings funds. As noted earlier, postal savings systems are typically restricted to investing in government bonds and government-guaranteed securities. In all cases the posts in the Asian countries discussed in this book were highly restricted in their investment options by their respective ministries of finance and/or central banks. Among Asian countries a commonly stated principle, if not explicit policy, is that savings mobilized through the postal savings system should be invested or intermediated to serve economic and social development goals. Frequently, mobilized savings funds are intermediated through government-sponsored development banks and national development fund programs in addition to government obligation bonds.

In the case of India, 100 percent of the funds collected are distributed by the Ministry of Finance to the State governments in which the deposits were made. Previously, until April 2002, the Union government had retained 20 percent. There is no specific oversight by the central government of the States' use of the borrowed funds once they are remitted to them, as they are viewed as general financing for the state budgets, the largest outlays of which are for civil service salaries, followed by debt service. Interest rates on some postal savings products ranged as high as 12 percent, and even 14 percent. At this level the debt service repayment rates were unsustainable and highlighted the fiscal adjustment challenge facing the States and the public policy implications came under review. More recently, interest rates have been reduced (author's interviews).

An alternative to placing mobilized postal savings in government securities is to place them at the central bank. In China, all funds until 2003 were transferred to the People's Bank of China, the central bank. In 2004 permission was granted to invest newly deposited monies into the interbank loan market. The creation of a postal bank has also been under discussion. Hotly debated, however, are the policy implications of individual ministries being permitted to create their own "money pot" of available funds by owning their own bank, and whether or not "market principles" would govern their lending policies. Similar concerns have been voiced in some CIS and other transition economies regarding the governance implications and the potential for misallocation of funds.

In recent years, alternative market-based philosophies for the investment of funds have been called for in some countries and have led to problematic attempts and mixed results, which we will discuss in the next two subsections.

Mobilized Postal Savings Funds and Economic Development

Since the 1880s, Japan's Ministry of Finance (MoF) has directed the use of postal savings funds toward national goals, at various times to remedy specific problems. For example, during the inflation following the First World War, saving was encouraged to absorb excess liquidity and curb inflation. Postal savings provided resources for public sector pump-priming for new and developing industries, and the development and modernization of infrastructure. Japanese postal savings funds have also been used to stimulate the economy during recessions or to stabilize financial markets when needed. Historically, their foremost goal has been economic development.

Beginning in the postwar period and until the end of 2000, the MoF's Fiscal Investment and Loan Program (FILP) had allocated the funds to meet national and regional development goals. In recent years numerous critics had questioned the efficacy of the FILP program. The question of optimal placement of postal savings resources has become a concern in recent years in Japan. The large volume of funds coming into the postal system has raised controversy over how they should be deployed, especially in light of the vast amounts of public debt generated in efforts to resuscitate the stalled Japanese economy.

In response, a partial market approach has recently been implemented. In the beginning of 2001, postal savings funds began to be managed by a reorganized Postal Savings Agency that had been given a larger measure of discretion over where to invest the collected funds. Current policy calls for purchasing Japanese government and agency bonds with 80 percent of the funds and allocating the remainder to a mix of domestic and foreign equities, and corporate and foreign-denominated bonds, thus subjecting a significant portion of the funds to market and foreign exchange risk for the first time. The Postal Life Insurance Welfare Corporation presently invests the funds. At the end of September 2001, unrealized losses in the stock market were already estimated at ¥6,600 billion ($54 billion) (*Nikkei Shimbun,* 25 December 2001) and continued to decline as the Nikkei Tokyo Stock Exchange average reached twenty-year lows. Domestic and foreign fund management firms currently handle *yu-cho*'s investment needs.

Is Financial Market Investment a Realistic Option for Placing Postal Savings?

Financial market investment is not a realistic option for most developing economies, which typically have shallow financial markets. Such markets are often subject to high volatility, speculative forces, and opaque operations, making placement in them highly risky and thus inappropriate for postal savings. Efforts to place funds in domestic markets in Malaysia and Sri Lanka typify the problem. Their respective national savings banks are required to invest a minimum of 60 percent of their funds, reduced in recent years from 100 percent, in government bonds and government-guaranteed securities, leaving the rest for other placements. However, they have found few prudent opportunities in which to invest the balance in local financial markets and achieve the same rate of return or safety that government securities offer. Malaysia's NSB offers its own credit products such as residential mortgage financing, small business loans, and consumer loans; however, as this market falls far short in absorbing their investment needs, 87 percent of Malaysia's NSB investments still remain in government securities. In Sri Lanka's case, 83 percent is invested in government bonds and treasury bills; 10 percent in short- and long-term lending to other financial institutions; 5 percent in housing lending, which more than doubled in recent years; and only 2 percent in equities that are held short-term, changed from the NSB's previous buy-and-hold investment strategy (author's interviews).

Some foreign financial institutions have suggested that the savings funds be invested overseas in wholesale banking markets or in foreign bonds and equities. Such investments would do nothing to satisfy the development needs of the country and also expose the postal savings system to various market risks.

Is Tax Exemption Necessary in Mobilizing Funds?

A further issue involving savings, not only postal savings resources and the national treasury, is the practice of offering tax-exempt savings products, as is done in China, India, and Vietnam as well as many economically developed countries, including Japan. Despite the costs of these products to the treasury, the volume of low-cost domestic funds mobilized may outweigh the costs. The funds are then lent to the government. For example, more than half of the savings products devised by India's National Savings Organization feature tax advantages, including tax-free saving certificates sold through the commercial banks and marketed to an economically advantaged population. In India, of the some 350 million non-agricultural workers, only 10 percent earn incomes high enough that would make them liable for income tax. Therefore the utility of these tax-free savings plans have been criticized by some as an unnecessary benefit to an elite sector of the population. Until recently an anonymous savings certificate was available that did not even require a designated owner's name or beneficiary for payment (its purpose was construed by many to be to attract money made in the black market). There is a price to be paid by the public treasury for tax exemption, however, and in India the Ministry of Finance estimates that the overall cost of tax incentives amounts to 16 percent of the value of the funds collected under the program. In China, until 2002 any number of savings accounts could be opened with fictitious names, and, as in Vietnam, it remains to be seen whether these funds could be mobilized otherwise. Income tax collection is no easy matter in most developing countries; the use of tax-exempt products, mainly benefiting the well-off, highlights the need for governments to devise and enforce equitable forms of taxation rather than promote schemes based on tax avoidance.

The issues raised in this chapter, together with the discussion in the preceding chapters, have addressed policy questions that reflect not only Asian experiences in postal savings, but also illustrate many of the problems common to small savings mobilization and postal financial services in other regions as well. In the chapters that follow, the case studies will delve more deeply into the individual characteristics of each country's postal savings experience. The purpose of this book is to assist in sharing postal savings practices among the developing countries, and we hope that the case studies that follow contribute to that exchange.

Part 2

Asian Country Case Studies

4
Developing Postal Savings in China
Peng Min'an

China's Postal Savings System

The postal savings system has a long history in China. In 1918, China Post started postal remittance services and in 1919 began postal savings under the Postal Savings and Remittance Bureau (PSRB). In the years following, postal savings services developed a great deal, earning a good reputation with the public and becoming an important part of the government's financial system. However, military actions, economic chaos, and political turmoil during the War of Resistance Against Japan (1937–45) and the Civil War (1945–49) caused serious setbacks in postal savings service.

In 1949 the People's Republic of China was founded and a program of socialist transformation was initiated in 1953. In the financial field, savings institutions were reorganized and restructured, and the People's Bank of China (PBC) was established as China's central bank. Among the financial policies implemented by the PBC was making interest rates for savings uniform throughout the country. China's postal savings program was closed down during this process of restructuring the financial system.

In 1978, China undertook policies intended to open up and reform the economy to meet fast-growing development needs. The government, however, lacked the funds to invest in major economic construction and development. In 1983 the PBC and the Ministry of Posts and Telecommunications (MPT) began preparations to restore postal savings services throughout the country through the use of the postal infrastructure. In 1986, postal savings was reopened with Chinese socialist characteristics, operated by the MPT and supervised by the PBC. All deposits were placed in the PBC to finance an integrated national investment plan. The success of this effort helped the government mobilize household savings for increased investment in social capital and provided funds for greater construction.

China Postal Savings System: 1986–2000

The Agency Phase: 1986–89

On 8 January 1986, the Steering Committee for Central Finance and Economy of the State Council decided that the main task of postal savings services should be to gather indigenous capital resources and develop savings deposit services for individuals and households for the benefit of the people and the nation. In this connection the MPT and the PBC jointly released a circular on the opening of postal savings. As an incentive, to initiate this effort, it was decided that China Post should be able to earn a net profit from the new service. It was agreed that postal savings services were to be formally opened on 1 April 1986 and that all deposits would be handed over to the PBC, which in turn would pay China Post a 2.2 percent commission on the average daily balance of accumulated funds as its agency fee. In successive stages, post offices nationwide opened postal savings services. The interest rate is set by and changes according to the PBC.

China Post has maintained a good reputation since the founding of the People's Republic of China. The importance of the post as a public service system was championed by Chairman Mao, who wrote: "People's Posts and Telecommunications—regularity, speed and accuracy are key to promote service and achieve the public's acceptance." From 1986 to 1989 the growth in postal savings greatly accelerated, reflecting the numerous promotional campaigns undertaken by China Post to get customers to make large deposits by advertising the advantages of postal savings. By the end of 1989, after three and a half years of operation, there were 15,609 postal savings branches and the balance of deposits reached RMB 10 billion yuan, making up 1.96 percent of total savings deposited in urban and rural areas (RMB is the *renminbi*, China's currency).

During the ten years of the "open up and reform" period from 1978 to 1988, China was in transition from a planned economy to a market economy. It therefore became necessary to restructure the financial system, which had been organized under the planned economy. The main institutions competing with China Post for retail savings deposits were the four largest state-owned commercial banks: the Industrial and Commercial Bank of China (ICBC), the Agricultural Bank of China (ABC), China Construction Bank (CCB), and the Bank of China (BOC). However, under the financial system reforms these four big banks were transitioning to commercial banking operations.

Postal Department Phase: 1989–99

In order to promote the further development of the postal savings service in the climate of economic reform, the MPT and the PBC in November 1989

Figure 4.1 **Comparison of Market Share of China's Postal Savings System and Other Financial Institutions (as of June 2002)**

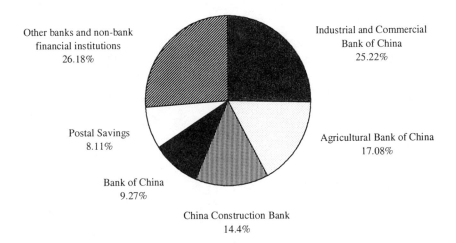

released a joint circular on "Further Developing the Postal Savings Service." Together they decided that henceforth postal savings would be run solely by the Postal Department, not as an agency of the PBC. Mobilized postal savings would be redeposited with the PBC, which would pay interest on funds to the Postal Department. The post, in turn, would pay interest to the postal savings depositors. The difference between the interest earned and interest paid would constitute operating revenues to be retained by the Postal Department. Detailed methods for handling redeposited funds were also formulated. The redeposit rate, however, was not a fixed rate, but would change according to periodic adjustments of the government's own unified interest rate. More than ten rate adjustments were made during this period, thus introducing the issue of rate risk and its management.

During the 1990–98 period there was competitive pressure from other financial institutions, including from the four large state-owned banks, which still accounted for over 90 percent of deposits in 2002 (see Figure 4.1: Comparison of Market Share of China's Financial Institutions). The Postal Savings Department adhered to the principle of "development on one hand, management on the other." While banks aimed at serving only the most profitable markets, postal savings aimed to serve the people, providing service to all who needed it. But the Postal Department also needed to earn revenues to maintain its services. Striking a balance between public service and profit was a difficult question for China's postal savings at the time.

Figure 4.2 **Balance of China's Postal Savings: 1986–June 2002**

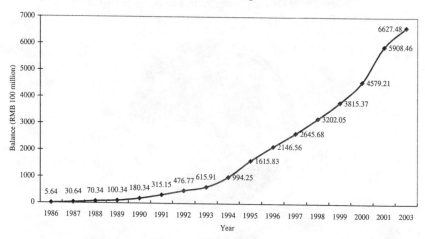

The postal savings system has had to compete intensely with commercial banks and non-bank financial institutions, including Agricultural Credit Cooperatives, and the Agricultural Foundation, both of which offer credit products. Nevertheless, strict management practices and good service have resulted in a dramatically increased market share for the postal savings system. The balance of deposits more than doubled from 1996 to 2000 and reached 663 billion yuan in 2002 (see Figure 4.2: Balance of China's Postal Savings: 1986–June 2002).

When this period began, it ushered in a new sense of competition to improve the level of service and to extend the postal network (see Figure 4.3: Branches of China's Postal Savings System: 1986–2001). The resultant rapid growth in postal savings service was achieved through measures such as: more effective staff training, standardizing service procedures, extending service hours, building new electronic networks, and, after 1995, the introduction of the capability for any depositor to make savings deposits and withdrawals anywhere in the country. Moreover, the Asian financial crisis in 1997 precipitated public distrust of banks. Use of the postal savings system dramatically increased so that by June 2002 postal savings' market share reached 8.11 percent, a 47 percent increase compared to 5.57 percent in 1996 (see Figure 4.4: Market Share of China Postal Savings: 1986–June 2002). Postal savings has continued to experience healthy development while deposits in other financial institutions have risen more slowly.

The number of postal savings branches reached 34,540 in 2001; 2,672 postal savings branches were added within the previous year. From cities

Figure 4.3 **Branches of China's Postal Savings System: 1986–2001**

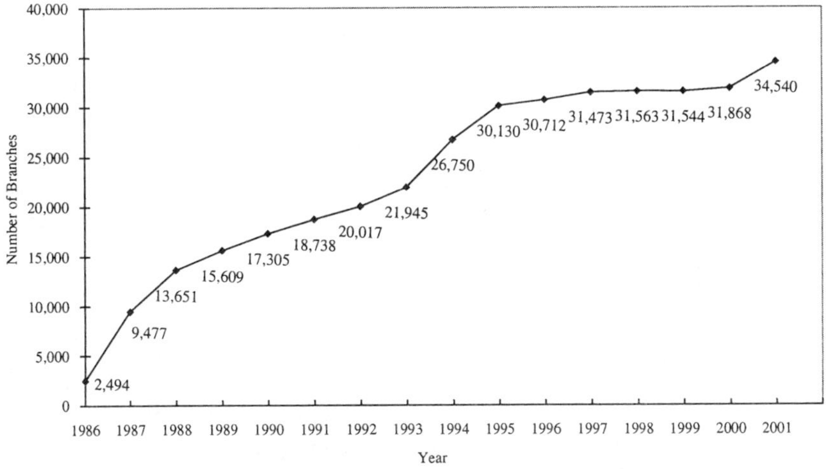

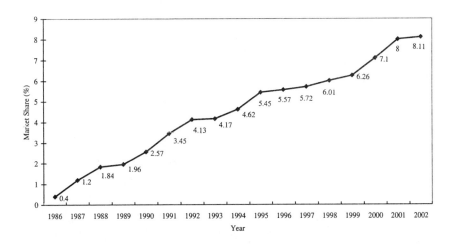

Figure 4.4 **Market Share of China's Postal Savings: 1986–June 2002**

and towns to rural areas across the country, the existing postal infrastructure is highly utilized by the postal savings network, greatly exceeding the range of the commercial banks' network. Eighty percent of postal savings branches are located in rural areas benefiting customers who otherwise would be without financial services. Between 1990 and 1998, many postal savings branches were opened, extending savings and remittance services to every province, municipality, and autonomous region. In addition, the Postal Savings and Remittance Service has opened multiservice counter centers in some cities, greatly improving the quality of service and availability of the postal savings network.

In China, 104 million households have postal savings accounts. Of those accounts, 70 percent of the balance of deposits are from urban areas, although they represent less than 30 percent of total postal savings branches. Why do 30 percent of the branches, which are in urban areas, hold 70 percent of the postal savings balance? Generally speaking, there are several reasons. The average income of residents in urban areas is two to three times the income of households in rural areas. Also, the financial awareness of urban residents is much higher than that of rural residents, who often keep their small savings in cash or in-kind. A third factor is the dominating role of rural credit cooperatives, which are also deposit-taking institutions but, unlike postal savings, offer credit facilities to their members. Access to credit is essential to agricultural production and hence to rural economic life. Nevertheless, postal savings continues to grow especially well in rural areas due to the strong promotional efforts by the entire postal staff.

In 2002, twenty-one provinces and municipalities (out of thirty-one) had a postal savings balance exceeding RMB 100 million yuan, an indication of how significant postal savings can be in a region compared to the commercial banking sector (see Figure 4.5: The Balance of Postal Savings by Region). Particularly significant is the well-above-average market share held for several years by postal savings in many of China's poorer provinces (see Table 4.1: The Balance, Market Share, and Income of Postal System, October 2000). This is indicative of China Post's commitment to serve populations in regions that are without many alternative means of access to financial services, such as banks.

Postal Savings with Chinese Characteristics: Organizational Structure and Operations

China's Postal Savings and Remittance Bureau (PSRB) is the leading subordinate enterprise of the State Post Bureau (SPB). The SPB's branches are distributed across three levels: county, provincial capital, and province. Attached to each of the thirty-one regional State Post Bureaus, including special municipal bureaus and bureaus for autonomous regions, is a PSRB department.

Within the Postal Savings and Remittance Bureau are eight functional divisions:

1. General Management Division—in charge of comprehensive affairs inside the PSRB, such as political, financial, personnel, and external affairs;

Figure 4.5 The Balance of Postal Savings by Region

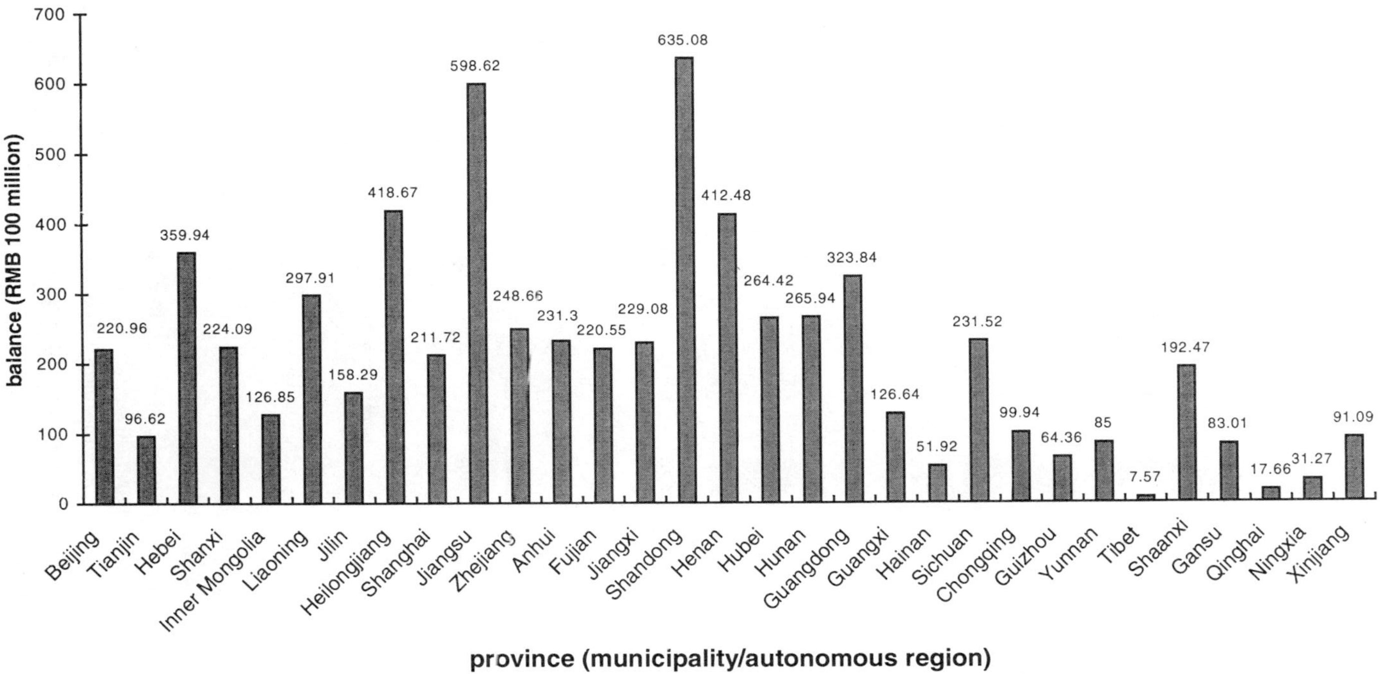

Province (municipality/autonomous region)	Balance (RMB 100 million)
Beijing	220.96
Tianjin	96.62
Hebei	359.94
Shanxi	224.09
Inner Mongolia	126.85
Liaoning	297.91
Jilin	158.29
Heilongjiang	418.67
Shanghai	211.72
Jiangsu	598.62
Zhejiang	248.66
Anhui	231.3
Fujian	220.55
Jiangxi	229.08
Shandong	635.08
Henan	412.48
Hubei	264.42
Hunan	265.94
Guangdong	323.84
Guangxi	126.64
Hainan	51.92
Sichuan	231.52
Chongqing	99.94
Guizhou	64.36
Yunnan	85
Tibet	7.57
Shaanxi	192.47
Gansu	83.01
Qinghai	17.66
Ningxia	31.27
Xinjiang	91.09

Table 4.1

The Balance, Market Share, and Income of Postal System, October 2000

Region	Balance of PSS	Position	Market Share (%)	Position	Income of PSS	% Total Postal Revenue
National Total	441,399		7.0		11,693	34.3
Beijing	16,762	10	5.9	28	465	19.4
Tianjin	6,997	22	6.1	25	189	36.2
Hebei	25,073	5	6.4	23	612	49.4
Shanxi	14,530	14	8.4	13	335	46.8
Inner Mongolia	8,824	21	10.3	5	232	38.5
Liaoning	21,996	6	5.9	27	555	42.7
Jilin	11,470	19	7.7	17	333	48.4
Heilongjiang	27,427	3	12.4	1	728	54.7
Shanghai	15,056	13	5.9	26	404	20.1
Jiangsu	37,881	2	8.7	12	903	34.8
Zhejiang	15,839	12	4.6	29	459	29.7
Anhui	14,458	15	10.1	6	343	32.2
Fujian	17,092	9	10.1	7	474	31.0
Jiangxi	12,837	17	10.4	4	301	32.7
Shandong	40,978	1	9.3	9	917	45.2
Henan	27,375	4	8.7	11	631	43.0
Hubei	14,044	16	7.5	18	331	25.5
Hunan	17,829	8	9.6	8	401	30.9
Guangdong	21,847	7	2.6	31	105	31.8
Guangxi	9,424	20	7.0	20	251	42.8
Hainan	4,218	28	10.5	3	122	44.6
Sichuan	16,161	11	6.2	24	428	37.6
Chongqing	6,821	23	6.5	22	167	35.4
Guizhou	4,455	27	8.4	14	136	26.4
Yunnan	5,017	26	4.5	30	157	29.3
Tibet	447	31	11.4	2	20	35.0
Shaanxi	11,574	18	7.8	16	290	37.2
Gansu	5,426	25	6.8	21	161	33.8
Qinghai	1,201	30	7.8	15	40	38.3
Ningxia	2,045	29	9.2	10	58	39.1
Xinjiang	6,298	24	7.2	19	180	39.4

2. Savings Service Division—in charge of savings and savings card business;
3. Remittance Service Division—in charge of domestic remittance business and interprovince settlement of electronic remittance funds;
4. Agency Service Division—in charge of development, planning, and administration of agency services;
5. Operation Development Division—in charge of development planning, statistics collection, information, and marketing of postal financial services;

6. Fund Clearance Center—in charge of settlement between second-level settlement center on the national postal savings computer network;
7. Audit Divisions—in charge of inspecting and auditing of postal financial services;
8. International Service Division—in charge of development and operation of international business, such as international remittances, Western Union money transfers, and so forth.

The Supervising Department regulates and controls the savings business. For the past sixteen years it has closely followed its mandate to "grasp both development and management." It has abided by the state financial laws and regulations together with Postal Savings Department regulations and its inner oversight mechanism. All levels of the control system are aimed at effectively strengthening risk management procedures, which include: authorization procedures; follow-up supervision and accounting systems; and improving technical staff training at the municipal, provincial, and national level.

Although the PSRB is a government-owned business, it is fiscally independent from other government entities and is required to operate in a profitable manner. Its provision of financial services is based on an ongoing analysis of public needs and the additional goal of reducing transaction costs to the public to the greatest extent possible.

China's postal savings system is an easily accessible institution that is highly regarded by its customers. Postal savings customers may make deposits and withdrawals at any computerized postal savings branch throughout the country. For example, money deposited into an account at any postal savings branch in Beijing may be withdrawn from that account at any postal savings branch in Guangzhou. In 2001 there were some 13.6 million transactions, valued at RMB 86.2 billion.

Postal savings deposits are treated as largely long-term funds by the PSRB, which redeposits them into the PBC. From May 1996 to December 1997, 80 percent of PSRB deposits in PBC were deposited as long-term and 20 percent on-demand. After 1997, both the long-term and short-term accounts were combined, with the PBC providing the necessary funds whenever needed to meet liquidity demands for withdrawals, thus freeing the PSRB from liquidity risk management. The interest earned on redeposits is used to pay the interest on customers' postal savings accounts. The surplus income goes into the general income account of the State Post Bureau.

The profits from operations of the postal savings system account for nearly one-third of all postal services revenues. In 2001 the total revenue of China

Post was RMB 47.09 billion, and income from the postal savings system was upward of RMB 14.82 billion. Philatelic sales and letter delivery accounted for 14.0 percent and 10.8 percent respectively in 1998, ranking a distant second and third place in the SPB's revenue stream. Therefore, the postal savings system makes an enormous fiscal contribution and is by far the largest source of income to China Post.

Deposit Base and Institutional Capacity

The inculcation of values of thrift and savings is a common attribute of Chinese culture, even among Chinese residing in other countries. Generally speaking, in China, middle-income and poor people, especially women, have better saving habits and attitudes than higher income groups and men. The postal savings system builds on this in its marketing strategy.

The rate of interest on savings is a negligible factor in attracting savings deposits, particularly since the rate of interest paid on savings by the postal savings system and the commercial banks is uniform and strictly regulated by the PBC. The public's confidence in postal savings is very high. Because the funds from postal savings households are redeposited, that is, invested, solely with the PBC, China's central bank, the principal and interest paid into postal savings accounts come from the PBC investment. The PBC in turn invests the funds with the State Development Bank.* The postal savings system does not provide commercial credit services, therefore there is no opportunity to incur bad assets, that is, non-performing loans. The public is confident that their savings will be available for withdrawal when needed, and this confidence is boosted by the government's guarantee on deposits and China Post's reputation of good service.

Therefore, the main marketing strategy of postal savings is to improve its level of service and promote those improvements. Since its inauguration in 1986, the postal savings system has launched various efforts to achieve the highest quality of service, including standardizing the operational methods of the postal sector and improving workers' attitudes, as reflected by the slogan "Service best and customers first." Also, China Post promotes the advantages of its longer business hours and the availability of its services during holidays and weekends when other financial institutions may be closed. Through its postal delivery operations to hundreds of millions of households, PSRB provides a set of special services, including door-to-door home service of remittances, and special services for handling large-scale remittances of

---

*Editor's note: Beginning in 2004 newly deposited postal savings monies may also be lent through the interbank market to other financial institutions.

business enterprises. These special services are used to provide greater customer convenience and are part of the process to increase the level of postal savings deposits.

The postal savings system has been able to extend its reach successfully into rural areas, especially the less developed regions of central and western China, which commercial banks and other commercial financial institutions have found to be unprofitable for their purposes. Postal savings is growing well in rural areas, although it represents only a 20 percent market share. This is mainly due to lack of credit facilities which PSRB's competitors, the Agricultural Bank of China and Rural Credit Cooperatives, offer their depositors. Furthermore, since China Post subcontracts much of its rural postal delivery services to the local People's Committee staff, this results in a smaller number of offices staffed by the postal administration who serve as retail sales persons for the post's financial services.

The postal savings system is not hampered by either postal or other governmental regulations or restrictions on customers, such as limiting the balances of individual depositors or limiting amounts of withdrawals from accounts. China's postal savings system also welcomes small account-holders.

The PSRB uses the media to promote postal savings, including television and newspapers, with advertising adapted to reflect local and regional needs and characteristics. Advertising its services helps raise the social reputation of the postal savings system. China Post also takes advantage of the special characteristics of its postal and telecommunications infrastructure to actively promote the postal savings service. Advertising has been instrumental in introducing and popularizing new services, including current account deposits that enable customers to deposit money in one place and withdraw it from another; also, etiquette savings—special deposit services for gift-giving at festivals, birthdays, and so forth, which have increased deposits overall. Among the agency services PSRB provides are salary payments for enterprises, receiving telephone bill payments, and periodical subscription services. Additional financial products include fixed-term deposits and agency sales by some local postal administrations of government bonds, insurance, pension plans, and so on. All of these operations add to the volume of financial transaction fee revenues.

As of March 2001, 28 million postal savings households had Green Cards, which gives them access to the postal system's forty-six hundred automated teller machines (ATMs) and are also debit cards. The cards are being used increasingly for point of sale payments in participating stores. Credit facilities are not offered by the postal savings system; therefore the Green Card is only a debit card and not a credit card.

Money orders are also an important product sold by the postal savings system. They are mainly a domestic service, although China cooperates actively with foreign postal authorities and has signed agreements on international money order service with over twenty foreign countries. In 2001, incoming international receipts numbered 162,317 with a total value of US$119 million while the outgoing orders numbered only 2,080, valued at US$654,809. This is in comparison to 22.6 million domestic money orders totaling RMB 293.4 billion yuan. International money orders have been declining in recent years as China's means of processing international services orders have not stayed current with new technology. China Post is currently focusing on its long-term goal of providing an efficient international electronic remittances service. More recently, China's post offices began to provide agency facilities for Western Union's twenty-four-hour money transfer business at 257 branches.

Technology and the Development of Postal Savings

Advanced technology has brought fresh vigor to the development of postal savings services, and the PSRB attaches great importance to investment in technology. In early 1994 the technical transformation project of the postal savings computer system, known as "the Green Card Project," was begun. In May 1996 an online postal savings computer system was put into operation connecting Beijing, Shanghai, and Dalian, which enabled customers to deposit money in these three cities and withdraw it from the ATMs and counters in any of these three cities. By the end of 1996, thirty provincial capitals and more relatively developed cities had joined this computerized system.

In 1998 the Postal Savings Online System was opened to the networks of commercial banks in Changsha, Shanghai, and Beijing, enabling commercial bank customers to use their cash cards at postal savings' ATMs to access their ordinary deposit account funds while postal savings customers were able to access their ordinary savings accounts via the banks' ATMs.

By 2000, approximately 21,000 computerized postal savings branches of the eventual 33,698 postal savings outlets had been built. There were also 17,839 offices or agencies providing online deposit and withdrawals in 1,316 different counties and cities in all thirty-one provinces and autonomous regions of China.

A New Phase: The Postal Savings Bank

As a state-owned institution dedicated to individual and household savings, the postal savings system is continuing to fine-tune its operations to meet the changing times. Toward this end the postal savings system is developing measures to further upgrade its operations to reduce costs and maintain healthy operations. These measures include improving the levels of operations management and risk management, upgrading and extending the computer network system, increasing the number of post office-based ATMs, opening more self-service automated banking centers with stand-alone ATMs, and developing and expanding telephone banking and debit card services. In addition, China Post provides agency services in some locations for other financial service companies; services include sales of insurance products, and possibly in the future mutual funds. The postal savings system is also currently facilitating the development of an electronic remittance project aimed at improving the efficiency of remittances.

Although the previous eighteen years witnessed rapid growth in postal savings, the development of a market economy in China has brought demands for a change in the current status of postal savings, more specifically that the PSRB become a formal financial institution under the supervision of China's central bank, the PBC. Under the supervision of the postal administration the PSRB's products are currently limited to a smaller range of services compared to the four state-owned commercial banks.

In accordance with a directive of the State Council to reform the postal savings system, in May 1999 the State Post Bureau began preparations to form the Postal Savings Bank of China. The new bank, whose functions are now carried out by the PSRB, is to be an independent corporation led by the China State Post Bureau. This will mark the entry of China's postal savings system into a new stage.

The creation of the new Postal Savings Bank is in part a response to fierce competition in recent years, especially in the urban market. A large number of the commercial banks' retailing outlets, which are concentrated in the big and middle-sized cities, have been losing market share in recent years to diverse alternate investment channels being offered to the public, including investing in the stock market. As a result the commercial banks have been losing their previous market share and have even shown negative growth in deposits. Although the PSRB has continued to retain its deposit levels in urban areas, it is working to maintain its competitive advantage by seeking to provide additional banking services through its transformation into a bank.

It is envisioned that the China Postal Savings Bank will be able to offer the following products and expanded services after its establishment: (1) savings and deposits in both Chinese currency (RMB) and foreign currency; (2) postal savings and remittances; (3) sale and payment of government bonds; (4) Agency services such as pension payments, and the sale of financial products for other institutions; (5) after setting aside reserve funds for management of savings operations, the funds obtained will be deposited in the PBC, the state-owned commercial banks, and policy based banks, or be used to purchase state bonds and some financial paper issued by state-owned banks and the three government-owned policy based banks: the State Development Bank, the Agricultural Development Bank, and the State Import and Export Bank; (6) finally, it will offer any other service permitted by the PBC.

Concluding Remarks

The Chinese postal savings system has made great contributions in facilitating China's economic construction and improving social welfare by collecting capital for national economic development and providing individual savings services for all households nationwide.

At present the postal savings system business products and operations are comparatively simple, mainly because the postal savings system does not provide credit facilities or its own insurance services. New challenges and opportunities are emerging with China's entry into the World Trade Organization and its implementation of complex institutional reforms. Foreign-owned financial institutions that are well capitalized and have advanced management skills and technology are expected to enter the market. Within five years they will be authorized to operate retail business in China's currency, the *renminbi* (RMB). In order to meet these challenges, China has been accelerating the momentum of reform and has increased the pace of upgrading financial technology, including the establishment of an electronic remittance system. At the same time, it has maintained its focus on the institutional transformation of the PSRB from a government bureau to a formal bank.

5
Postal Savings as a Financial Intermediary in the Republic of Korea
Chan Ki Nam

Introduction

Postal savings in Korea began in 1905 under the Ministry of Posts, Telephone, and Telegraph. Postal money order and life insurance services were initiated in 1929. These services were directly administered by the Ministry of Posts and it successor, the Ministry of Information and Communication (MIC), which encompassed telecommunications, postal operations, and postal banking. In 1977 postal banking and insurance operations were ended, and these services were handed over to the Bank of Agricultural Credit (agricultural cooperatives). The purpose of this changeover was to relieve post offices from banking and insurance businesses so that MIC could concentrate on the telecommunications business.

The Postal Financial System of Korea

By 1983, postal financial services were reintroduced. While not a major part of the Korean financial sector, they were found to be an effective way to fill a niche. In 1982 the operation of the telecommunications business was taken away from the posts and handed over to a government-sponsored corporation, the Korea Telecommunications Authority (KTA). This change was largely the result of market liberalization initiatives and the need to efficiently meet the rapidly increasing demand in telecommunications services. At the same time, MIC came to realize that there was considerable merit in managing postal savings and insurance businesses together with postal business as complementary operations. It saw the potential benefits from economies of scope by utilizing the same post office facilities and employees in running the three businesses together. Thus, MIC made full efforts to reinstitute the postal savings and insurance business and was able to resume their operations on 1 January 1983, when the Postal Savings and Insurance Act (PSIA) went into effect.

Figure 5.1 **The Organizational Structure of the Postal Savings System in the Republic of Korea**

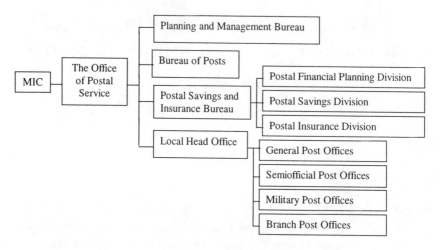

The nation's postal savings and insurance business has grown continuously over the last two decades. Viewed qualitatively from a service perspective, there has been major progress in computerization with online real-time processing of savings, giro accounts, and money order transactions throughout the post office's nationwide network. With more than twenty-eight hundred post offices, even small post office branches are connected through the online system. The postal banking system is connected to the Korea Financial Telecommunications & Clearings Institute operated by the Bank of Korea, the central bank. The outstanding balance of postal savings deposits reached about 24.5 trillion won at the end of 2000 and has shown unusually rapid growth in the volume of deposits since the 1997 financial crisis.

The Office of Postal Service in MIC is in charge of running both the postal and the postal savings businesses, as shown in Figure 5.1: The Organizational Structure of the Postal Savings System in the Republic of Korea. It was set up on 1 July 1999 to introduce more commercial concepts to the management of the postal business. The president of the Office of Postal Service is responsible for managing both postal operations and postal banking services. Three vice presidents are responsible for the Planning and Management Bureau, the Bureau of Posts, and the Postal Savings & Insurance Bureau. Within the Postal Savings & Insurance Bureau are the following three divisions: the Postal Financial Planning Division, Postal Savings Division, and the Postal Insurance Division.

The net income from postal savings in Korea increased modestly from 89 billion won in 1997 to 103 billion won in 1998, and dramatically increased to 297 billion won in 1999, as shown in Table 5.1: Income Statement. While

Table 5.1

Income Statement (in billions of won)

	1997	1998	1999	2000	2001
Revenues	953	1,176	1,467	1,709	2,094
Expenses	864	1,073	1,170	1,401	1,663
Net Income	89	103	297	308	431

Note: Revenues are interest income plus other income, and expenses are interest expenses plus other expenses. However, the interest portion is dominant.

the interest paid to depositors remained level, interest from investments increased sharply, resulting in the large increase in net income. In 2000, as a result of a mismatch on interest rate movements, investment returns lagged while rates on time-deposit funds remained fixed over the year. The interest paid out increased more sharply than interest revenues, resulting in a big decrease in net income from savings. The large decrease in net income was due to the fact that a large portion of postal savings funds were collected in fixed-rate time deposits whose maturity is relatively long and bear a fixed interest rate until the product's maturity, while government fiscal policy at the time was to reduce interest rates overall.

Nevertheless, the positive net incomes during the last four years indicate the soundness of postal savings so far. Also, no serious problems have arisen in managing the funds raised by postal savings.

Role of Postal Savings

The role of postal savings and insurance services is set forth in Article 1 of the PSIA, which states that the aim of offering postal savings and insurance services through the post office network is to enhance national economic stability and public welfare. In addition to their traditional roles as financial institutions, postal savings and insurance services focus on mobilizing savings nationally at a relatively low overhead cost compared to commercial financial institutions. The funds mobilized are invested mainly in policy-based financial institutions (including government accounts), which make loans to small businesses and give support to developing the social infrastructure. The interest rate paid by the government account is directly linked to the interest rate of the National Housing Bonds issued by the government, with a maturity of five years. The interest rate paid by policy-based financial institutions is determined in relation to the rate of government bonds that have similar maturity.

In general, the role of financial institutions is to efficiently intermediate

Table 5.2

The Distribution of Post Offices (31 December 2000)

	Number of Post Offices	Percent Distribution
Metropolitan Cities*	742	26
Other Areas	2,074	74
Total	2,816	100

*There are six special metropolitan cities and eight provinces in the Republic of Korea. In each province there are several cities and *kun*. Usually the population of a city is greater than 100,000. Each *kun* consists of 10 to 15 *myun*. In each *myun* there exist about 10 *dong* (villages). About 45 percent of the total population lives in special metropolitan cities.

funds between savings surplus units (savers) and savings deficit units (borrowers). Savings surplus units are usually individual households while savings deficit units are usually firms and the government. In other words, financial institutions collect funds from individual households and invest them in firms and the government. Firms usually use these funds to finance production, and the government uses them for social overhead capital projects such as airports, railroads, harbors, and the like. In this context, we can divide the role of postal savings into two different aspects: the deposit-taking side and the investment side.

First, if we look at the deposit-taking side, the role of postal savings is not only to promote the importance of household savings as a prerequisite for a stable national economic life, but also to provide convenient banking services through the nationwide post office network.

Postal savings services are widely used by the Korean people throughout the country. As shown in Table 5.2: The Distribution of Post Offices, of the 2,816 post offices, only 26 percent are located in the largest metropolitan cities. Nearly three-quarters are located outside the major cities, particularly in the countryside where only post offices and agricultural cooperatives maintain branches that provide financial services. While commercial banks sometimes maintain branches in downtown areas at the *kun* (county) level, the postal banking service maintains branches at the *myun* (township) level. This indicates that post offices provide savings services in rural areas where commercial banks do not have branches due to low profitability. The reason the number of post offices in metropolitan cities is relatively small is that post offices in large cities were established, not based on the need for financial services, but on the need for postal services.

More than half of the deposits to postal savings are made in small cities and rural areas, as shown in Table 5.3: Deposits by Region. The relatively low market share of postal savings in metropolitan cities, 3.4 percent, re-

Table 5.3

Deposits by Region (as of 1999, in billions of Korean won)

	Metropolitan Cities	Other Areas	Total
Postal Savings	8,260.6 (49.5%)	8,427.4 (50.5%)	16,688.0 (100%)
Deposit Money Banks	236,831.3 (73.2%)	86,579.8 (26.8%)	323,411.1 (100%)
Share of Postal Savings	3.4%	8.9 %	4.9%

Table 5.4

Number of Postal Savings Accounts (as of 31 December 2001)

Number of Active Accounts (thousands)	20,261	71.3%
Number of Dormant Accounts (thousands)*	8,153	28.7%

*If no transactions have been recorded for an account in ten years, it is considered dormant and the balance is transferred to the government's account at the Bank of Korea.

flects the keen competition among a large number of different kinds of financial institutions in the metropolitan savings market. However, postal savings has a much higher market share in the other areas, 8.9 percent, even though the Bank of Agricultural Credit is a strong competitor in rural areas. In addition, postal banking services focus on individual customers while banks emphasize both individual and commercial customers in conjunction with providing loans. From this point of view, postal savings is a complementary institution to commercial banks; by providing universal financial services through its extensive system of post offices, it thereby improves the quality of the national financial system as a whole.

Table 5.4: Number of Postal Savings Accounts, shows that the number of active accounts reached 20.3 million by the end of 2001, however, 28.7 percent were dormant. Considering the number of households (nearly 13 million), and the population of Korea (47.3 million), approximately every two or three persons on average has at least one postal savings account, and every household averages more than one and a half accounts.

Second, if we look at the investment side, the role of postal savings is an important source of government funding. The funds raised from repurchase agreements (see below) are invested in government bonds. The funds raised from postal deposits are redeposited into either Treasury Loans and Investment Special Accounts (TLISA) or into other financial institutions, such as trust accounts of commercial banks. The Postal Savings & Insurance Bureau cannot make loans directly to individual customers under the PSIA.

The funds placed in government bonds and TLISA are utilized for investments in social infrastructure in accordance with government programs and intermediated through public policy-based institutions, such as small business lending institutions. While more than half of the proceeds from savings and time deposits are invested in TLISA, the remaining funds are usually redeposited into other financial institutions. In this sense, postal savings services help the funding of both government and commercial financial institutions.

Deposit-Taking

Savings products offered by Korean post offices include ten categories of postal savings deposit accounts, and repurchase agreements (RPs); these are in addition to remittance products such as postal money orders, postal giro accounts, cashier's checks, and a range of insurance products. Table 5.5 provides a summary of postal savings products.

The individuals who seek higher interest rates for relatively large amounts of money usually use time deposits, while those with regular income who want to accumulate funds for a specific purpose prefer installment deposits. Ordinary deposits and savings deposits are usually used for transaction purposes since there is no restriction on the number of transactions. Preferred savings are used for specified groups of depositors, such as workers and families to whom the government wishes to give special incentives like interest rates on limited amounts of deposits. Finally, short-term investors use RPs because of relatively high interest rates combined with very short-term maturity. RPs are financial contracts in which the seller of a government security agrees to buy back the security within a specified period of time at a stated price. They are usually used as short-term investment vehicles by financial institutions and corporations. RPs are also used by central banks to fine-tune the money supply. With the Korea Post's special RPs, investors can buy these instruments in small denominations typically not available in the financial market and withdraw funds without penalty after a week, the minimum period of deposit.

The balance of postal savings deposits increased rapidly from 1995 to 2000 as shown in Table 5.6, Deposit Balances. In 2000, deposits grew 46.8 percent, and the average annual growth rate from 1996 to 2000 was 29.3 percent, despite four reductions in interest rates on time deposits (on July 1, August 7, August 21, and September 1, 2000). These reductions were the cause of the mismatching problem of payouts versus investment income mentioned earlier. The deposit balance of postal savings did continue to grow, and increased further in 2001.

Table 5.5

Postal Savings Products Summarized (as of 31 December 2001)

Kind	Maturity	Interest rate (%)	Maximum amounts of deposit (Korean won)	Characteristics
Ordinary Deposit	–	1.0	None	
Savings Deposit	–	2.0	None	
New Savings Deposit	Less than 3 months 3–6 months More than 6 months	2.0 2.5 2.5	50 million	• One account per person
Time Deposit	30 days 3 months 6 months 1 year More than 2, less than 3 years	4.1 4.6 4.7 5.0 5.5 5.5	None	
Installment Deposit	6 months–1 year 1–2 years 2–3 years	4.8 5.5 5.4	None	
Family-Preferred Installment Deposit	6 months–1 year 1–2 years 2–3 years	4.9 5.1 5.5	30 million	
Student Installment Deposit		5.5	Middle/high school: 2 million Kindergarten elementary school: 1 million	• Join through school • No income taxes on interest earned
Worker's-Preferred Savings	3 years 5 years	6.0 6.0	Minimum of more than 10 thousand and maximum of less than 500 thousand per month	• Workers whose annual income less than 20 million won • 1 account per household • No tax on interest earned
"Full"-Preferred Savings	Less than 5 million 5 million–10 million 10 million–50 million 50 million–100 million Over 100 million	1.0 3.0 5.0 5.5 6.0	Minimum deposit of 5 million	
Repurchase Agreements	7–15 days 16–30 days 31–60 days 61–90 days 91 days–180 days 181 days–1 year	1.0 3.5 4.1 4.3 4.6 4.7	More than 50 thousand	

Table 5.6

Deposit Balances (in billions of Korean won)

	1995	1996	1997	1998	1999	2000
Postal Savings	6,986.3	7,952.1	9,291.2	13,584.1	16,688.0	24,496.3
(Growth Rate)		(13.8%)	(16.8%)	(46.2%)	(22.8%)	(46.8%)
Deposit-taking Banks*	154,136.1	181,720.8	198,197.4	251,794.5	323,411.1	404,660.9
(Growth Rate)		(17.9%)	(9.0%)	(27.0%)	(28.4%)	(25.1%)
Total		161,122.4	189,672.9	207,488.6	265,378.6	340,009.1	429,157.2
Market Share of Postal Savings	4.3%	4.2%	4.5%	5.1%	4.9%	5.7%

Source: Bank of Korea, *Survey and Statistics Report,* November 2001.
* Aggregated accounts of commercial and specialized deposit-taking banks, excluding trust accounts and accounts at their overseas branches.

This high level of growth can be explained by the change in the savings behavior of depositors during the financial crisis in Korea, which started at the end of 1997 (see chapter 6 by J.S. Park and C.K. Nam). At the time of the crisis, a large number of financial institutions closed, and the depositors of those institutions suffered when they could not withdraw their deposited funds from these banks. Although small deposits in private banks are safe, customers experience inconvenience when attempting a withdrawal if the bank gets into financial difficulty. As a result, depositors sought safer places to make their deposits. Postal savings was a good choice since there was no chance of bankruptcy of postal savings due to the government's guarantee of both the principal and the interest on deposits. Deposits in private banks are not guaranteed by the government but are insured by the Korean Deposit Insurance Corporation.

In addition to the change of savings behavior of depositors during the financial crisis in Korea, there were also marketing campaigns to increase outstanding savings balances. Rather than increasing interest rates on deposits, the campaigns focused on incentive schemes for postal savings employees that provided commissions and bonuses based upon their performance evaluation. These evaluations rated the amounts of savings maintained over a period of time. As a result, large numbers of post offices started to build closer relationships with their depositors, by introducing new products and providing both friendly counter service and convenient electronic service transactions. Customer satisfaction has im-

Table 5.7

Share of Major Types of Postal Savings Products
31 December 2000 and (1999) percentages

Time Deposit Accounts	Installment Deposit Accounts	Savings Deposit Accounts	Repurchase Agreements (RP)	Other Products
52.6%	20.6%	10.9%	9.5%	6.4%
(53.4)	(14.6)	(12.4)	(9.8)	(9.8)

Table 5.8

Percentage Share of Repurchase Agreements (RPs)
(in postal savings instruments)

1995	1996	1997	1998	1999	2000
23.7%	19.1%	21.5%	15.3%	9.8%	9.5%

proved so much that the post office is now ranked first among public enterprises according to the results of a survey conducted by the Korea Management Association.

The market share of postal savings also increased from 4.3 percent in 1995 to 5.7 percent in 2000 as shown in Table 5.6: Deposit Balances. This increase in market share is due to postal savings' larger rate of growth in comparison to other deposit-taking institutions.

If we look at the relative importance of postal savings products as shown in Table 5.7: Share of Major Types of Postal Savings Products, we see that time deposits are the largest financial instrument, followed by various installment deposit accounts, savings deposit accounts, and repurchase agreements. A special marketing campaign in 2000 was a factor in increasing the balance in Family-Preferred Installment Deposit accounts.

While the percentage share of RPs decreased to 9.5 percent in 2000, it has been traditionally a more important savings instrument in terms of the amount of funds mobilized, as shown in Table 5.8: Percentage Share of Repurchase Agreements. This product may be considered uniquely characteristic of Korean postal savings. Although RPs are usually a wholesale financial instrument, Korean post offices offer retail RPs. In contrast to the wholesale RP, which is denominated at over 50 million won with a liberalized interest rate, the minimum denomination of retail RPs offered by postal savings is 50 thousand won. Thus postal savings RPs provide customers with short-term retail investment opportunities at competitive interest rates. Although the relative importance of the RP has been on the decrease since 1997 due to new competing short-term financial products, such as the CMA (cash management account) offered by merchant (investment) banks, it still plays a significant role in funding postal savings.

Investment

The investment side of the banking business is as important to a commercial bank as the financing side because the difference between the investment yield and the funding cost is the main source of bank profit. However, in the case of postal savings, profitability is not the single most important criterion in making investment decisions. The investment of postal savings funds has two objectives, which are pursued simultaneously: public welfare and profitability.

While postal savings funds are either invested in securities or redeposited in other financial institutions and the TLISA, the investment of these funds can be divided into two categories according to the two objectives. If we look at Table 5.9: Percentage Investment of Postal Banking Funds, the portion invested with the purpose of raising public welfare is 64.8 percent while the amount invested for profitability is 32.8 percent (commercial bank paper plus cash). This indicates that Korean postal banking makes its first investment priority public welfare, and then profitability. Although this has sacrificed some yield, it has also reduced risk.

One thing to note is that, by the nature of the RP instrument, all of the funds raised by RPs are invested in government bonds. The funds raised by postal savings, with the exception of RPs, are mainly redeposited with TLISA and commercial financial institutions. Postal savings funds are also channeled to public policy-based banks, such as the Korea Development Bank, which in turn make loans to small businesses.

While public responsibility is emphasized in the investment of postal savings funds, the fact that the postal savings operations have to earn appropriate profits to avoid financial distress should also be recognized. Therefore, when postal savings funds are redeposited in TLISA, the most important consideration is securing an appropriate interest margin. The yield on the redeposit to TLISA is determined by the five-year interest rate of government bonds. Since the interest rate on government bonds is not fixed, the yield may sometimes be lower than the highest interest rate on a particular postal savings instrument, thereby resulting in a negative interest margin on that particular savings instrument at that time.

Underlying this problem is the fact that TLISA is not able to satisfy postal savings' need for a higher yield. This is because TLISA operates at a deficit due to the negative spread and is thus subsidized by the state. The main reason for the

Table 5.9

Percentage Investment of Postal Banking Funds
(31 December 2000 and 1999)

	Investment of Postal Savings Funds	
	2000	1999
Total Public Welfare Investments:	64.8	59.3
TLISA	24.2	26.9
Government Bonds	22.2	11.4
Small Businesses	14.9	21.0
Other		3.5
Total For-Profit Investment:	32.8	36.5
Commercial Financial Institutions	32.8	36.5
Cash	2.4	4.2
Total	100.0	100.0

negative spread is that TLISA makes loans at below-market interest rates. There may be several ways to solve this problem, but one possible way is for TLISA to make loans at the market interest rates, thereby satisfying the fund suppliers, or make the subsidy explicit to the borrower instead of hiding it in a below-market interest rate. Lending at a market interest rate also contributes to a more efficient allocation of funds, since the acceptance of projects to be funded should not be based on lower interest rate costs but on market evaluations.

Regulation

Postal banking is a deposit-taking financial institution that raises funds from depositors and invests them in government securities and wholesale lending. If we use a balance sheet concept, the right side of the balance sheet represents the sources of funds and the left side represents the usage of funds. Regulatory restrictions are imposed on both sides of the balance sheet: the funding and the investment sides.

The law governing postal banking and insurance operations is the Postal Savings and Insurance Act (PSIA), mentioned earlier. The key regulatory constraints are on the funding side, as stipulated in Article 10, which states that MIC should consult with Ministry of Finance and Economy (MoFE) before making any changes to the following items:

1. Types of deposits, terms of maturity, and interest rates;
2. Service procedures and interest rate on RPs;

3. Types of insurance, maximum amount of insurance coverage, insurance premium and payment conditions, insurance period, age of the insured, and other service procedures.

Consultations are not required, however, with MoFE if the changes are within the range of conditions determined by the National Finance and Monetary Committee. This partial deregulation was applied to the liberalization of the financial services industry as a whole.

The constraints before the partial deregulation indicate that, without the agreement of MoFE, it would be difficult for MIC to expand its postal banking and insurance operations by introducing new savings and insurance products or changing the terms on existing products. Since the growth of depository financial institutions largely depends upon the growth of deposit volume, the requirement of MoFE's approval implies that the growth of postal savings is, at the very least, under the indirect control of the MoFE.

Concerning the investment side, Article 18 of the PSIA states that funds raised by postal savings can be managed in the following ways:

1. Redepositing to other financial institutions;
2. Purchasing securities issued directly or guaranteed by the central government, local governments, public organizations, and financial institutions established under the Banking Act;
3. Purchasing stocks issued by government corporations or those designated by MIC.

While the above items broadly define how postal savings funds should be invested, there is a requirement that 80 percent of the funds raised by postal savings, except demand deposits, be deposited into TLISA. However, the investment portfolio of postal savings and the portion deposited to TLISA also depends on the MoFE's funding plan. If government bonds need to be issued to finance airport construction or railroads, for example, then postal savings might participate in providing funds.

All in all, there has been a considerable change in the Korean regulatory system on postal savings since the 1990s. While regulation on the funding side has moved from heavy regulation to partial deregulation, investment-side regulation is moving toward a more restrictive policy. This is indicative of the increasing importance the government has begun to place on postal savings as the volume of postal savings funds has grown. Partial deregulation positively impacted the growth of postal savings volume by allowing significant autonomy to funding-side operations. Korean postal savings must now pay attention to the heavy regulatory restrictions on investment-side operations since this has often resulted in the past in negatively impacting profitability.

Selecting the most efficient regulatory system often depends on the specific financial conditions of a country. Both profitability and growth are necessary factors for postal savings to continue to be financially successful in the future. A correct balance in the regulatory regime of both the finance side and the investment side of operations needs to be appropriately maintained, since one side cannot be pursued extensively at the cost of the other.

Human Resource and Technology Development

The training of employees is another very important factor in providing efficient transaction services. The Office of Postal Service maintains the Information and Communication Officials Training Institute that has a comprehensive training program covering post services, postal savings, and postal insurance operations. In 2001 the number of persons who had been trained by the Institute reached 16,261, and 126 courses are currently available to the trainee. A cyber remote-site training program utilizing the computer network was also introduced in 1999. The main objective of these training programs is to improve the management and operation skills of postal employees.

Providing convenient transaction services through a computerized network is an important tool in improving competitiveness in the quality of services. Since the postal savings computer network was connected to the Korea Financial Telecommunications & Clearings (KFTC) Institute in 1995, postal savings customers have been able to transfer their money electronically to all financial institutions and utilize cash dispensers and giro service facilities at other financial institutions. Thus, postal savings transaction services are not only accessible through post offices around the nation, but also at a large number of commercial banks. This is a result of mutual agency relationships that provide over-the-counter transaction services through the commercial banks' KFTC network. These arrangements indicate that the Korean postal savings system has chosen a strategy that is complementary and cooperative with the banking system, taking into account that while the postal savings service can successfully compete against any one bank, it can hardly confront the entire banking system as a whole. Furthermore, in June 2000, Korea Post's own new computer system for postal savings operations was launched and is now regarded as one of the most advanced online banking systems in Korea.

In addition, the Korean postal savings service proposes to cooperate with some commercial banks in sharing counter facilities. This cooperation would benefit both the banks and postal savings. The banks would benefit because the costs of establishing branches are much greater than the costs of agency fees paid to Korea Post. The postal savings service also would benefit from this cooperation because the marginal costs of dealing with the additional work as agents are lower than the fees it would expect to receive from banks. Recently these kinds of cooperative relationships in transactional services were extended to a credit card and a securities company.

Conclusion

Since the Korean postal savings service started again in 1983, it has played two important roles as a state-owned retail financial institution. The first is as a provider giving equal access to financial services to both rural and urban areas throughout its nationwide post office network, thereby stabilizing the economic life of the people and improving the quality of the national financial system as a whole.

The second role of the postal savings service is as a source of funds for government projects that are designed to improve the public welfare. When postal savings funds are invested in government bonds and TLISA, these funds are utilized to increase benefits to the general public through investments in the social infrastructure. Thus, the second role is to mobilize personal household savings for societal use through government bonds and TLISA.

To perform these roles more successfully in the future, the postal savings service, as a matured state-owned public entity, should improve its competitiveness in terms of price and service quality in the savings markets. Since it is very often difficult to sustain a higher rate of return than other financial institutions, Korean postal savings tries to develop its competitive advantage in the quality of service it provides its customers.

Finally, regarding regulation, Korean postal savings should not only make an effort to obtain proper autonomy on the funding side, it should also continue its intentions to participate in government funding. Since these efforts cannot bear fruit without the mutual cooperation of MoFE and MIC, both sides need to make mutual concessions. One possibility is for MIC to gradually increase the amount of funds redeposited in TLISA, and for MoFE to allow the gradual introduction of new financial services to postal savings. If MoFE allows MIC to increase its market share in the individual/household savings market, MIC can increasingly channel funds to MoFE, which needs financing for public policy purposes.

References

Bank of Korea. 2000. *Statistics of Bank Management.*
——. 2001. *Economic Statistics Yearbook.*
Ministry of Finance. 2000. *Financial Savings Statistics.*
Ministry of Information and Communication. 2000. *Statistics of Postal Banking and Insurance Services.*
Nam, Chan Ki. 1989. "Cash Flow Analysis of Postal Banking Service," *Research Report* 89–06, KISDI.
——. 1989. "Net Interest Margin Analysis of Commercial Banks," *Journal of Finance & Economics* (spring), Korea Investors Service.
——. 1990. "Survey on the Behavior of Postal Banking Customers and Its Applications," *Research Report* 90–I-10, KISDI.
——. 1991. "Strategy for Postal Banking Service in the Wake of Liberalization," *Research Report* 91–36. KISDI.
——. 1992. "Comparative Analysis of Postal Banking Service Between Korea and Japan," *Telecommunications Policy Issue* (February), KISDI.
Nam, Chan Ki, and Sang Yirl Nam. 1990. "Comparison of Performance Between Commercial and Local Banks in Terms of ROE," *Journal of Finance & Economics* (summer), Korea Investors Service.
Sinkey, J.F., Jr. 1989. *Commercial Bank Financial Management*, 3d ed. New York: Macmillan.

6

Postal Banking and the Financial Crisis in the Republic of Korea

Policy Strategy Proposals for the Postcrisis Era

Jae Seog Park and Chan Ki Nam

Introduction

On 21 November 1997 the government of the Republic of Korea was forced to request bailout loans from the International Monetary Fund (IMF) in the face of unmanageable external liabilities. Within a few days the government signed an agreement for a financial aid package totaling $58.3 billion, subject to a broad range of conditions, including macroeconomic stabilization and structural reform. Since then the Republic of Korea has undergone far-reaching and drastic changes in all aspects of its economy. In the aftermath of the crisis, major structural reforms in the midst of severe economic contraction reshaped the economic landscape in Korea. The postal savings system played an important stabilizing role during the crisis and transition period that followed.

The Financial Crisis

Underlying the financial crisis was the massive insolvency declared by large corporations, usually members of *chaebol* (conglomerates) from the mid to late 1990s. This undermined the soundness of most financial institutions, which had been their creditors. Non-performing loans (NPL, interest not paid for more than three months) of commercial banks and merchant (investment) banks, including substandard, doubtful, and estimated loss loans, stood at about 13 trillion won at the end of 1996. Due to the financial crisis a large number of financial institutions closed. Without direct access to their funds because of the bank crisis, a large number of borrowers were unable to meet their debt-servicing obligations, nor could ordinary depositors withdraw their funds. See Table 6.1: Non-Performing Loans at Financial Institutions. The

Table 6.1

Non-Performing Loans at Financial Institutions
(in trillion won)

	December 1996	December 1997	March 1998	June 1998
Precautionary	—	42.8	57.7	72.5
Non-Performing Loans	13.5[2]	43.6	59.6	63.5
Bank	12.2	31.6	38.8	40.0
NBFI[1]	1.3	12.0	20.8	23.5
Total Loans	434.4[2]	647.4	668.7	624.8
Percentage of NPLs	3.1%	6.7%	8.9%	10.2%

Source: Ministry of Finance and Economy.
Notes: 1. Non-Bank Financial Institutions; 2. Commercial Banks only.

NPLs thus almost tripled to about 43 trillion won by December 1997. Of these, merchant banking corporations, which had originated large amounts of new loans funded from abroad, recorded NPLs of 3.9 trillion won at the end of October 1997, nearly three times the previous year's 1.3 trillion won. These institutions had been under lax supervision by financial authorities due to their recent upgrade from small finance companies. Non-performing loans of the entire financial sector amounted to 59.6 trillion won at the end of March 1998, equivalent to 13 percent of gross domestic product. Lack of international competitiveness further weighed down the already fragile financial sector with huge NPLs.

By its acceptance of the financial aid package from the IMF on 3 December 1997, the government agreed that it would pursue an economic reform program focused on macroeconomic stability and reforms in the financial, corporate, and labor sectors as well. Accordingly, a policy stance was adopted that made paramount the issues of reviving the financial system through restructuring and providing a safety net for the newly unemployed through increased public budget spending, including an increase in social welfare expenditures.

The short-term objective in restructuring the financial sector was to stabilize the financial system, and the long-term goal was to enhance the soundness and efficiency of financial institutions. However, speed was of the essence in the restructuring process in order to alleviate the credit crunch that had been stifling the entire economy and eroding long-term growth potential.

To achieve swift and prudent reform, the Financial Supervisory Commission (FSC) was established as an independent and consolidated supervisory authority. As a result, domestic banks cleaned up their balance sheets and through recapitalization adopted capital/asset ratios ranging from 10 to 13 percent, that is, above the Basel Committee standard of 8 percent. The government supported these rehabilitation efforts with approximately 64 trillion won of public funds.

At the end of 1997, of the twenty-five troubled commercial banks, only thirteen were able to satisfy the 8 percent minimum Basel Committee capital adequacy requirement. Reviewing the rehabilitation plans submitted by the other twelve unsound banks, the FSC classified them into three categories: "rejected," "conditionally approved," and "approved." The FSC rejected the rehabilitation plans of five banks and conditionally approved the plans of the additional seven, depending on their fulfillment of the conditions imposed by the FSC. None of these banks were initially classified as "approved."

The government recapitalized two troubled banks, Korea First Bank and Seoul Bank, to prevent any systematic risk that could endanger the payment settlement system. The five banks whose plans were rejected (Kyungki, Donghwa, Dongnam, Daedong, and Chungchong) were closed and merged with healthier banks. Two other troubled banks, Korea Commercial Bank and Hanil Bank, announced a merger on 31 July 1998. Like commercial banks, insolvent non-bank financial institutions such as insurance companies and security brokerage firms were suspended or closed.

As shown in Table 6.2: Status of Restructuring in Financial Institutions, the number of financial institutions that closed from the start of the crisis until August 2000 was 485, or 23 percent of the total number of financial institutions.

Another major task has been the disposal of non-performing loans (NPLs). The government injected fiscal resources to dispose of NPLs and recapitalize banks. As a part of financial restructuring, the government provided fiscal support for the purchase of NPLs through the Korea Asset Management Corporation (KAMCO). At the end of 2001, according to statistics provided by the FSC, NPLs totaled 35.1 trillion won after the introduction of forward-looking criteria. The amount of unsound credit still held by Korean banks was estimated at 18.8 trillion won.

The Effects of the Financial Restructuring Program on Postal Savings

During this period there was unusually strong growth in the postal savings system (see chapter 5 by Chan Ki Nam). The effects on postal savings of positive and negative perception and fears for the financial sector restructur-

Table 6.2

Status of Restructuring in Financial Institutions (August 2000)

Financial Institutions	Total Number of Institutions (end of 1997)	Closure	Closure Rate (%)	Comments
Banks	33	11	33.3	License revoked 5, merger 5, foreign loan 1
Merchant Banks	30	21	70.0	License revoked 18, merger (business closure) 3
Securities Companies	36	6	16.7	License revoked 6
Investment Trust Companies	31	7	22.6	License revoked 6, merger 1
Insurance Companies	50	13	26.0	Contract transfer 5, merger 1, sale 5, business transfer and withdrawal 2
Leasing Companies	25	9	36.0	Withdrawal 9
Mutual Savings and Finance Companies	231	78	33.8	License revoked 43, merger 19, acquisition by 3rd party 16
Credit Unions	1,666	340	20.4	License revoked 2, merger 201, liquidation 97, bankruptcy 40
Total	2,102	485	23.1	

ing are summarized in Table 6.3: Effects of Financial Sector Restructuring on Postal Savings.

Fund-Raising Strategy

Owing to the crisis, the criteria of depositors in selecting a financial institution shifted from an emphasis on profitability to stability and transactional convenience, as many bank depositors had found it difficult to withdraw

Table 6.3

Effects of Financial Sector Restructuring on Postal Savings

Positive	**Soundness of Postal Savings** • Confidence levels in private financial institutions fell while confidence in the stability of government-owned postal banking rose. • Postal savings was at an advantage with a nationwide postal network whereas the branch networks of private financial institutions were reduced. **Image Promotion of Postal Banking** • Postal banking strengthened its level of competitiveness by providing a combination of services and products from the three businesses: postal services, postal savings, and postal insurance services. • Postal banking helped meet the increased demand for public policy-based funds.
Negative	**Difficult Business Conditions** • Possible shrinkage of postal banking business was feared due to diminishing savings potential with the increase in unemployment and the slowdown in economic growth. **Intensified Market Competition** • Intensified competition for attracting banking customers was done through the restructuring of private financial institutions. • Relatively weak competitive ability of postal system compared to the active offerings of new financial services by both domestic and foreign financial institutions. **Difficulties and Limitations Confronting the Management of Postal Banking Funds** • Difficulty in reacting promptly to changes in the financial markets compared with other financial institutions due to regulations in the Postal Savings and Insurance Act (PSIA). • Low profitability due to interest rate increases on deposits and consequent decreases in net interest margins. • Increase in the risk of fund management for postal banking due to the insolvency of other financial institutions, since some portion of postal banking funds were invested in commercial financial institutions.

funds from their commercial bank accounts during the crisis. Therefore, postal savings considered the following when formulating marketing strategies to attract potential customers.

In view of the volatility of the financial market, postal banking remained attractive as a stable and reliable government-operated financial institution. Second, the products offered by post offices, such as postal services, postal savings, postal insurance services, and related products, needed to be further developed and expanded. A program was thus begun that provided greater benefits to customers who make large amounts of deposits by introducing relationship banking principals. Third, it was recognized that postal banking had to specialize in retail banking.

It was expected that once the restructuring of the financial sector was realized, postal banking would have to compete with the universal banking system that would emerge to handle all related businesses such as banking, insurance, and securities. Although some financial institutions would specialize in certain businesses, postal banking needed to create a market strategy that would focus on a wide range of retail financial services.

Lessons Drawn from Funds Management

In the midst of uncertainty in the financial markets, postal banking increased the stability and liquidity of its management of funds. Implementation of a partial deposit insurance system had created a "moral hazard" condition for the banks (reducing their fear of the consequences of bad debt), and subsequent large government investment in unhealthy financial institutions led to an even greater risk of bad debt. When forced mergers of banks and bankruptcy resulted, the withdrawal of deposits, except from the postal savings system, became nearly impossible for a certain period of time.

Considering as well the risk in the stock market and real estate market, it would have been appropriate to increase the proportion of low-risk investments such as government bonds and beneficiary certificates. This does not necessarily mean that postal savings should have withdrawn funds entirely from the private sector. However, postal savings should have reduced its risk in its investments by restructuring its portfolio through diversification and decreasing its position in high-risk investments. In addition, there should have been some flexibility in the selection of target financial institutions for postal savings. More generally, a proactive evaluation of postal savings' investments in financial institutions, rather than just relying on the periodic announcements of institutional credit rating agencies, is needed when evaluating portfolios. The structure of fund management should reflect changes in actual economic conditions.

Change in Postal Banking during the Three Years of the IMF Program

Analysis of Deposit Trends

After the financial crisis, the criteria many Koreans used when selecting a financial institution and financial products changed from chasing profitability to choosing stability. While deposits in commercial banks continued to rise, due to an emergency guarantee by the government on their safety, nevertheless, deposits in postal banking, increased more rapidly.

Figure 6.1 **Growth Rate of Deposits**

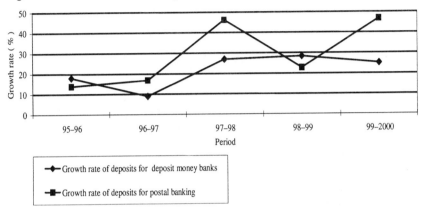

See Figure 6.1: Growth Rate of Deposits. In 1998 the balance of deposits in money banks (commercial banks and specialized banks) increased 27.0 percent, whereas it increased 46.2 percent for postal banking. After 1997, deposits in deposit money banks showed modest growth while there was a sharp rise in postal banking deposits. In particular, in 2000, deposit-money bank deposits rose 25.1 percent while postal banking deposits grew 46.8 percent.

Market Share for Postal Banking

After the financial crisis, the market share of postal banking deposits increased from 4.5 percent to 5.7 percent at the end of 2000. See Figure 6.2: Market Share of Postal Banking Deposits. In addition to the public's perception of safety and stability, the increase in market share reflected an increase in the competitiveness of service of government-run postal banking. Because postal banking's stability and convenience will continue to be maintained, the increase in postal banking's market share is expected to continue in the future. The following are the factors that have contributed to the growth of postal banking's market share in deposit-taking.

First, the net interest margin in postal banking is relatively large due to an absence of bad debt. Since postal banking puts an emphasis on transaction services, such as giro and remittance services, the portion of funds raised through the transaction services is larger for postal savings than for deposit money banks. In addition, the portion of invested funds is over 90 percent of the total funds raised, due to postal operating costs being significantly lower than those of deposit money banks.

Second, because postal banking runs three businesses—postal services,

Figure 6.2 Market Share of Postal Banking Deposits

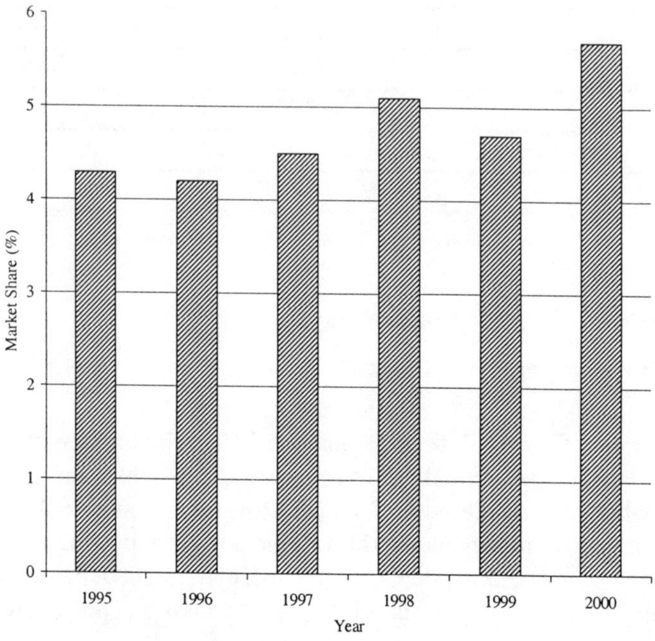

Source: Bank of Korea, *Survey and Statistics Report*, November 2001.

postal insurance, and postal savings—the sharing of joint overhead costs keeps operating costs for each line of business low.

Third, as a government-run business, postal banking is highly reliable. Banking customers feel secure about the safety of their savings because the government guarantees the payment of principal and interest.

All three of the above factors gave postal savings customers' good reason to have confidence in its system, thus increasing the percentage of its share of deposits over the commercial banks.

Role of Postal Banking in the Financial Crisis

During the financial crisis, the survival of many private financial institutions was threatened. Banks were forced to restructure in order to clean their balance sheets of excessive bad debt and raise their existing capital backing. As a result, surviving banks that had previously been primary fund suppliers to industry did not completely recover and sharply reduced their lending. By comparison, the government-owned postal banking system was and continues to be strongly regulated with the requirement of full disclosure of infor-

Table 6.4

Public Funds and Their Major Sources (2001, in trillions of won)

Total Amount of Fund	Postal Banking	Public Pension	Miscellaneous Fund
78.6	10.8 (13.7%)	29.4 (37.4%)	38.4 (48.8%)

mation regarding the management of funds. As a result, its operation is healthier and more transparent than that of the private financial institutions. Private financial institutions needed more careful monitoring to reduce risky investment as their management was tainted by moral hazard problems.

With virtually no insolvent claims to burden its financial operations, the first role of postal banking during the financial crisis was to invest a portion of its deposits in the budgetary account of the government.

Second, with the bankruptcies of financial institutions following the financial crisis, there occurred a massive withdrawal of deposit funds from the banking system. Even though the government propped up the remaining banks with deposit guarantees, still, a large portion of those funds were moved to postal banking. Therefore, the second role of postal banking during the financial crisis was to recapture funds from within the financial system.

Third, large portions of the funds raised by postal banking were used as social overhead capital to help build national economic development. This capital was allocated to construction by way of a public fund. The size of the public fund is presented in Table 6.4: Public Funds and Their Major Sources. Postal banking's contribution to public funds has steadily increased, from 2.9 trillion in 1998 to 5.1 trillion in 1999, 6.8 trillion in 2000, and to 10.8 trillion won in 2001. In 2001 there was also a massive increase in the amount and percentage of "miscellaneous funds," that is, 3.3 trillion (8 percent) in 1999 to 38.4 trillion (48.9 percent) with a corresponding decrease from the public pension fund from 31.8 trillion (79.3 percent) to 29.4 trillion (37.4 percent) in 2001. The sources of the increased "miscellaneous" funds include the National Debt Management Fund, the Economic Development Corporation Fund, and so on. The shift in funding was an outcome of the liberalization of the public pension fund's investment policy.

Proposals for Developing Postal Savings in the Postcrisis Era

In the Republic of Korea the main competitors of postal banking are commercial banks and the Bank of Agricultural Credit (agricultural cooperatives). Both of these criticize postal banking for unfair competition due to both the

Table 6.5

Mid- to Long-Term Business Strategy for Postal Banking

	Providing Universal Services	Strengthening Its Role as a Public Organization
Existing Strategies	*Offering comprehensive financial services:* • Development of joint services between its postal, banking, and insurance divisions • Expansion of business cooperation with other financial institutions • Improvement of service quality	*Supporting public funding:* • Purchasing government bonds • Supporting government policy-based funds, such as providing financing to new business ventures through venture capital fund companies
New Strategies	*Expansion of electronic banking:* • Expanding Internet banking • Providing advanced transaction services such as electronic money, EBPP (electronic bill presentment and payment), etc.	*Providing a national financial infrastructure:* • Opening the network to other financial institutions by sharing retail counters • Providing private financial institutions with agency services in collecting deposits

government guarantee on the payment of principal and interest, and the use of post offices as retail outlets. To ameliorate this criticism, postal banking needs to develop new strategies for the future with other financial institutions in order to strengthen its role as a public organization, as shown in Table 6.5: Mid- to Long-Term Business Strategy for Postal Banking.

Concerning universal services, in addition to offering joint services of posts, banking, and insurance, one of the important strategies will be the expansion of electronic services such as Internet banking and EBPP (electronic bill presentment and payment). Regarding its role as a public organization, postal banking, in addition to supporting public funding, should also act in concert with the national financial infrastructure by sharing its retail counters and opening its network to other financial institutions.

Through the use of the post office network as a financial infrastructure, a new strategy needs to be developed that encompasses the role of postal banking from the perspective of the consumer, the national economy, and financial intermediation as summarized in Figure 6.3: The Role of Postal Banking.

Figure 6.3 **The Role of Postal Banking**

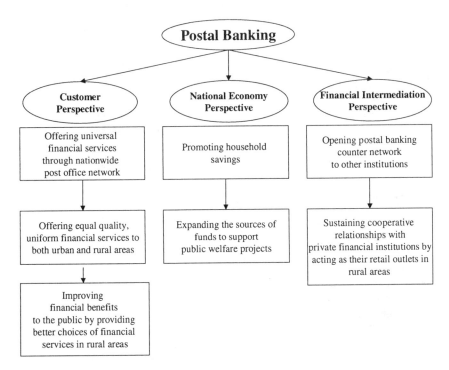

Conclusion

The use of the post office network has both advantages and disadvantages for the postal savings business. The advantages are economies of scope for the post's three businesses: postal services, postal savings, and postal insurance services. The primary disadvantage experienced by the post is that its product line is limited in accordance with regulatory restrictions. To overcome this, postal savings should develop cooperative business ties with other financial institutions that are not similarly constrained. For example, through mutual cooperation with private financial institutions the post bank could provide counter services for other banks, thereby increasing its own competitiveness. Since restructuring, private banking institutions are closing unprofitable branches in order to reduce costs and improve efficiency; the use of the postal branch network by these institutions would therefore be beneficial to both sides. The private institutions would receive the benefit of postal savings' network, and postal banking would be able to increase its revenues in the form of agency fees and service charges to be paid by the private institutions. By so doing, postal banking can help the structural reforms of these financial institutions, and their using the branch network of postal banking would then be a shared benefit to both.

From the customer's perspective, by offering equal quality financial services to both urban and rural areas through its nationwide network, postal banking can provide better choices in rural areas and thereby improve financial service benefits to the public as a whole. From the perspective of the national economy, by promoting household savings postal banking can expand the sources of funds for public welfare projects. From the perspective of financial intermediation, postal banking can sustain cooperative relationships with private financial institutions by acting as their retail outlets in rural areas as the commercial financial sector undergoes restructuring.

References

Bank of Korea. 2000. *Economic Statistics Yearbook.*
———. 2000. *Statistics of Bank Management.*
Choi, Gongpil. 1999. "The Korean Experience with Financial Crisis: A Chronology," *Financial Research Paper* 99–05 (June), KIF.
Don Hanna and Suktae Oh. 2000. "Korea's Financial Restructuring Efforts: Where to from Here?" CID/KIF Conference (October).
Lee, Jang-Yung. 2000. "Monetary and Financial Policies in Korea After the Crisis," KIF (January 7).
Ministry of Finance. 2000. *Financial Savings Statistics* (December).
Ministry of Information and Communication. 2000. *Statistics of Postal Banking and Insurance Services.*
Nam, Chan Ki. 1990. "Survey on the Behavior of Postal Banking Customers and Its Applications," *Research Report* 90–I-10, KISDI.
Park, Jae Seog. 1997. "Business Study on Postal Savings in the Era of Paradigm Shift," *Research Report* 97–23, KISDI.
Park, Jae Seog, and Jung Kwon Park. 2000. "Survey on the Behavior of Postal Banking and Its Direction of Development," *Research Report* 00–29, KISDI.

7

Policy Challenges and the Reform of Postal Savings in Japan

Mark J. Scher and Naoyuki Yoshino

Introduction

Japan's postal savings system (*yubin-chokin*, popularly called *yu-cho*) with 240 trillion yen (July 2002) is not merely the world's largest postal savings system in volume of deposits, but is also the world's largest financial institution, with more individual and household savings deposits than all of Japan's commercial banks combined. As *yu-cho*'s deposit base has steadily increased over the past decade, largely as a result of the public's fears over the uncertainty of the commercial banking sector, there have been repeated calls from *yu-cho*'s critics for it to be privatized, if not entirely abolished. Japan took its first steps of reform in April 2001 when *yu-cho* was reorganized to give it autonomy over its investment policy and to achieve a partial "market solution" for the investment of postal savings funds. At the same time the intermediation of postal savings funds was partially delinked from the policy-based objectives of a key government loan program. With more changes on the horizon, the post office, which had been a government department, in April 2003 became a separate, government-owned public corporation, an event that may change the entire postal savings system.

Privatization of *yu-cho* is being fiercely advocated not only by banking industry critics but also by important members of government reform advisory committees. These include leading academic figures, who have put forth substantive recommendations for *yu-cho*'s privatization, and government policymakers, including Prime Minister Koizumi, who has made market liberalization of all postal services one of his chief policy objectives (Koizumi interview, *Financial Times,* 13 May 2002).

In this chapter we will examine from a public policy perspective the issues related to the privatization of Japan's postal savings system and assess to what extent, if at all, privatization is likely to improve on government-run postal savings. We will also examine the social and economic effects of privatization and/or termination of Japan's postal savings system within the context of the competition in Japan's financial sector for savings funds, and the possible effects on *yu-cho*'s organizational strategy of a changing regulatory framework, market liberalization, and privatization. Postal savings in Japan has had a profound effect as a means for social growth and economic development. It still continues to serve this purpose by delivering financial services, often otherwise unavailable, to all segments of the population without discrimination, most notably the poor, as well as middle-income savers, pensioners, and rural and low-population areas. Nevertheless, just as several European countries have privatized their systems, some important large business and financial organizations, such as Keidanren (Federation of Economic Organizations) and Zenginkyo (Japan Bankers Association), are advocating the same course for Japan.

Postal Savings and Japan's Development

Origins: Inculcating Values of Thrift

Since its origins in the nineteenth century, Japan's postal savings system has played a significant role in economic growth. It has done so by serving as a collector of domestic savings and a provider of financial services for middle-income and poor people, and at the same time by serving as a means to build the nation's capital resources. When Japan's postal savings system was introduced in 1875, saving was not socially condoned according to the prevalent effete moral attitudes of the feudal aristocracy of the late Edo period of the nineteenth century. A popular saying of this elite class admonished "trying to get one *sen* (cent) to last from one day to the next was shameful." At that time there were no savings banks or commercial banks in Japan for personal savings, either in the cities or the rural areas. Households saved in cash or kind to meet emergencies or special events. Despite such conditions, Maeshima Hisoka, who had founded Japan's national postal system in 1871, at the beginning of Japan's modern period, the Meiji Era (1868–1912), introduced a postal savings system in Japan that he based on his own firsthand observations of the British postal savings system. Maeshima had been greatly impressed with the positive role he perceived the postal savings system to be playing in English society. Through his efforts, including the organization of schoolchildren's savings programs to inculcate thrift, post office branches for the first time began accepting deposits at eighteen locations in downtown Tokyo and at one office in Yokohama in May 1875. The number of post offices taking savings deposits rapidly expanded to rural regions soon thereafter, aided by the fact that Maeshima had previously charged all village headmen throughout Japan to establish local post offices and serve as postmasters in their villages. This step created an extensive nationwide network of post offices within a year or two of the institution of a national postal system. Japan was the fourth country to establish postal savings and the first in an Asian economy.

Japan's postal savings system was initiated at a time when Japan was moving out of centuries of feudalism and isolation. Unequal treaties had been earlier imposed by foreign naval forces, granting Britain, France, and the United States extraterritorial rights that also restricted Japan's rights to collect customs duties to 5 percent. By comparison, the United States' own tariffs were 45 percent and the main source of revenue for the U.S. government, as were Great Britain's tariffs during its Industrial Revolution. Japan's Meiji-era leaders were acutely aware of the political dismemberment of China by the same Western imperialist powers. Eliminating the unequal treaties and restoring Japan's economic sovereignty were their prime concerns.

The government's leaders had also taken note of the foreign indebtedness of the Ottoman and Chinese Empires to European bankers. The Japanese government decided to turn to mobilizing its domestic savings for building its industries, railroads, shipping, communications, and, most significantly and not least, its military. Japan was thus able to forswear almost all foreign borrowings for its military and infrastructure development for the next twenty years (until the advent of the Russo-Japanese War). It can be said that the establishment of a postal savings system at such a critical juncture in its history provided Japan with a significant resource in its future economic and social development. The history of Japan's economic and financial development in the 1870s offers some interesting parallels to problems confronting developing economies today. With unfettered and untaxed access to Japan's domestic markets, foreign traders and mercantile banks also took advantage of the disparities between Japan's and other nations' fixed gold and silver exchange rates and were able to completely drain Japan's gold reserves, not unlike the 1997 Asian financial crisis, which also drained the reserves of several Southeast Asian countries that hopelessly tried to defend their currency's overvalued fixed exchange rates. Faced with runaway inflation from the government's issue of inconvertible notes that in turn bankrupted the government's efforts to collect taxes, Japan's banking system collapsed. This was then followed by an ill-fated experiment in adopting an American-style national banking system. Some 153 newly formed banks issued their own banknotes, further exacerbating inflation, with taxpayers again passing the depreciated banknotes at face value for payment of taxes. The public then, as now, had no confidence in the banking system. Against this historical background, with the banking system in complete collapse, the new minister of finance, Masayoshi Matsukata, took charge in 1881, overturning previous monetary policy.

The postal savings stamp deposit forms and promotional posters of the late Meiji and Taisho eras (1900–25) document the appeals used by the post office to encourage individuals to save, both for their personal future prosperity and for the prosperity and development of the nation. One of the postal savings system's unique attributes, and the probable basis for its early mass appeal, was the fact that at one time it accepted deposits as small as one-half a *sen* (100 *sen* = 1 yen).

The State Harnesses Savings for Development

In 1885, Meiji finance minister Matsukata brought postal savings funds under the control of the Ministry of Finance and directed their use toward the goals of building the nation's industrial, transportation, and military infrastructure, and carrying out anti-inflationary policy. Already by 1883, as the success of the system was growing, the cumulative total of these small savings deposits had reached 9 percent of Japan's ordinary bank deposits, and by 1897 postal savings were nearly 13 percent of ordinary bank deposits. Taxation riots following the Russo-Japanese War (1905) further strengthened the government commitment to mobilize savings to serve its financing needs. Campaigns to increase postal savings deposits and promote thrift resulted in postal savings deposits increasing 390 percent from 1905 to 1914, compared to a 120 percent increase in ordinary bank deposits during the same period. Postal savings depositors increased from 12 percent to 23 percent of the population.

Postal savings deposit campaigns were later initiated at various times to remedy specific problems. For example, during the inflation following the First World War, a campaign was launched to encourage savings to stem spending and absorb the excess liquidity that had resulted from the war. Postal savings represented 13 percent of total commercial banking deposits. In 1919 postal savings deposits became the largest resource of direct government financing, as direct taxation had proved unreliable and counterproductive, sparking periodic riots and agrarian tax rebellions.

As the Japanese economy developed, the postal savings system was able to respond to the changing circumstances. Some of the issues, besides inflation, that the postal savings system helped the government confront included providing pump-priming private sector support to new and developing industries, developing and modernizing the infrastructure, pumping up the economy during recessions, and at times stabilizing capital markets and providing non-inflationary funding of government deficits. Postal savings deposits grew especially during deflationary periods, 1881–87, 1925–31, and 1990–92. Historically, however, its foremost goal has been to sustain economic development.

The Early Modern Period and the Development of Savings Banks

The development of the Japanese banking system coincided with the early growth of the postal savings system. In 1880, five years after the establishment of postal savings, Japan's first private savings bank, the Tokyo Savings Bank, was established, and by 1890, when the Savings Bank Act was passed to protect small savers, there were twenty-three savings banks. Both the number of savings banks and the volume of deposits grew rapidly, doubling every four years or less. By 1920–21 the number of savings banks and their branches reached its zenith, with 2,128 savings bank branches holding 95 percent of all bank deposits (including all private/ordinary banks). Alarmed at the deteriorated condition of the commercial bank sector, the government moved to reverse this trend through the Savings Bank Act of 1921, which converted 77 percent of the savings banks into commercial banks. Postal savings, a non-bank institution, continued to grow, and in 1937 it had on deposit nearly one-third of the amount of deposits in commercial banks. Although the government had repeatedly sought to consolidate the savings banks, it was not until 1943 that the Ministry of Finance ordered almost all of them closed and the personal savings they held transferred into commercial banks to intermediate funds to munitions industries for financing the war effort.* Postal savings, however, was left intact. By the end of the war only five savings banks remained, which were ultimately merged with or converted to commercial banks in 1949. At this point, individual and household savings became a large component and foundation of the profits of the main bank system (see Scher 1997, 1998).

Today, besides the postal system the only remaining non-bank savings deposit–takers are the *shinkin* (non-profit financial cooperatives), which have some 40 percent of the volume of deposits by individuals compared to the postal savings system. Viewed from the perspective of total deposits raised

---

*Some trace the origins of Japan's main bank system to the wartime period. However, the system's origins were evinced in the dedicated financing by their industrial conglomerates, known in the prewar period as *zaibatsu*, which owned commercial banks. These conglomerates were in turn prefigured by the earlier *zaibatsu*-group accounting houses of the seventeenth century, such as those owned by Sumitomo and Mitsui. See Scher, 1997, 1998.

by all of Japan's deposit-taking institutions (1,202 trillion yen), the postal savings share of 20.8 percent slightly exceeds the 20.6 percent total share of Japan's seven existing city banks. Regional and second-tier regional banks make up another 19.8 percent share. The balance of funds raised (18.5 percent) are deposited in private sector trust banks, long-term credit banks, and foreign-owned banks, and 19.6 percent is held in government-owned policy-based financial institutions that specialize in lending to small and medium-size businesses, agriculture, forestry, and fisheries (Zenginkyo, 2001). From the perspective of small individual and household savings, the end of March 2000 saw 260 trillion yen in personal savings on deposit in the postal savings system, representing 36 percent of all personal savings on deposit in Japan, an amount nearly equal to the combined personal/household savings deposited among all private sector commercial institutions. (The balance of small savings is mainly in *shinkin*, non-profit financial cooperatives, and mutual credit cooperatives.) Deposits of individuals/households represent 54.9 percent of total deposits in city banks, 67.0 percent of deposits in regional banks, 69.6 percent in second-tier regional banks, 75.3 percent in *shinkin* banks, and 99.6 percent in postal savings deposits (*Economic Statistics,* Bank of Japan, 31 March 2000).

Fiscal Investment and Loan Program: From Postwar Development to Structural Readjustment

Starting in the postwar period and until the end of March 2001, postal savings funds deposited into the Ministry of Finance's Trust Fund Bureau were in turn lent to the Fiscal Investment and Loan Program (FILP) (*zaisei toyushi*—the so-called "*zaito* system"), also managed by the Ministry of Finance. Major recipients of FILP funding during the 1950s through the early 1980s included policy-based financial institutions such as the Japan Development Bank (JDB), which allocated funds for industrial development to meet national and regional development goals. In the 1950s, FILP provided funding for the reconstruction of the electric power, coal mining, ocean shipping, and iron and steel industries. In the late 1950s to the early 1960s the emphasis shifted to catching up with advanced countries in the synthetic fiber, oil refinery, nuclear power generation, machinery, and electronics industries. By the late 1960s and into the early 1970s, FILP's policy emphasis was redirected toward social welfare and environmental considerations in urban and residential land development, pollution prevention, welfare facilities, private railroads, and further development of new technology. In the late 1970s and early 1980s, energy policy received priority from FILP, with lending for energy conservation and the development of alternative energy sources.

Other public policy-based institutions that received FILP funds during the postwar period included the Japan Import-Export Bank; regional development finance institutions, such as the Hokkaido-Tohoku Development Corporation and the Okinawa Development Finance Corporation; the Japan Finance Corporation for Small Businesses and the People's Finance Corporation, which provide loans for small and medium-size firms; and the Housing Loan Corporation for housing finance. By the 1990s, however, JDB and other policy-based institutions were no longer a major recipient of FILP funds.

The character of the FILP program changed in the early 1990s in response to the economic crisis following the collapse of the bubble economy. FILP's key mission was redirected toward promoting structural adjustment of industry and maintaining employment through the funding of infrastructure and other construction projects aimed at providing economic stimuli to ailing sectors of the economy, the chief beneficiaries of what has come to be called "Japan's second budget." Whatever the policy intention, political trade-offs were involved in the FILP system. During the 1990s the overwhelming majority of FILP funds for developmental purposes were no longer channeled through the JDB or other government-owned banks and policy-based financial institutions. Instead they were directly parceled out to designated quasi-governmental companies such as the Japan Highway Company and other politically well-connected recipients of local infrastructure development funds, particularly those tied to the construction and real estate industries interests, which were also key borrowers responsible for the non-performing bank loans that still plague the banking industry. Political considerations were also never far from such an investment/disbursement system that favored rural provincial areas rather than urban industrial centers.

Reform of FILP and Its Relation to Postal Savings

The 1990s economic crisis accelerated the movement for reform of Japan's financial system, the so-called "big bang," which was modeled after the U.K. market liberalization reforms of the same name. There was already a growing demand that financial markets be liberalized, halfheartedly begun in the 1980s, to respond to new domestic and international monetary and structural environments. The state-led development model of postwar Japan came under criticism as being incompatible with a liberalized financial system. Among the policies criticized were what some critics termed "government intermediation," referring specifically to the use of postal savings funds by the FILP. Nevertheless, following the burst of the bubble economy in 1989 and the ensuing domestic banking crisis, the government's need for state-directed credits to small businesses and housing lending overrode market liberalization concerns when the commercial banks ceased to lend. This further enhanced the FILP's role as a policy instrument in revitalizing the economy.

Some economists and financial industry critics have questioned the continued need for and efficiency of FILP types of development-lending practices in the presence of a developed capital market. Others have seen the disbursement function of FILP as the underlying cause of fiscal inefficiency and have argued that the disbursement function should be kept separate from the collection function of the postal savings system. Critics have emphasized a political rationale behind what they term to be "government intermediation" of the postal savings funds to FILP to finance *tokushu hojin*—various governmental and quasi-governmental financial institutions and infrastructure agencies that finance housing, highways, and small businesses. The majority of these enterprises have been criticized not only for being inefficient and debt-ridden but also for undertaking unnecessary investment, as exemplified by bridges and rural highways that lead to nowhere and nearly vacant government-financed resort facilities. Often justified as public works projects to create jobs to sustain the ailing economy, their political raison d'être is, however, feeding pork-barrel projects for politicians' local districts and generating employment opportunities for higher-level retired bureaucrats. In 2002 the largest recipients of FILP disbursements were local governments (28 percent), the Government Housing Loan Program (19 percent), the National Life Finance Corporation (13 percent), the Japan Highway Public Corporation (8 percent), the Japan Finance Corporation for Municipal Enterprises (6 percent), and the Japan Finance Corporation for Small Businesses (5 percent).

Indignant public outcry challenging the misuse of funds had become a staple of the press, and a new term, "MoF-bashing," became a mainstay of public debate. Taxpayer outcry had its effect: the FILP program was reformed, and its direct financial ties to the postal savings funds through the Trust Funds Bureau of MoF were severed. However, FILP is still quite relevant to *yu-cho* since the postal savings funds and other postal administered funds are expected to be major investors in the bond issues of FILP and its related agencies through 2006. In 2001, 76 percent of FILP bonds, some 33.3 trillion yen, were purchased either by postal savings (41 percent), postal pension plan reserves (27 percent), or postal life insurance funds (8 percent).

Another outcome of the reform program was that after several years of lobbying, the Postal Savings Bureau was finally granted the authority to invest the funds it collects in the financial markets on its own, thereby bypassing the MoF/Trust Fund Bureau in the designated-finance FILP system. In April 2001 the reorganized Postal Savings Agency was given discretion over the investment of collected funds, thereby opening itself to market risk.

The Fundamental Reform Law and the Changing Role of the FILP

FILP-related programs are now required to meet the following criteria to qualify for support:

1. Individual FILP institutions will be assessed by an independent policy assessment organization;
2. Each FILP operation will be either terminated or privatized unless its necessity as an activity of the government is convincingly proven;
3. Each FILP institution will utilize the private capital market to raise funds for the operations it supports;
4. If the FILP institution's activity is deemed necessary for policy purposes, its funding will be covered by bonds issued by the relevant sponsoring agency;
5. The FILP institution will focus on guaranteeing and refinancing through market mechanisms such as securitization.

Intermediation of Postal Savings Funds: The Search for a Market-Oriented Solution

One result of the Reform Law and its changes with respect to the intermediation of funds to the FILP has been that the MoF Trust Fund Bureau was deprived of direct access to the postal savings funds. Now, governmental financial institutions and agencies (GFIA) have to issue their own bonds (agency bonds), participate in issuance of Trust Fund bonds to finance their own lending, or issue government-guaranteed bonds. Among these three classes of financial instruments, FILP bonds are the major source of funding for the new FILP system. In the case of agency bonds, each GFIA has to obtain a credit rating to issue bonds whose yield properly reflects its investment risk. Given MoF's willingness to require all GFIAs to issue their own bonds, instead of piggybacking on government bonds, the GFIA bond rating was not questioned (Shigeru Itose, *Keizai Koramu*, No. 10, 6 December 2001).

While markets foresaw a Darwinian evolution in the FILP bond system, problems have been alleged in the credit rating process. It is said that rating agencies evaluate the solvency of the GFIAs based on a GFIA's "closeness" to the government. The closer a GFIA is perceived to be to the government, the better the rating it receives (Cargill and Yoshino 2003). If such practices really dictate the ratings and the ratings determine the yield, then the yield of a FILP bond will not truly reflect its risk based upon financial fundamentals. For a genuinely free and fair market, FILP-related bonds must be rated based on the same rating criteria applied to private corporate bond issuers.

MoF sharply reduced the 2002 budget for FILP by 18 percent from the previous year to 26.8 trillion yen (*Asahi Shimbun,* 19 December 2001), expecting the GFIAs to fill the gap by issuing their own bonds in the market, totaling 2.7 trillion yen, albeit all with government guarantees and therefore without credible risk. This was a 270 percent increase in GFIA bonds over the previous year. As of November 2002, 14 out of 33 FILP agencies have issued their own agency bonds. In what seems to be a variation of Gresham's Law, of "bad money driving out the good from circulation," the weaker-rated, high-interest guaranteed bonds work to exclude better-rated bonds from the market, a case of "junk bonds" driving out good bonds. New accounting rules will be also applied to FILP projects. Each government entity will disclose its "policy cost" (i.e., state subsidies) and show the discounted present value of the project to be financed. In this way it is expected that an accurate estimate can be made of future demand for a given public project and the future profitability of the project.

This appears to be a good prescription for the financial health of postal savings and other purchasers of the bonds. It is especially significant for postal savings because, even though the postal deposit funds were officially severed from the controlling hand of the MoF in April 2002, the Postal Savings Bureau is expected to continue to finance FILP in the form of direct purchase of FILP bonds, and those issued by GFIAs, until the end of fiscal year 2006. As the major buyer of FILP bonds, *yu-cho* needs to be informed of the risks of the bonds and the solvency of GFIA bond issuers.

Commercial Banks versus Postal Savings

Besides reproaching postal savings as the prime channel for financing highly political FILP projects, the postal savings system has been attacked for its savings mobilization function itself. Envying for many years the huge amount of deposits the postal savings system continued to garner, Japan's private banking sector has called for the system's privatization, if not the abolishment of postal savings. In March 1998 postal savings represented a 36 percent share of all household deposits, exceeding the combined household deposits in Japan's city banks (banks with a national franchise), making the Japanese postal savings system the largest financial institution in the world. Since the Japanese banking crisis began in 1990, there has been a flight to safety by individual/household customers at commercial banks. The contraction of commercial bank deposits and marked increases in the size and number of depositors in postal savings accounts reflect the crisis of public confidence in Japan's banking system. This trend is likely to increase as the government intends to reduce the ceiling on government guarantees on bank deposits, further fueling the rise of postal savings deposits. While it thus remains popular with the Japanese public, we should examine the charges that have been leveled by *yu-cho*'s critics.

Does Postal Savings Have an Unfair Competitive Advantage?

Critics from the banking industry have complained of the unfair advantages given the postal savings system by its exemption as a government-owned institution from national and local taxes of all types and from the requirement to insure its customers' accounts with payments to the Deposit Insurance Corporation. *Yu-cho* is also exempt from Bank of Japan's reserve requirements and the payment of dividends that private banks make to their shareholders. On the other hand, the chronic losses experienced by banks over the last decade have also resulted in the banks' not paying taxes and issuing only minimal or no dividend payments to their shareholders. Furthermore, the huge portfolio of non-performing loans held by the banks is in stark contrast to *yu-cho*'s investment portfolio of government-guaranteed bonds, which obviates the need for deposit insurance.

The banks' main argument, and some economists' as well, is that *yu-cho*'s success in mobilizing deposits deprives the banks of these funds for intermediation. If this argument is to be considered, we should first ask what in fact are banks doing with their funds? In 1999, 8.4 trillion yen (US$80 billion) in public funds were spent in recapitalizing the commercial banks so as to provide them with adequate capital reserves to resume their lending to small- and medium-size enterprises (SME). Instead, banks have chosen to purchase Japanese government bonds with their funds rather than lend to SMEs, thus violating the spirit and intent of the government's bank recapitalization program. Meanwhile, for the SMEs, publicly owned policy-based finance companies that are funded in part by postal savings deposits must fill the needs left by the commercial banks' lending gap. This role reversal, where postal savings must indirectly take up the bank's role as a supplier of credit to SMEs, highlights a key policy failure in resolving Japan's long-ongoing banking crisis.

Is Postal Savings Cross-Subsidized by the Posts?

Cross-selling of financial products has become a commonplace strategy in recent years in the global financial sector and has provided the motivation for many of the megamergers in the banking, securities, trust, and insurance industries as a result of the market liberalization in financial services that has taken hold in most developed countries. As discussed in chapter 2, similar cross-selling opportunities have also taken place in the private sector express package delivery services, which have reconfigured and market themselves as fully integrated logistics services, not only delivering parcels, but also offering warehousing, product fulfillment, and financial service components such as billing, and factoring as newly formed logistics services. Despite the prevalence of cross-selling practices in the private sector, when government-owned institutions, such as the post, make use of their own facilities for multiservice activities, the charges of anticompetitive cross-subsidization are heard from the private sector.

Some critics of *yu-cho* have argued that revenues from postal operations subsidize the postal savings system; however, the Ministry of Post's own cost analysis shows there is no such subsidy. As discussed earlier in chapter 2, postal financial services provide a substantial portion of the post's revenue and typically support mail delivery, which operates at a loss in many countries. In fact, without the multiple use of the existing infrastructure, the Japanese postal system would find it difficult to sustain mail delivery operations in many rural areas if left on its own. Postal savings officials also counter criticisms of a supposed competitive advantage by pointing to the costs they must bear in providing postal, savings, and life insurance services in rural areas to fulfill their official mandate to serve all markets, rural or urban, whether profitable or not.

The Marketing Failure of Commercial Banks

The commercial banks rely chiefly on the employee accounts of their client firms for individual and household savings. These employee accounts have historically been part of a package of rewards to the main bank, in which such accounts provide cross-subsidization of the bank-firm relationship. These accounts are the mainstay of a bank's deposit base under Japan's so-called "main bank system," whereby corporate finance in Japan has been largely mediated by the banking sector, especially within groupings of affiliated companies (see M.J. Scher 1997, 1998 *Japanese Interfirm Networks and Their Main Banks*, Palgrave-Macmillan and Toyo Keizai Shimposha). With captive employee accounts as their prime source for retail banking fees such as bill payments, ATM transactions, and other profitable services, including consumer lending, the City banks have had no incentive to improve retail client services and products since these employee accounts are an expected component of the bank's commercial relationships with its corporate clients.

In contrast, the popularity of postal savings is due in large measure to the capabilities of postal savings and from the tremendous economies of scale provided by the post office network to reach out to rural areas and urban/

suburban neighborhoods where there would be little profit margin for a stand-alone institution such as a bank. In addition, the popularity of the postal savings products and services is another crucial aspect in its ability to mobilize savings.

The ongoing shift of household deposits out of the employee accounts into postal savings has become a significant loss to the commercial banks and is thus a factor in the declining efficacy of the corporate lending system and weakening of the so-called main bank relationship. This tendency is likely to continue in the face of corporate downsizing and layoffs, which have fueled employee distrust in the corporate system in general, and the profound fear by depositors of the lack of safety and security of the banking system in particular.

Attractiveness and Cost of Savings Products

Postal savings has captured a substantial part of the retail market with its *teigaku chokin*, a ten-year time deposit with an early withdrawal option. Although the private banking sector has the right to issue the same product, virtually no banks do. Indeed, since the 1980s a level playing field has existed for both the type and features of financial products, including tax exemptions, that postal savings offers.

A case can also be made that the postal savings system helps keep the private sector honest, and that even with the competitive pressure from the postal savings system, private sector banking has shown little innovation on its own and made few efforts to provide competitively priced retail banking services and products for the general public (see Table 7.1: Comparison of Convenience: Postal Savings vs. Banks). Government even aids the private banking sector by restricting *yu-cho* from making any comparison to banks in their advertising and by restricting postal savings interest rates to the levels of commercial banks' offerings.

Indeed, the programs and plans offered by the postal service have materially improved the quality of financial services available to the general public. The post office has long offered products such as life insurance (since 1916) and pension plans (both managed separately from postal savings), and payment services (giro, since 1906; money orders, 1875), although it is only in recent years that Japan's private sector institutions have begun to compete in the cross-selling of products such as insurance and pension plans. Postal savings maintains a nationwide network of automatic teller machines that can be used to make deposits, withdrawals, credit card payments, or to pay utility bills or transfer payments to anywhere in Japan without the fees exacted by banks.

Table 7.1

Comparison of Convenience: Postal Savings vs. Banks
(as of January 2001)

		Postal Savings	Bank of Tokyo-Mitsubishi
Annual Interest	Regular	0.12%	0.10%
	CD	0.15%	0.15%
Transaction Fee	Teller	¥ 140	¥ 315–840
	Internet		¥ 0–367
ATM Fees (weekend and nighttime)		No Fee at Post Office ATMs	¥ 105
No. of Office Branches		24,768*	316*
No. of ATMs		25,184*	3,873*

Source: Shukan Daiamondo, 20 February 2001.
* = 31 March 2000 *Annual Reports*: Postal Savings Bureau; Bank of Tokyo-Mitsubishi.

Banks are only now beginning to compete in these areas in response to consumer pressures. The number of postal savings ATMs also overwhelms those of any single private bank, with 25,184 machines (March 2000). This number is 6.5 times as many as those of Bank of Tokyo-Mitsubishi, one of Japan's "big four" banks. Postal offices' ATMs are more depositor-friendly than those of banks, charging no transaction fee for after–6 P.M. and weekend use. The number of postal savings ATM outlets continues to expand, with tie-ins to several private sector financial institutions adding 2,152 ATMs as of December 2000. Recently some city banks have begun to charge depositors a minimum account fee, while postal savings depositors can keep a minimal balance, even as low as ten yen, without any account maintenance charges.

Accessibility of Locations

The success of the postal savings system can be chiefly attributed to the fast and consumer friendly ease of counter service (average wait time 2 minutes 40 seconds), and the fact that Japan's widely dispersed 24,737 post offices function as collection points for its savings system, far outstripping the 16,000 branches of all 110 banks, savings and loans, and other financial institutions in Japan. In fact, Japanese people on average live within 1.1 kilometers of a post office, while bank branches are typically found clustered in the cities' commercial business districts. Of the 3,235 cities and municipalities that have post offices, 567, that is, some 18 percent, are without banks. The wide-based infrastructure of post offices offers tremendous economies of scale, especially in reaching out to rural areas where there would be little profit margin for a stand-alone institution such as a bank.

Postal Reform and the Future of *Yu-cho*

The Creation of Japan Post in 2003

In December 1997, then–prime minister Ryuichi Hashimoto's final report on proposed ministerial reform, *The Fundamental Reform of the Central Government Ministries and Agencies Law (Chuo shocho to kaikaku kihon ho)*, defined the future shape of the postal organizations. The former Postal Agency was incorporated in April 2003 as an independent public enterprise known as Japan Post. The new entity administers postal services, postal savings, and postal life insurance businesses. The regulatory provision governing the Japan Post requires an annual financial audit by the Financial Service Agency. Under the old rules, each one of the three postal businesses had what was called a "special budget" (*tokkai*) that was independent of the general accounts and operated within a special, regulation-free framework (*Shukan Daiamondo*, 20 January 2001, pp. 32–33). Even though opaque accounting frameworks are hardly unique among government agencies, the new accounting rules, which we discuss later in more detail, are expected to eliminate the obscurity of the postal accounting system, render the corporation subject to an independent audit by an external authority, and improve its accountability and transparency, thus eliminating the very points upon which many privatization advocates hang their arguments.

Junichiro Koizumi, then health and welfare minister in the Hashimoto cabinet and an adamant postal reformer, reluctantly endorsed the 1997 proposals, although they fell far short of his ultimate goals of privatization of the posts, with the following conditions:*

1. Mandatory deposit of postal savings funds with the Trust Fund Bureau (TFB) under management of the Ministry of Finance (MoF) would be abolished, and the savings and life insurance funds would be independently managed (as discussed later, in more detail).
2. The postal delivery business would be deregulated, and private companies can enter the market. This was more controversial.

---

*Koizumi obtained the support of the Mori faction in exchange for approving the Postal Corporation initiative when Koizumi ran for LDP chairman in April 2001. Ushio Shioda, "Focus Seiji," in *Shukan Toyo Keizai*, 26 January 2002, pp. 104–5.

First-class mail delivery in urban business areas, a profitable monopoly of the Postal Agency, is the main target of deregulation. The scope of deregulating this sector is still under discussion. While Koizumi pushes for full, unconditional deregulation, the Ministry of Public Management, Home Affairs, Posts, and Telecommunications (MPT) attempts to maintain some regulatory control through the partial deregulation of the posts by weight of the mail. The MPT is concerned that a full deregulation of the market may destroy the existing "universal service" principle, which guarantees impartial delivery across the nation with equal service quality at the flat rate. Once the free market principle rules the industry, postal service companies—whether a privatized Japan Post or a parcel delivery firm like Yamato—are likely to stop service or raise fees in unprofitable areas. Such was the case in Finland and Sweden (see Chapter 2).

Japan's postal delivery already suffers from severe loss of market through regulatory evasion. Liberalization typically brings new entrants into markets, thereby causing loss of market share in formerly highly regulated service industries, especially banking, but also in telecommunications, electric power generation, and other utilities that are obligated to provide the public with certain basic, if not universal services, as does the posts. For example, far from enjoying a monopoly position in the market, advertising circulars and utility bills bypass the postal system and are routinely deposited by independent carriers directly into the letterboxes of households and businesses. Non-priority mail (advertising, etc.) accounts for only 12 percent by volume of the Japanese post office business compared to the U.S. Postal Service's 48 percent, the U.K.'s 69 percent, and France's 74 percent. Japan also has the lowest number of average post deliveries per capita among the major industrialized countries, at 206 pieces per annum, compared to in the U.S., 734, France with 447, the Netherlands' 442, and the U.K.'s 336. The loss of these revenues is partially compensated for by Japan's high postal rates. The high rate of mail delivery in the United States stems from the U.S. Postal Service rigorously enforcing its legal control of exclusive access to letterboxes for advertising as well as all other mail. This factor keeps U.S. first-class postal rates the lowest of all industrialized countries, and less than half of Japan's letter rate. Prime Minister Koizumi's proposed introduction of competing private sector postal delivery companies to cherry-pick the market even further will likely result in making the postal system's urban deliveries unprofitable as well (see *Financial Times,* 13 May 2002 interview with Prime Minister Koizumi). Koizumi already met partial defeat of his agenda when the Japanese parliamentary committee recently required any new entrants to the mail delivery market to provide as many letter collection boxes throughout Japan as Japan Post provides, some 175,570, thus making his proposal a non-starter (*Financial Times*, 4 July 2002).

In spite of strong political pressure within his own party opposing privatization, Koizumi has not given up his postal privatization stance. Yet after more than three years after entering the prime minister's office, Koizumi's personal advisory group, which consists mainly of intellectuals and policymakers who have been studying and discussing a postal privatization strategy, has yet to make public any specific plans.

Nevertheless, business groups, including the Keizai Doyukai, have proposed a privatization blueprint to create a postbank separate from the postal service. The proposed postbank would first be 100 percent government-owned, with its financial products sharply reduced to only postal savings and life insurance; privatization would follow as soon as possible. Some private think tanks have suggested a hybrid approach, breaking up the privatized postal savings entity into prefectures and turning them over to the severely ailing regional banks. Since a straightforward privatization of the Japan Post, which dominates in the three postal-related businesses, would not remove the threat of monopoly to other private competitors, it is argued by the business sector that the postal savings and postal life insurance businesses should be privatized and partitioned. The business groups' complaint about the size and scope of the post's "monopoly" seems disingenuous when private sector financial megagroups have been formed in recent years between commercial banks, securities firms, trust banks, and insurance companies, such as the Mizuho Group (centered around IBJ, DKB, Fuji Banks), Sumitomo-Sakura Bank Group, and the forthcoming merger of the UFJ Group (Sanwa and Tokai Banks) with the Mitsubishi-Tokyo Bank Group.

Funds Management and the Privatization Question

Some of the rationales for privatization of the postal system pertain to its financial activities per se:

1. The Japan Post lacks the ability to independently manage the enormous amount of funds on deposit, 255 trillion yen in postal savings and another 112 trillion yen in postal life insurance. A failure in funds management would be a costly liability that would ultimately be borne by taxpayers.
2. The amount of funds is so large, it may distort the market. Of particular concern are the so-called PKO (price-keeping operations) in equity markets, that is, government intervention that buoys the stock market. The existence of PKO is frequently referred to in financial circles and the press, yet is flatly denied by postal savings officials.
3. Japan Post deprives markets of business opportunities by "monopolizing" retail savings, a chief complaint of private sector financial institutions.

Is Postal Savings to Blame for Bad FILP Performance?

The above points highlight a significant conceptual problem in public debates over postal savings reform, namely the failure to distinguish between the function of the postal savings system (i.e., savings collection) with that of funds management. In particular, privatization advocates tend to focus on past mismanagement of funds as a major reason for liquidating the entire postal savings system. In a press interview in 2001, Mr. Koizumi argued:

> Why do we need a privatization of the three postal businesses? The answer is simple. A downsizing of public employment, an elimination and/or reorganization of the GFIAs, and a reform of the FILP system. All these reforms, which are the focal point of administrative and financial reforms, are in essence linked to a postal reform. . . . The financial source of the GFIAs is postal savings and postal insurance. We cannot make progress in rationalization of the GFIAs and reduction of public service workers unless we privatize the postal businesses and sever this flow of funds. (*Shukan Daiamondo*, 20 January 2001, p. 46)

Savings collection and funds management, however, are independent functions, and until 31 March 2001 had been administered by different ministries. Management of funds is guided by the investment practices of fund managers, and institutional channels give discretionary access to funds. Past investment and financing losses are more properly attributed to the Ministry of Finance, whose Trust Fund Bureau (TFB) had abused the funds by financing fruitless government-sponsored projects and/or investing postal pension plan funds in volatile financial market operations. This confusion over the domains of responsibility and authority among government institutions is a misconstruction that harms serious consideration and discussion of institutional reforms of the postal savings system.

How Should Funds Be Invested?

This leads to a critical question that needs to be addressed: How should funds raised through the postal savings system be managed for better performance? The past poor performance of the postal savings funds has come from, among other things, mismanagement by FILP as mentioned above, a lack of transparency and accountability under accounting rules used for postal savings funds, and poor investment by the TFB in equities and land. We have already discussed how political considerations have wasted postal savings funds under the FILP program. The old accounting rules, which kept postal businesses untouched by external scrutiny, continued to coverup the underperformance of investments. For example, the postal savings system was not obliged to report its financial statements based on market value (which was also the case until recently for commercial banks). Inadequate accounting and reporting frequently led to calls for a "market solution" for what was essentially a governance problem. Whether or not the market can provide any better governance mechanism or safety in preserving postal saving funds' assets we will examine next.

The Mode of Funds Management and Market Risk

Under the new law, the Postal Administration Council, an advisory group to the Minister of Public Management, approves the portfolio structure of the postal savings fund. As of 2002 the fund guidelines are as follows: 80 percent of funds is in domestic bonds that are almost entirely invested in Japanese government bonds and other government-guaranteed securities; 10 percent is divided equally into domestic and foreign securities, including some corporate bonds of foreign companies; 5 percent is in bonds of foreign governments and international organizations; and 5 percent is in the overnight interbank market. The basic composition of the portfolio has varied little in the past few years.

Since the government is prohibited from investing directly in stocks, the Postal Savings Bureau manages and invests the equity portion of the investment funds indirectly, through 15 or 16 private trust banks. The market keeps an eye on this type of investment because some analysts allege that the funds are being used as the source of the government's PKO operations. Responding to these concerns, the MPT has pledged to "conduct a market-neutral fund management" (*Nikkei Shimbun*, 25 December 2001). Nevertheless, Japan Post will become a major market player with its 2–3 trillion yen in investments, which represents about 20 percent of the 16 trillion yen traded through the market.

The MPT also expects that in the future, when market demand by city banks for overnight interbank loans recovers this demand will help further diversify its portfolio structure to mitigate risks and better enable more stable investment returns (*Nikkei Shimbun*, 11 February 2002). Several asset liability management and portfolio diversification techniques are employed when 20 trillion yen are invested in equities together with life insurance in order to reduce exposure to volatile securities markets at home and overseas. The fundamental issue, however, is whether a market-vulnerable portfolio is desirable or necessary when Japanese government bonds are a risk-free alternative.

Since Japan Post has not publicly reported its investment performance to date, we do not know the specific performance of each class of investment or the amount of loss or gain associated with a specific class of investment. However, given the burst bubble and the stagnant Japanese equity market since then, coupled with the volatile U.S. and global markets, it is probable that postal investments have accumulated losses. As of the end of September 2001, unrealized losses in stock market investments were estimated to amount to some 6.6 trillion yen (*Nikkei Shimbun*, 25 December 2001). In a highly volatile market environment, it would therefore seem more prudent for postal fund managers to concentrate on low-risk investments, especially government bonds, that are virtually risk-free. Riskier investment requires fund management expertise and financial techniques, the very tools the postal savings system lacks. Moreover, poorer fund management may cost not only investment performance, but, more important, credibility and safety—two major advantages postal savings has over commercial banks. Postal savings depositors today do not expect higher returns but rather the safety and security of their deposits.

Even with a portfolio of only government and government-guaranteed securities, the postal savings system needs a viable internal risk management system, and especially for the existing portfolio strategy. Effective asset and liability management is essential to any financial institution entering into investment activities. The system helps mitigate various kinds of risks inherent in financial markets and allows the financial institution to take proper and quick action whenever risks come to a dangerous level. An improved internal control system needs to be the first step toward an accurate, market value–based accounting practice, which the current system lacks.

The savings fund intends to invest 10 percent in stocks. Foreign denominated bonds for which 5 percent of the fund will be allocated are subject to foreign exchange risk, and even sovereign-risk bonds are not risk-free, as was recently seen in the Argentine debt default. The fund must also pay attention to solvency of its borrower banks in the call market. The exposure to volatile equity, bond, and call markets requires the postal savings fund managers to reinforce their risk management system and strategies.

An area that threatens consumer confidence in savings instruments is Japan Post's intention under its new business plan to sell a defined-contribution pension plan, a Japanese version of the U.S. 401(k) plan. This type of product would require a sufficiently competent sales/postal counter staff to explain the risks involved in this and other investment fund products to its customers. The stunning loss of retirement savings facing U.S. defined-pension planholders owing to the U.S. stock market collapse and the attendant fraudulent reporting activities of companies whose stocks were held in their employee plans should give pause to Japanese public policymakers, as if the 1989

Japanese market's collapse should not have already given enough of a clear warning to policymakers of the public's concern over losing their retirement savings. Until now, post offices have sold only principal-guaranteed products such as time deposits and life insurance accounts.

Conclusion

Depositors in fear of a financial meltdown continued to shift their assets from private banks, equity, and real estate into postal savings, and to a lesser extent to foreign currency accounts, mainly at foreign-owned banks, and more recently into gold bullion. With seemingly no headway in resolving long-standing banking issues, the popular distrust in banks was at a high point. The bankruptcies of major and smaller banks, slow progress in writing off non-performing loans, and the limitation on deposit guarantees on bank accounts to 10 million yen, originally slated for 1 April 2003 and further postponed, have further heightened the public's sense of insecurity about the banking industry. With the possible loss of deposit guarantees at banks, postal savings stands as a harbor of safety and trust for an apprehensive public. Although the maximum amount in a postal savings account is 10 million yen, one can deposit an unlimited amount in a non-interest-bearing arrangement. Even with no interest income, Japanese depositors find comfort in the safety provided by the postal savings system. Thus, postal savings is the most popular form of savings nowadays.

Japan has a highly risk-averse culture, where safety and stability are the most crucial elements in people's savings decisions. While commercial banks underwent reorganization through mergers and acquisitions, with changes in ownership, bank names, and brands, postal savings maintained its original brand identity. The long-term penetration of the postal savings system in every locality helped assure confidence, trust, and familiarity among people. Bank mergers and ownership changes confused and worried many ordinary Japanese who prize what is old, large, and stable, and are not used to the constantly changing "M&A" (merger and acquisition) culture and constant morphing of financial and non-financial institutions of all types. One cannot find a safer investment than postal savings in today's Japan.

Critics acknowledge an "evolutionary" process of financial reform, including a continuation of postal savings, as the "second best option" as opposed to radical change of the system (Cargill and Yoshino). Any radical transformation in this huge savings system is viewed as too risky for a society undergoing critical structural changes, such as a decreasing working population, an increasing percentage of older people in the population, and a mounting public debt that now exceeds 140 percent of annual GDP. As discussed earlier, the system needs to improve accountability and transparency in its accounting and investment practices. It should also review its internal risk management system and its portfolio structure against market risks. On the other hand, the postal savings system cannot, indeed should not, take for granted its portfolio management capacity. Maintaining depositors' confidence in the system matters most.

Depositors' Confidence

Many Japanese and foreign-owned financial institutions anticipated massive redemptions upon the maturity of the ten-year *teigaku* postal savings time deposits in FY (fiscal year) 1999 and FY2000, and began to introduce all sorts of attractive market-based financial products. Nevertheless, 84.9 percent of the maturating deposits were rolled over into new certificates, and the remaining balance went into Ordinary Deposit postal savings accounts. The much-anticipated flow of funds to the commercial financial sector never materialized. Unlike savers in 1875, who had little choice but postal savings, or those in wartime who had to show patriotism in the form of postal savings, today's depositors *choose* to put their money into postal savings.

Postal Savings as a Catalyst for Better Service in Banking

For many years banks have been allowed to offer the same products that postal savings offers its clients, but have not done so. Postal savings officials counter criticism of its supposed competitive advantage by pointing to the costs they must bear in providing postal, savings, and life insurance services in rural areas to fulfill their mandate. A good case can also be made that the existence of the postal savings system may raise the quality of private banking services available to the general public. The postal savings system has been a catalyst for keeping the private sector competitive and better qualified in the services offered. The consumer-oriented Japanese postal savings system offers products such as life insurance and a nationwide ATM network that can be used to make deposits, withdrawals, credit card payments, or to pay utility bills or transfer payments to anywhere in the country at lower fees than charged by banks. Since the 1980s its inexpensive international giro payments service has become very popular for sending overseas remittances. Banks, especially the large city banks, have long taken their retail clients for granted. Banks now have come to realize the profitability of the retail banking market, especially its income from transaction fees. In fact, banks' revenue from retail fees is larger than profits from corporate lending, especially in light of Japan's huge problem in non-performing bank loans. Only recently have banks begun to respond to the competitive pressures of the postal savings system. It would be instructive for banks to revisit their client strategies and examine why the people prefer postal savings. The postal savings system's attributes of safety, accessibility, and convenience of service, and the ease of comprehension and use of its financial products, are a clear advantage of the system over banks. It is hoped that banks will get some clues from these attributes and use them to provide better and more competitive services and products in the future.

Important policy implications are at issue in the intermediation of *yu-cho*'s funds that go well beyond the exposure to market risk. At issue is differentiating the intermediatory roles of savings institutions, such *yu-cho*, that were created for individual and household thrift, and charged with the prudent safeguarding of savers' deposits as compared to the designated role of commercial banks of financing business enterprises with creditors' risk. A considerable amount of public funds has been spent in recent years by the Japanese government to recapitalize the banks, some 8.4 trillion yen (US$80 billion) in 1999, to provide the banks with adequate capitalization to resume financing small and medium-size enterprises (SME). Rather than providing credits to SMEs, banks have instead invested their funds in the safety of Japanese Government Bonds (JGB). On the other hand, policymakers have moved to increase postal savings funds' investment-risk profile in equity markets instead of government-guaranteed securities, thereby giving it greater risk exposure. By not addressing the wishes of postal savings depositors, whose primary concern is safety, a major reversal of the primary roles of commercial banks with that of savings institutions is taking place. Government-owned, policy-based finance companies must now provide small business loans while commercial banks avoid credit risk by buying risk-free JGBs. With the huge amount of public debt that needs to be underwritten, some 140 percent of GDP, there is no reason not to provide postal savings depositors with the security they are seeking by investing in the safety of government bonds. Commercial banks that rely on client companies' employee deposits as a cheap source of funds, on the other hand, have all but abandoned commercial lending and depend instead on fee income and government largesse. Unless banks that have accepted government injections of capital are proscribed from purchasing JGBs, there will be no way that the Japanese economy can recover based on its bank-centered financing regime.

The Politics of Privatization

When Maeshima first established the Japanese postal service, he appointed prominent individuals in rural areas as local postmasters who in turn provided postal station facilities at little or no cost. Even today some 80 percent of Japan's post office buildings are privately owned by their postmasters, most having inherited their positions over many generations. Needless to say, these postmasters are a powerful force in regional and national politics, with support from former Prime Minister Hashimoto's faction within the ruling Liberal-Democratic Party. Working together with the Postal Workers' Union, which supports the Democratic Party, the main opposition party, they have been able to foil Prime Minister Koizumi's plans to privatize the postal sector and banking industry efforts to marginalize or abolish Japan's postal savings system.

Japan Post would like to see postal savings operations fully privatized as a bank, which would make Japan Post not only the owner of the largest bank in Japan but in the world. The commercial banking sector, on the other hand, wants to see the postal savings system totally abolished. Both outcomes are unlikely. Compromise positions that take into account the fiscal needs of Japan Post would include agency agreements for over-the-postal-counter sales of the financial products of commercial sector institutions. Japan Post would unlikely be able to survive if deprived of the income it receives from its own financial products and services, such as postal savings, postal life insurance, and national pensions plans. *Yu-cho*'s critics are suggesting further limitations on the size of accounts and on the sale of the popular *teigaku* savings product. Other limitations they propose are to restrict the geographic scope of operations to commercial unviable remote regions and to reduce the postal workforce by as much as 30 percent. What all of the proposals of the contending groups share is a fundamental lack of respect for the needs and concerns of the many households and individuals who are seeking a safe and convenient place to make deposits and withdrawals without placing their life savings in jeopardy of bank failure and financial market risk.

Acknowledgments

Mark Scher would like to thank Toake Endoh for her contributions to earlier drafts of this chapter. He would also like to thank the members of the Japan Economic Seminar for their comments on an earlier version of this chapter presented as a paper at its November 2002 meeting in Washington, D.C. In particular, he would like to thank Patricia Kuwayama for comments as discussant and to Kazuo Sato for his extensive written comments following the JES meeting.

References

Anderson, Stephen J. 1990. "The Political Economy of Japanese Saving: How Postal Savings and Public Pensions Support High Rates of Household Savings in Japan." *Journal of Japanese Studies* (winter): 61–92.

Calder, Kent E. 1990. "Linking Welfare and the Developmental State: Postal Savings in Japan." *Journal of Japanese Studies* 16: 31–59.

Cargill, Thomas F., and Naoyuki Yoshino. 2000. "The Postal Savings System, Fiscal Investment and Loan Program, and Modernizations of Japan's Financial System." In *Crisis and Change in the Japanese Financial System*, ed. T. Hoshi and H. Patrick. Boston: Kluwer.

———. 2003. *Postal Savings System and Fiscal Investment in Japan.* Oxford: Oxford University Press.

Doi, Takero, and T. Hoshi. 2002. "FILP: How Much Has Been Lost? How Much More Will Be Lost?" Unpublished paper.

Kuwayama, Patricia Hagan. 2000. "Postal Banking in the United States and Japan: A Comparative Analysis." *Monetary and Economic Studies* (Bank of Japan).

Scher, Mark J. 1997. *Japanese Interfirm Networks and Their Main Banks.* London and New York: Palgrave-Macmillan and St. Martin's (U.S. and Canada).

———. 1998. *Mainbank shinwa no hokai (Collapse of the Main Bank Myth)*. M.J. Scher, with postscript by Hiroshi Okumura. Tokyo: Toyo Keizai Shinposha Ltd.

———. 2001. "Postal Savings and the Provision of Financial Services: Policy Issues and Asian Experiences in the Use of the Postal Infrastructure for Savings Mobilization." *Discussion Paper Series*, no. 22, United Nations Department of Economic and Social Affairs (December).

———. 2002. "Postal Savings System." *Encyclopedia of Japanese Business and Management*, ed. Allan Bird. New York: Routledge.

Tamaki, Norio. 1995. *Japanese Banking: A History, 1859–1959.* Cambridge: Cambridge University Press.

Zenginkyo (Japanese Bankers Association) 2001. The Banking System in Japan. Tokyo.

8

The National Savings Organization* and the Status of Small Savings in India

Dhirendra Swarup and Anil Bhattacharya

A Brief History of Savings in India

In India, savings based on a legislative framework of government banks has a history of 130 years. Some historians trace the genesis of the savings movement to 1834, when the first savings bank was established in Calcutta by the government. However, the Government Savings Bank Act was passed in 1873, and it was in 1882 that the Post Office Savings Bank of India came into existence. In 1886 the Government District Savings Banks were merged with the Post Office Savings Bank (POSB). While under British rule the Government of India had also set up the National Savings Central Bureau with the objectives of promoting thrift, containing inflationary trends in the economy caused by the Second World War, and mobilizing funds to finance the war. It is said, however, that this drive did not gain momentum, as the people were not enthusiastic about funding an alien war effort.

After independence in 1947, it was felt that more of an impetus had to be given to the savings movement, and the National Savings Organization (NSO) was created in 1948. The words of then Prime Minister Pandit Jawaharlal Nehru signify the crucial role envisaged for the national savings movement in the context of domestic savings as a force for national development:

> I attach great importance to the movement of National Savings. It is important not only because we want people to save and to apply these savings for our development plans, but also because it reaches a large number of people. It is not enough merely to make appeals. There must be organization be-

---

*The National Savings Organization was reorganized in 2003 and renamed the National Savings Institute to focus on designing savings products and on research and development of the savings market. Direct supervisory functions of its agents were transferred to the State Small Savings Organizations.

hind it also so as to reach every village. . . . Every person who participates in this campaign and adds to the savings not only helps in the fulfillment of our Second Five Year Plan but also becomes in a sense a sharer in it. . . . I wish this campaign every success.

Small savings were considered a priority concern of the government. The Constitution of India, adopted in 1949, lists the Post Office Savings Bank in its Seventh Schedule, Item No. 39. Utilizing the Government Savings Certificates Act of 1959 and the Public Provident Fund Act of 1968, the Ministry of Finance (MoF) framed numerous small savings plans under these acts.

The primary objective of the small savings program has been to promote the habit of thrift and savings among citizens of the country. The emphasis, as the words "small savings" suggest, is to bring the small depositor into the fold of the savings movement. The Post Office Savings Bank has been the main vehicle for these plans across the length and breadth of India since its establishment 120 years ago.

The Demographics of Household Savings: Urban and Rural

Recent estimates indicate that the population of India has surpassed 1 billion. Assuming an average family size of five, there are some 200 million families in India. As of 31 March 2000 there were 114 million accounts under small savings, and it is estimated that some 50 million households were small savings depositors. Small savings collections represent about 3.5 percent of the GDP of India. Total deposits under small savings plans were on the order of US$40 billion in 2000.

Building a Deposit Base for Postal Savings

The NSO has taken as its motto "Torch Bearers of Household Savings" for more than five decades. As part of the Golden Jubilee celebration of the National Savings Organization in June 1998, a pair of postage stamps was issued. The theme depicted on the stamps was "Collective Thrift in the March of the Nation." The NSO's marketing strategy for small savings is two-pronged: promoting household prosperity and "building the country."

The NSO emphasizes plans that help develop financial stability and prosperity for the individual and his family. Its small savings plans facilitate long-term planning by encouraging saving small sums of money to reap larger benefits for future occasions. Subscribers' savings also represent a major resource for financing development. The NSO logo of a honeybee is symbolic of collective saving for the future. World Thrift Day and other publicity campaigns inform the public of the developmental projects by State governments. Indeed, in many States there is a direct flow from the State's share of collections under small savings plans to the local areas in which the collections were made.

Saving is an inherent trait in the Indian psyche; families tend to save. Traditionally, grain had been saved by households to tide over difficult periods, and gold is saved after the birth of a child, looking especially toward the future marriage of a daughter. The *hundi* (small pot), a traditional form of piggy bank, is still used in rural India. Nevertheless, Western influences toward consumption rather than savings are now beginning to take hold in society.

The Public's Confidence in Postal Savings

The government's sovereign guarantee is the most important reason for the consumer confidence that small savings plans enjoy. Many subscribers prefer the government's NSO plans over venturing in capital markets, which are associated with some risk. Small savings collections in India have grown consistently in recent years, with no sudden rush of withdrawals at any point in time. As a result, net collections, after deducting payments to cover maturity withdrawals, have also consistently increased.

The small savings system is extremely robust. In the last decade there have been several repeated instances of uncertainty in the capital markets, with investor confidence being rudely shaken. By contrast, the NSO's small savings plans are seen by the public as zero-risk investments, which provide additional benefits such as attractive interest rates and, in some plans, substantial tax incentives. In addition, these plans are sold mostly by the post office, a government institution in which the public has much faith, and the public sector's nationalized banks, autonomous institutions wholly owned by the government that offer three of these savings plans.

Small savers generally invest their money in savings plans according to their present circumstances and future needs. Senior citizen pensioners like to invest their savings and retirement benefits in plans that generate periodic income, such as the Monthly Income Account and Deposit Plans for Retiring Employees. A large section of savers are income tax payers who invest in plans having tax concession provisions such as National Savings Certificates, the Public Provident Fund, and so on.

Among the plans that are very popular in rural areas is the Kisan Vikas Patra (Farmers Development Certificate). This plan is based on a deep discount bond in which the principal invested doubles in seven years and eight months, an implied interest rate of 9 to 10 percent. The maturity period is determined by the prevalent interest rate structure at the time of deposit. This plan is of particular appeal to rural savers and uneducated urban people in that it provides a readily understandable option in which the rate of interest does not have to be reckoned. The Post Office Recurring Deposit Plan has also acquired immense popularity as it helps savers save small sums of money over a long period of time in a phased manner.

The NSO under the Ministry of Finance has been entrusted with the work of promotion and publicity of these plans. The organization also provides training and support to agents, state government officials, and postal authorities. In 2001 there were eight plans in operation, including two plans introduced in 1989 and 1991 for the benefit of retiring government employees and the retiring employees of public sector companies. (See the appendix to chapter 8 for details.) All these plans are specifically designed to serve the different needs of small depositors. These plans are operated through the network of over 154,000 post offices, and some are offered as well in the 8,000 branches of the public sector banks. In addition, an agency force of over 500,000 freelance NSO agents has been appointed to facilitate subscriptions to these plans at the grassroots level; nearly one-third of the agents are women. Some 90 percent of the POSB accounts are serviced by NSO agents.

Outreach Efforts to Women and Disadvantaged Groups

Because it functions as a field organization, the NSO as well as the Department of Posts provide inputs for the development of new savings products and the improvement of existing plans. Recently they conducted a survey to ascertain the differences in the nature of collections in rural versus urban post offices. New surveys are being planned in consultation with the National Small Sample Survey Organization under the Ministry of Statistics and Programme Implementation.

In addition to savings products, the government of India has also devised extension agencies, which reach out to subscribers all over this large country. There are three agency systems that authorize agents to canvass for small savings on a commission basis. One of these agency plans, the Mahila Pradhan Kshetriya Bachat Yojana (Women's Savings Agency Plan), enables housewives to collect monthly deposits under the Post Office Recurring Deposit Plan in their locality. Women are considered thrifty and are known to systematically put away some of the household budget for a rainy day. In 1972 the government introduced the Post Office Recurring Plan targeted specifically to women to help them save small, fixed sums of money each month.

This plan has been hugely successful in certain parts of the country, particularly in rural areas and in certain States like Kerala, where women are known for being progressive. Under the Mahila Pradhan Kshetriya Bachat Yojana plan, women agents canvass house to house to collect savings from women at their doorsteps for deposit into the Post Office Recurring Deposit Plan. Women are sometimes shy about talking to men and often find it easier to talk to NSO's women agents, who are specially trained to promote this savings plan. The vast savings potential of women in villages and towns is thus being tapped by these female agents.

Collections under the Post Office Recurring Deposit Plan represented more than 11 percent of the total gross collections of small savings in 1999–2000, thus underlining the contribution of women agents in mobilizing resources for the country. The NSO is planning to broaden its servicing of rural clients. India's rural population, about 70 percent of the nation, has varied cultural backgrounds and many different languages. The educational level in the rural areas is not high and people require counseling about their finances. To spread its program of small savings plans among the rural population, the NSO requires its local workforce of agents to have an aptitude for working in such areas. Such help is essential for servicing rural clients and potential depositors. Plans sold by NSO agents are designed to reach the small depositor at the grassroots level in order to facilitate regular subscriptions.

This agent system for women was started in 1972, and now the agency force consists of over 150,000 women agents. This program also provides income for the women agents and thus empowers them as well. Agents are authorized to collect money from savers and deposit it within a stipulated time at post offices where the accounts are maintained. However, agents cannot make withdrawals on behalf of their clients. In the case of a depositor appointing the sales agent as her messenger, the withdrawal form is brought to the savings sales counter and payment is made by the Post Office Savings Bank. The government, however, bears no responsibility for misappropriation of withdrawals by a messenger because it is deemed to be an individual assignment from the account-holder.

The last fifty years have seen tremendous growth in India's industrial sector. Most industries are labor intensive, and large numbers of workers earn their livelihood in this sector. In 1958 the Pay Roll Savings Group Plan (PRSG) was introduced in private sector enterprises and later extended to government offices in 1962. Under this plan the worker joins a group and authorizes his employer to make a regular deduction from his monthly salary income for deposit in the various postal savings plans, depending on the worker's capacity to save as well as his future needs. Savings products offered by the PRSG include the Recurring Deposit Plan, Two-year, Three-year, and Five-year Time Deposit Plans, National Savings Certificates (VIIIth Issue), and the Public Provident Fund. The group leader authorized to operate on behalf of the employees is also paid an agency commission as an incentive.

Commissioned agents are also appointed to service other specific plans with a view to reach each and every group of society, including the poor, slum dwellers, and the like. For example, Extra-Departmental Branch Postmasters, who are under contract to the Department of Posts and generally based in rural and remote areas of the country, are also authorized to canvass and collect deposits for small savings plans. As an incentive they are further compensated by being paid commissions for their savings collection activities.

The basic philosophy of the concept of saving is taught to children by a program of the NSO. School Savings Banks, called Sanchayika, have been set up for schoolchildren. Introduced in 1968, the plan requires every schoolchild in selected schools to contribute a small amount out of his pocket money for deposit in Sanchayika. Primary training in savings education is given to the schoolchildren, and the children administer the bank under the guidance of their teachers and the school principal. The entire interest on the total deposits is shared by the children and the school. The Sanchayika board of trustees has authorized that 25 percent of the interest earned be put toward student welfare, by remunerating teachers and students engaged in Sanchayika work through incentives in the form of bonuses and by awarding token prizes to members for the promotion of Sanchayika in schools and colleges.

Promotion of Plans and Services

The NSO is entrusted with the work of promoting the plans and services, as are the individual State's Small Savers Organizations. Publicity is undertaken in the print and electronic media, in printed literature, and in short documentary films, released to 13,500 cinema theaters. Publicity is prepared in English, Hindi, and regional languages. Seventy-five newspapers, including two regional newspapers for each State, are used for the release of NSO advertisements. Publicity is also present at village exhibitions, market gatherings, local fairs, and religious festivals.

The small savings plans of the Government of India are designed in the Ministry of Finance. The National Savings Organization provides valuable input into this process. Although there is no organized market research carried out at present by the NSO, the District Savings Officers, Deputy Regional Directors, and Regional Directors interact intensively during the course of their duties in the field with various segments of subscribers, nodal associations such as the Lions Club and Rotary Club, women's associations, State government officials, and postal officials. This field experience is used by the Ministry of Finance in designing products.

Reaching the Rural Population

The real challenge that emerges in the small savings movement in India today is penetration into the rural and far-flung areas of the nation. The savings movement has caught on in the urban areas but rural populations too often still lack information and facilities to implement small savings plans. The National Savings Organization has been spreading the message through its administrative units and through nodal organizations. It is felt that we must strengthen the outreach abilities of this organization. Similarly, the NSO's sales agent force and postal personnel need to be trained more extensively to meet the needs of rural clients.

It is observed that the small savings plans are very successful in certain States, including West Bengal, Uttar Pradesh, Punjab, Maharashtra, Bihar, and Gujarat. These are among the more populous States, and the attention given by these State governments to small savings plans largely contributes to their success. In certain areas, such as the North East Region, collections under small savings plans are not significant. Population density in these areas is significantly lower than elsewhere, and lack of development may also be a factor. In 1999–2000, by States (excluding Delhi), the ratio of deposits to population ranged from a high per capita ratio of Rs. (rupees) 1,702 per person in some States to a low of Rs. 145 in others.

The present information base does not yield any data on separate groups of subscribers. We hope in the future to design detailed surveys in consultation with the National Sample Survey Organisation (NSSO), a field organization under the Ministry of Statistics and Programme Implementation. A questionnaire will be prepared by the NSO, which may be fielded by the machinery of the NSSO. This synergy is expected to create a regular mechanism for the collection of data on subscribers of small savings and their preferences so as to more accurately identify customer needs in designing savings products and the delivery of services. In 2004, this project was in a nascent stage.

Affordable Pricing of Savings Plans in the Development of Savings

Every citizen of India is eligible to subscribe to small savings plans. Small savings products are designed to make them accessible even to subscribers in the poorer regions. Therefore, the minimum amount of subscription required is only a token amount. Unlike instruments offered in the securities market, small savings plans are easily affordable by the smallest investor, and the minimum deposit is very low so as to attract the small investor. For example, the Post Office Recurring Deposit requires a minimum monthly deposit of only Rs. 10. The minimum subscription in a Savings Account is Rs. 20, while in some other plans, such as Time Deposits, National Savings Certificates, and Kisan Vikas Patras, the minimum amount is Rs. 50 or 100. For Monthly Income Accounts, where interest is paid out each month, a higher minimum deposit amount of Rs. 1,000 is required.

Defaults in the Recurring Deposit Plan are permitted for six months, and a nominal default fee is charged. In addition, keeping in mind the requirements of the small investor, every attempt is made to ensure liquidity in the savings instruments. Most instruments have an exit provision in the early period. Some plans, such as the Recurring Deposit Plan and Public Provident Fund, do not permit borrowing against deposits. Partial withdrawals, however, are permitted in the Public Provident Fund whereas the savings certificates (Kisan Vikas Patra and the NSC VIII Issue) can be pledged as collateral for loans in banks. To help the salaried class save, most of the plans offer significant tax credits, as described later in this chapter.

Small savings plans are accessible all over the country in over 154,000 post offices. Deposits are transferable from one post office to another. The Public Provident Fund (PPF), which permits limited withdrawals, is offered both in post offices and nationalized banks and is transferable between these two networks. Eighty-six percent of PPF accounts are held at nationalized banks. A high-level committee recommendation that the Kisan Vikas Patras plan and the National Savings Certificate should also be authorized to be sold at the banks is under consideration. No privately owned banks are authorized to sell the NSO's small savings plans.

In addition to plans for the individual small saver, selected plans are available for group accounts, such as the Public Provident Fund, superannuities funds, security deposit accounts, and trusts. Recently it was decided to open access in certain plans to farmers' and laborers' cooperatives and other self-help groups for the investment of their surplus funds.

The postal savings system has been able to extend its reach to small depositors in all the areas of the country, including the urban market. Although the presence of public sector banks and other chartered financial institutions, including those with a nationwide franchise, are particularly strong in the urban and semi-urban areas and have more attractive premises, deposits into small savings plans of the post office are significantly higher in these areas as well. Urban savers often prefer the various small savings plans of the NSO for their deposits, in view of their tax concessions, regular Monthly Income plans, and the safety of their deposits combined with advantageous returns.

Social and Cultural Factors in Designing Small Savings Products

The different maturity profiles of the various small savings products make it easy for the small depositor to save for different social occasions. Both availability of cash and end use reflect different requirements, and the small savings plans are designed to cater to the varying needs of subscribers in these respects. Educating children, house-building, and marriages of children are some of the events for which a plan such as the Recurring Deposit is designed. The plans allow depositors to save small sums on a monthly basis, which arrive in a lump sum. Farmers have access to large cash surpluses at harvest time, and Kisan Vikas Patra is a handy plan in which they can invest this surplus. Saving for festivals is possible through the Savings Account.

The maturity period of small savings plans differs from Savings Accounts (with no expiration) to One-, Two-, Three-, and Five-Year Time Deposits (fixed deposits), ranging to four- to six-year plans with different features, and a Public Provident Fund with a term of fifteen years. The basket of plans offered with a variety of maturities ensures that the differing requirements of subscribers are met. For instance, the Monthly Income Account provides interest each month to meet the consumption expenditure of savers, in particular, retired people; the Savings Account helps subscribers bank with the post office on a day-to-day basis.

The Kisan Vikas Patra (KVP), or Farmers Development Certificate, designed for farmers as a rainy-day fund, is a deep-discount bond that is also extremely simple to invest in. A onetime investment doubles after a fixed period. The concept of "doubling of capital" is comprehended easily by rural and semiliterate subscribers. Because farmers are not liable for income tax, this savings certificate does not offer any tax-free concessions or withhold taxes at payout. The KVP is available to any saver in addition to farmers. Those non-farmer savers, however, would be liable for paying income tax on their interest earnings as ordinary taxpayers.

There is also a small savings plan (the Protected Savings Plan, under the Post Office Recurring Deposit Plan), which provides optional insurance to beneficiaries in case of the death of the subscriber to a Post Office Recurring Deposit Plan. This is available in monthly denominations of Rs. 50, and in the event of death of the subscriber, the designated beneficiary receives the maturity payment.

Tax Incentives on Deposits

There are substantial tax incentives in many of the small savings plans. Certain plans allow for a deduction from taxable income to the extent of 20 percent of a saver's investment in the plan.

For example, the interest income from a Post Office Savings Account, Public Provident Fund Account, or a Deposit Plan for Retiring Employees of government or Public Sector Undertakings (PSU), such as companies and enterprises in which the government holds equity, are entirely exempt from income tax. The interest income from a National Savings Certificate is deemed to be reinvested, as is interest income under other plans, including Post Office Time Deposits, Post Office Recurring Deposits, Monthly Income Accounts, and National Savings Plans. Any interest income from these plans or other similarly designed plans offered in the banking sector and securities markets are tax-free on amounts below Rs. 12,000 (approximately US$250), and therefore are targeted to benefit only the small saver.

Favorable Interest Rates Are Intended for Small Savers Only

These small savings plans are designed to serve the basic needs of small depositors. Some of these plans have an edge of about 0.5 percent per annum interest rate over similar plans offered by public sector banks and nationally chartered financial institutions. These plans, however, contain provisions for maximum deposit limits. Deposit ceilings are stipulated in the Public Provident Fund Plan and Monthly Income Plan.

The potential loss of revenue from small savings plans with higher interest costs is significant; therefore, the government stipulates a ceiling on the amounts in these accounts so that they are not misused as an avenue of investment by wealthy individuals. For the same reason, institutional investment in small savings plans is also banned. The government's aim is not to stimulate borrowing but rather to encourage the habit of saving and offer the small saver a range of safe savings instruments.

User-Friendliness of the System

The system is already quite helpful to savers, and steps have been taken by the government to make the system more user-friendly. For instance, linkages are available between plans so that the Monthly Income Plan payments to the account-holder can be credited each month to his or her savings account.

The Postal Savings Bank payout system is well established and enjoys the confidence of the public. Customer withdrawals and redemption of certificates are made across the counter. Smaller post offices generally require a day or two to prepare checks for large amounts because the check must be sent to the Head post office for signature. The availability of funds, however, is not an issue, as the amount is debited to the Public Account of India National Small Savings Fund (NSSF).

Post offices situated in rural areas are generally one-person post offices. Often the villager asks the help of the postmaster, who is an authorized NSO agent, for advice. The NSO agents are trained to counsel subscribers about the plans to enable them to make suitable choices. Local postmasters typically perform other favors as well, such as giving help by reading or writing a letter.

Computerization of savings bank operations in the post offices is in progress. About 300 Head post offices have already been computerized, and the computerization of 15,000 major post offices is under way. Eventually the entire network will be online through a dedicated very small aperture terminal (VSAT) network.

Although credit is not available in post offices, postal savings certificates can be pledged to a public sector bank as security to obtain a loan. Post Office Recurring Deposit Plan and Public Provident Fund (PPF) rules also permit the issuance of advances against deposits. This can be done in post offices for both plans and in banks for the PPF.

Utilization of the Postal Infrastructure: Efficiencies and Convenience

Out of a countrywide network of more than 154,000 post offices, 137,847 are located in rural areas. Each post office has the facility to maintain small savings plans. As the infrastructure of post offices exists in every nook and corner of the country, the public has easy access to them. The operational as well as procedural rules followed by POSB are simple and customer-oriented. Procedures have been designed to fully serve all of India's diverse population, irrespective of socioeconomic caste or class. Furthermore, as small savings plans are uniformly operated without distinction between rural and urban areas, all the plans are available without restrictions. The minimum entry subscription is also very low in contrast to instruments in the securities market and encourages even low-income depositors to save. The Department of Posts recently started selling a brokerage-based product under an agency agreement with a private sector financial firm. The response of savers to this product so far has not been encouraging. Although the minimum entry level amount for the new POSB-based brokerage account is Rs. 1,000 (approximately US$20), it has not made any major inroads among small savers as the brokerage plans have been less rewarding than the NSO Small Savings Plans.

In certain States, collections are favorably skewed toward collections in urban post offices, as there is a tendency on the part of the rural rich, including prosperous farmers, to travel to the nearest city to deposit their savings. A recent study, based on a sample survey conducted by the NSO of collections in rural and urban branch post offices, suggests that in most States, some 65 percent of collections are in urban post offices. However, before any sound conclusions can be drawn, it is necessary to conduct a more detailed study of postal counter transactions.

Some problems of dormancy exist in savings account plans. According to the Post Office Savings Accounts Rules, accounts in which there have been no transactions in the last three years are considered dormant. To bring down the inefficiencies associated with such accounts, a token annual maintenance charge has been introduced. It is hoped that this will act as a deterrent as well as weed out accounts that have only a small amount on deposit and have not been utilized for a long period. A revival fee has also been stipulated.

The Organizational Structure and Distribution of Postal Saving Funds

The postal savings system is an agency function performed by the Department of Posts on behalf of the Government of India's Ministry of Finance. The Department of Posts is also a part of the Government of India. Keeping in view the fact that assisting small savings is an important function of the Department of Posts, there is an organizational structure that provides both unity of command and functional autonomy. All savings mobilized under this arrangement are credited to the National Small Savings Fund (NSSF) in the Public Account of the central bank, the Reserve Bank of India.

The POSB as well as public sector banks are remunerated at a fixed annual rate, which is adjusted from time to time based on the average number of account transactions. The Department of Posts and the banks are compensated on the basis of the number of accounts opened and serviced, that is, Rs. 25/- for each new opened account and Rs. 20/- for old accounts. This agency fee is not, however, based on the value of the funds collected. Calculating the remuneration to the Department of Posts as a commission based on present levels of collections, the rate of compensation amounts to some 1.6 percent of the value of the collections. A similar calculation for banks that also handle NSO products would show the level of compensation at 2.2 percent. The Department of Posts, however, is an intrinsic part of the Government of India, which discharges savings bank operations on behalf of the Ministry of Finance, and therefore the relationship cannot be compared to other institutions, such as banks.

As far as operations are concerned, the Director General, Department of Posts, is the Chief Executive of the POSB. However, within the Headquarters of the Department of Posts, the POSB is under the control of the Member (Development) of the Postal Services Board, a group headed by the Deputy. The Director General (Savings Bank) assisted by the Director (Savings Bank) is responsible for the smooth functioning of POSB operations.

At the operational level, while the territorial jurisdiction for all post office functions includes postal savings banks, each head post office dedicates personnel to exclusively service the POSB customers. This arrangement is also found in most of the sub-post offices. However, for the purposes of audit and accounts, specialized savings bank units have been created that consolidate account records and cross-check the veracity of each and every transaction at all levels.

Management of Savings Assets and Liabilities

The Post Office Savings Bank collects money on behalf of the Ministry of Finance. As of 31 March 2000 there was an aggregate balance under all the plans of Rs. 1.875 trillion (approximately US$40 billion) placed on deposit in the central bank. This arrangement was made more market-oriented and transparent by the establishment in April 1999 of the "National Small Savings Fund" (NSSF) to account for all transactions relating to the small savings plans and the utilization of funds mobilized.

All of the net collections are presently used to purchase long-term (twenty-five-year) investments in special securities of the State governments in proportion to the collections mobilized within each State's respective jurisdiction. The State governments are expected to utilize the sums provided to them for development purposes and pay interest to the NSSF, currently at the rate of 12.5 percent per annum. If a State defaults on a payment of prior debt to the Central Government, the defaulted amount is adjusted during the next month's release of the State's share.

The costs of managing the small savings plans and paying interest are borne by the NSSF. The interest paid by the Central and State Governments on special securities is the Fund's income, and the securities held by the NSSF are its assets.

At the local level, collections made from small savings plans are first deposited by the post offices into the Government Account at local branches of the accredited public sector banks, which in turn transmit the receipts to the NSSF account at the central bank. Similarly, withdrawals, when needed, are made from the Government Account through local accredited public sector bank branches by the post office. As the Central Government's small savings plans are borrowing short and lending long, the costs of maturity mismatch and conversion are borne by the Government Account, and a new interest rate regime needs to be worked out. Although two models exist for such computation, an improved model is needed to obtain more robust estimates of the actual costs when compared to current administrative and relational benefits with the public sector banks. Therefore, the small savings plans' interest rate structure is under constant review. Within the last two years interest rates have been revised three times to reduce the risk of a mismatch of maturities compared to the prevailing cost of funds. The public sector banks also manage risk along similar parameters.

Training Program for Commissioned Sales Force

Introductory training as well as refresher courses are conducted to acquaint and update the staff in the Department of Posts on all matters including savings bank plans, rules, and regulations. The NSO also undertakes training programs for Extra-Departmental Branch Postmasters as well as the NSO's own appointed agents.

Training of agents is an ongoing activity of the NSO. Three agency plans for this purpose are Mahila Pradhan Kshetriya Bachat Yojana, the Public Provident Fund Agency Plan, and Standardized Agency System. The training program for commissioned sales agents is conducted on a weekly, fortnightly, or monthly basis depending on the number of agents appointed in particular areas of operation. The training comprises (a) preappointment training, (b) induction training, (c) foundation training, and (d) refresher training.

When prospective agents approach field officers or when field officers visit a particular place and observe that a particular person is capable of canvassing a POSB plan, a brief outline of how to sell government small savings plans is given. Once the prospective commissioned sales agent accepts the philosophy, agent status is granted. After commissioned sales agents are appointed, they are trained in the rules, regulations, procedures, marketing skills, and communication skills by field officers of the NSO.

In the foundation training program, the commissioned sales force is given detailed training in opening accounts, filling out forms, checking passbooks, rendering satisfactory service, delivering documents to savers, and following procedures to claim their commission, and they learn about the postal sales counters set aside for operating agency functions.

In the refresher training course, commissioned sales agents are updated on various changes in the plans, rules, and procedures, and are introduced to the latest technological developments in POSB operations. Recently a program for computer registration of NSO agents and issuance of identity cards has been launched to dovetail with the computerization program of the POSB network's operations.

Postal Savings and the Public and Private Sector Banks

Bank deposits by households are significantly higher than those under the small savings plans and hold 45 percent of the financial savings in the country. It should also be mentioned here that most of the chartered commercial banks are owned by the public sector. The number of branches of the largest public sector bank, State Bank of India, is about 9,000. Other financial institutions, such as the Life Insurance Corporation and General Insurance Corporation, have about 2,000 to 5,000 branches. The Reserve Bank of India has also emphasized the opening of rural branches, but, as may be seen from the number of post offices, no bank can match the Department of Posts in terms of the sheer size of its network and geographic scope. Moreover, as mentioned earlier, opening a savings account in a post office is a much simpler activity than opening an account in a public sector bank.

Deposits in public sector banks in 1999–2000 amounted to Rs. 7.373 trillion out of total deposits in commercial banks of Rs. 9.003 trillion, representing 81.9 percent of the total. Total household domestic savings in 1997–98 was Rs. 2.078 trillion, of which the commercial banking sector's share in household savings was Rs. 765.9 billion, 36.9 percent, and the collections under small savings in 1997–98 was Rs. 548.3 billion, comprising 25 percent of the nation's household financial savings. The balance of Rs. 793 billion consists of savings in public sector banks and other banking channels.

Direct and Indirect Subsidies to the Savings System

It has been suggested that the government gave two kinds of subsidies to the system of small savings. First, it was charged that the rate of interest paid by small savings plans was generally higher than that offered by public sector banks or nationwide financial institutions. In view of the zero risk to deposits in the central bank, this differential can hardly be classified as a subsidy.

Nevertheless, the government has recently accepted the recommendation of a high-level committee to benchmark the rate of interest paid on small savings plans to match the rates prevalent in banks and in other nationwide financial institutions. It was suggested that the rate differential was adversely affecting the interest rate structure of the banks and other financial institutions, even though banking system rates had been deregulated in the early 1990s. Preferential rates are being given to large depositors, and some nonbank and private institutions offer products that involve much greater risk but carry a more attractive return. Accordingly, in January 1999 and January 2000, rates of interest on most small savings plans were reduced by 1.0 percent, although the Reserve Bank of India also suggested in a recent credit policy statement that banks can offer a higher interest rate of 0.5 to 1.0 percent to senior citizens.

Second, it is suggested that the tax concessions to subscribers are a significant implicit subsidy. A valuation of the tax revenues lost on the small savings plans needs to be determined. Sensitivity analysis will be required, as the level of taxation of the subscriber is difficult to ascertain and has not been quantified so far, but it should be acknowledged that these incentives attract a lot of deposits into the NSO's savings plans.

The decision to reduce the interest rates on small savings plans has partially stemmed from the desire to channel household savings into the banking sector and capital markets. It should be observed, however, that small savings plans were started at a time when the banking and securities markets were relatively undeveloped and limited to a few urban areas. People looked to the government as a reliable trustee with whom they could lodge their hard-earned savings. That fiduciary confidence is still intact, but now the banking sector and the securities markets are developing and have reasonably wider coverage. Therefore, it is now considered necessary to wean savers away from looking to the government to provide assured high-yield, risk-free avenues for their savings. As a result, the returns on small savings plans are now being linked to market rates. Savings services will still be available to the citizens, but gradually the implied subsidized elements of the plans will be eliminated.

References

Annual Finance Accounts, Controller General of India.
Data compiled in NS II Section, Budget Division, Department of Economic Affairs, Ministry of Finance.
Handbook of Statistics on Indian Economy. 1999. Reserve Bank of India.
National Accounts Statistics 2000. CSO.
Report on Trend and Progress of Banking in India, 1999–2000. Reserve Bank of India.
"Supplementary Memorandum on Small Savings," Ministry of Finance to Eleventh Finance Commission.

Appendix*
National Savings Organization Plans Offered through the Post Office Savings Bank

1. Post Office Savings Bank Ordinary Deposit Account

This product was introduced to inculcate the habit of thrift among the masses and to put their idle cash to productive use. POSB Ordinary Deposit Accounts for individuals have a deposit ceiling of Rs. 100,000; joint accounts have a ceiling of Rs. 200,000. Institutions and certain government offices may also open POSB accounts without any limits on the size of their deposits. This type of account also has a checking feature available to the accountholder, with checks similar to those offered by commercial banks. Furthermore, a POSB account offers liquidity and can also be linked to other accounts. As the interest received under this plan is fully exempt from taxes, the effective yield is significantly higher for subscribers in upper tax brackets, as are the other plans that have tax-free benefits.

2. Post Office Time Deposit Plan

This product has specified rates of interest for One-year, Two-year, Three-year, and Five-year Deposit Accounts. No restrictions are imposed with respect to the invested amount. This account is also available to trust and regimental funds of the army and for welfare funds. The interest yield is linked to the duration of the deposit, with a longer duration returning higher yields. This product holds a special appeal because of the range of shorter maturities offered and the annually paid interest.

3. Post Office Recurring Deposit Plan

This product caters to small savers such as industrial workers, unorganized wage earners, and business owners who wish to save in regular increments

---

*Compiled by Mark J. Scher.

on a monthly basis. This deposit plan has a specified payout at the conclusion of five years, which may be extended to ten years. Only individuals can open accounts, but there is no limit on the amount to be invested. A unique social benefit is an optional life insurance feature in which the saver's dependents can receive the entire payment that is due on maturity, even if the account has not run for the entire five years. However, this product is only for the needs of those who wish to make an investment in a product with a five-year time horizon. Also, the account can be pledged as collateral for a loan from a bank.

4. Post Office Monthly Income Plan

In this six-year plan the saver makes a lump-sum investment, and monthly interest is accrued and is either paid to the saver or credited to the savings bank account. The plan is popular with farmers, recent retirees, and others who have seasonal income as well as those who receive a large lump-sum payment upon retirement and need to generate a regular income for their day-to-day expenditures. Investments under this plan also carry a 10 percent benefit bonus at maturity. The plan is available individually or jointly to those who make deposits with an investment ceiling of up to Rs. 300,000 and Rs. 600,000 respectively. Tax benefits are an additional feature of this plan.

5. National Savings Certificate

In this product there is no maximum ceiling of investment, the accrued interest is reinvested, and a specified lump-sum payment is repaid to the saver after six years. Presently in operation in its VIIIth Issue, these certificates are available to individuals, singly or jointly, and to trusts. This product has significant tax benefits and may be pledged as collateral for a bank loan.

6. Public Provident Plan

This product is intended primarily for individuals who are not covered by pension benefit plans, particularly the self-employed. Under this plan a specified amount (maximum contribution of Rs. 60,000 per year) must be deposited each year for a continuous period of fifteen years or more in additional five-year increments. The interest income is entirely tax-free, and limited withdrawals may be made after an initial period. The Public Provident Plan is designed to meet the needs of non-resident Indians (NRIs) who are working abroad. It is also available to those who are regularly employed in the government and private sectors as well. A unique feature of this product is that the court cannot garnish the amount invested under the plan.

7. Kisan Vikas Patra *(Farmers Development Certificate)*

These certificates are available to individuals, singly or jointly, and in trust. They are very popular with farmers and rural savers because of their simplicity. The principal invested is doubled in the specified period (in 2001, seven years and three months), and as it is designed for farmers and other non–income tax payers, its yield is higher than the tax-free products. The liquidity requirement of the savers is taken care of by an option for prematurity encashment. The certificate may also be pledged as collateral for a bank loan.

8. National Savings Plan 1992

Introduced in 1992 for savers seeking tax-free benefits and willing to keep their funds invested for a longer period (four years). The product has no investment-ceiling amount and interest is payable annually. It is available at all Head post offices and selected Sub-head post offices. This product has special appeal to high-income groups.

9

The Post Office Savings Bank of India
Ashok Pal Singh

The Post Office Savings Bank (POSB) of India is an institution steeped in history. The POSB originated in the Government Savings Bank Act of 1873 with the mandate of providing facilities for the general population to invest their savings. It opened its first branch on 1 April 1882, and by the end of 1883 the POSB was showing significant growth, registering 4,066 branches, 39,129 accounts, and deposits totaling Rs. 2,796,796. At that time the POSB was then open for transactions on all weekdays between 12 noon and 4 P.M.; however, a depositor could withdraw money only once a week. The rate of interest was 3.75 percent, subject to no higher monthly interest than Rs. 9.6 being allowed on any account. By 1886 the success of the POSB had convinced the government to amalgamate the District Treasuries Banks with the Post Office Savings Banks. From that point on the Post Office Savings Banks really began to come into their own.

The POSB today has a countrywide network of more than 154,551 post offices. Of these, as many as 137,847 are located in rural areas of the country. The network is not only extensive, but also user-friendly and accessible to the general population. Currently it is the largest mobilizer of individual savings in the country. The fundamental role of the POSB is to encourage the habit of thrift and to provide all of India's people with facilities in which they can deposit their savings, no matter what the size. In a larger context, the POSB is also being viewed as a way to mobilize resources for financing the development programs of the government.

Organization of the POSB

The POSB today is an agency function of India Post operated on behalf of the Ministry of Finance. All the savings mobilized by the POSB are credited to the Public Account controlled by the Ministry of Finance. India Post is remunerated on the basis of a fixed yearly rate based on the average number of transactions taking place per account and is adjusted periodically when the total number of transactions has changed.

The POSB is an important component of India Post, and its organizational structure reflects both its unity of command as well as its functional autonomy. The Director General of India Post is the Chief Executive of the POSB. However, POSB headquarters is under the control of the Member (Development) of the Postal Services Board, which is composed of a group headed by the Deputy Director General (savings banks) and assisted by the Director (savings banks) who is responsible for savings bank operations in the country.

At the operational level, India Post's territorial jurisdiction encompasses all post office functions, including savings banks; however, each Head post office has a staff dedicated to exclusively servicing POSB customers. This arrangement is also in place at most of the Sub-post offices. Auditing and accounting functions, however, are carried out by specialized Savings Bank Units, which consolidate accounts and cross-check the veracity of each and every transaction.

Placement of Mobilized Funds

As the POSB is an agency of the Ministry of Finance, all deposits are credited to the National Exchequer. Currently, 100 percent of these funds are used for long-term loans (twenty-five years) to the State governments in proportion to funds collected within their respective jurisdictions. Prior to 1 April 2002, the Union government utilized 20 percent of the funds for budgetary purposes. The State governments are expected to utilize the loans for developmental purposes and pay interest at the rate of 12.5 percent (as of 2001) to the National Exchequer for these loans.

Proposals are now being considered to make these loans more market-oriented. Under the proposed system, rather than offering equivalent long-term loans, the savings mobilized by the POSB in the concerned states would be earmarked for the purchase of state securities. This change is expected to induce greater financial discipline among the states and at the same time prove beneficial to the POSB in the long run as the new plan is designed to align the asset management of the POSB to the market.

The Scale and Scope of the POSB

The POSB network of 154,149 branches is justified by the size of its clientele and business. The POSB had nearly 110 million account-holders and its total deposits were over Rs. 1.8 trillion (in excess of US$38 billion) in 1999–2000. The average yearly collections of the POSB are Rs. 700 billion (US$14.5 billion) (see Figure 9.1: Number of Accounts at the POSB).

Figure 9.1 **Number of Accounts at the POSB** (in millions)

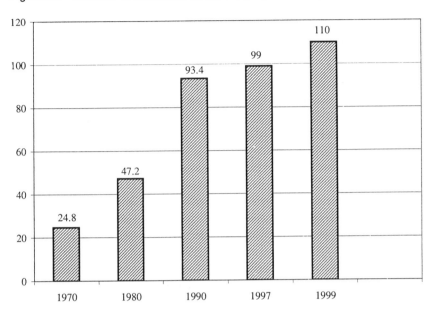

Analysis of the POSB's business profile shows that the number of account-holders has doubled in every decade between 1970 and 1990. Thereafter, however, the rate of growth has slowed, registering only a 20 percent increase from 1990–2000. This slowdown is partly attributable to the deregulation of the banking sector in India in the 1990s. During this period, growth of the POSB network also decelerated due to the government's decision to restrict the opening of new post office branches.

At the beginning of the decade (fiscal 1990–91) the balance of deposits stood at Rs. 501,090 million. This figure increased to Rs. 1,822,048 million in the year 2000. See Table 9.1: Outstanding Deposit Balances with the POSB.

One of the chief reasons for continued growth of deposits with the POSB during the past decade were higher rates of interest paid on most products compared to the commercial banks and tax incentives. During 1995–1996 there was a fall in the value of deposits, as during that time a decision was taken by the government to disallow corporations and institutions from investing in POSB plans. However, despite this continuing restriction there has been a steady resurgence in POSB deposits in subsequent years.

A comparative analysis of deposits in the Indian banking system shows that the POSB accounts for a 20.7 percent market share. See Figure 9.2: Deposits in the Indian Banking System.

A comparative analysis of the POSB vis-à-vis commercial banks clearly

Table 9.1

Outstanding Deposit Balances with the POSB
(in millions of rupees)

1990–1991	501,090
1991–1992	557,640
1992–1993	601,360
1993–1994	679,915
1994–1995	827,464
1995–1996	663,083
1996–1997	1,057,734
1997–1998	1,267,542
1998–1999	1,519,570
1999–2000	1,822,048

Figure 9.2 **Deposits in the Indian Banking System, 31 March 2000** (Rs. in millions)

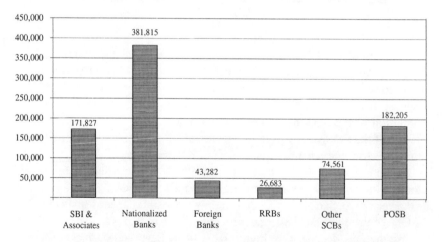

brings out the advantage that the POSB possesses in terms of branch network. Table 9.2: Branches in the Indian Banking System, shows that the POSB has almost 70 percent of the bank branches in India. The emphasis is in the rural areas, which account for 90 percent of the POSB network, and it can reasonably be concluded that the strength of the POSB lies in the rural sector (see Figure 9.3: Urban versus Rural Distribution of Branches).

Nearly 90 percent of POSB branches are in rural areas of the country, yet the ratio of rural to urban deposits is 16.1 percent. See Figure 9.4: Percentage of Rural Deposits in the POSB by States.

Table 9.2

Branches in the Indian Banking System, March 2000

Bank Group	Number of Branches	Percentage
A) All Scheduled Commercial Banks		
State Bank of India and Its Associates	13,374	6.06
Nationalized Banks	33,400	15.1
Foreign Banks	184	0.08
Regional Rural Banks	14,640	6.63
Other Scheduled Commercial Banks	5,079	2.3
Subtotal	66,677	30.2
B) Post Office Savings Banks	154,000	69.8
TOTAL	220,677	

Figure 9.3   **Urban versus Rural Distribution of Branches, 2000**

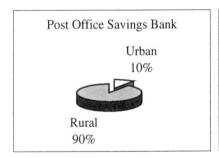
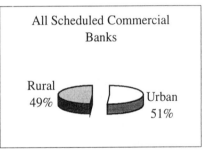

This is explained by a number of factors. Rural areas of India are relatively less affluent than urban areas, therefore deposits to rural accounts are lower than to urban accounts. A key attraction of the POSB plans are tax incentives provided to the depositors. In rural areas, however, there are fewer numbers of income tax payers, and thus many of the POSB plans do not provide any special attraction. Also, the POSB does not undertake lending functions. In rural areas credit is often an important inducement for farmers to open bank accounts in the institutions from which they draw loans. The implicit state guarantee of banking with the POSB is also nullified by the fact that the Government of India also owns a large number of the commercial banks functioning in rural areas.

In addition to differences between rural and urban uses, an analysis of POSB deposit balances also shows regional differences in terms of per capita deposits, with southern India accounting for the highest balance per account. See Table 9.3: Regional Distribution of POSB Deposits.

Figure 9.4 **Percentage of Rural Deposits in the POSB by States, 1998–99**

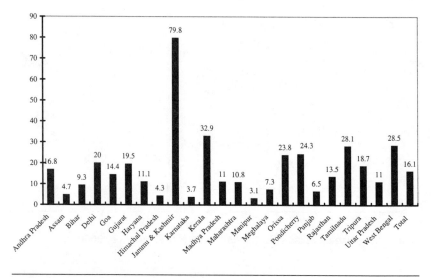

Table 9.3

Regional Distribution of POSB Deposits

Region	Number of Accounts (in millions)	Outstanding Balance (in millions)	Average Balance per Account
Northern	17.5	Rs. 244.772	Rs. 1390
Western	6.2	Rs. 114.823	Rs. 1862
Eastern	27.6	Rs. 137.017	Rs. 496
Southern	6.5	Rs. 349.534	Rs. 5366

Although its mandate requires the POSB to gear its efforts to meeting the needs of small savers, over time the rationale for providing an exclusive infrastructure for mobilizing small savings has diminished as a result of the rural expansion of commercial banks.

Use of Information Technology

An increasingly competitive environment coupled with the need to serve a very large customer base spread over the entire country has made it necessary for the POSB to upgrade its use of information technology. With a view to bringing about a qualitative improvement in customer service, an ambitious program of computerizing the post offices has been undertaken. Nearly two thousand computer-based, multipurpose postal counter terminals have been installed that enable customers to transact business conveniently and expeditiously within the branches. Within the branches this system uses a comprehensive savings bank software called Sanchay Post, which has been developed in-house and is already operational in nearly three hundred branches of the Post Office Savings Bank. This user-friendly software instantly facilitates all types of personal customer bank transactions. It is programmed to accept transactions according to the features of the different savings plans so that the chances of error are reduced.

Online help is integrated with the program to assist the post office staff in using the software. The software integrates front and back office operations so that ledger agreements, balance sheets, and other accounting requirements are accurately maintained without any time lag. Customer-specific information can be retrieved easily. Post Office Savings Bank control and audit offices have been computerized to enable more effective monitoring of these operations. The net result of the introduction of new technology has been the streamlining of account transaction and verification procedures. The previous system of multiple cross-checks and balances that dominated manual transactions has been replaced by automatic online verification processes, which has considerably aided the work of the internal audit departments.

India Post is currently in the process of establishing a dedicated VSAT (very small aperture terminal), the first phase of which will connect most of its fourteen thousand urban post offices. It is expected that in the near future the VSAT network, coupled with computerization of Post Office Savings Bank services, will facilitate the introduction of online banking and other new services to customers. The VSAT network is also being used to transmit Money Orders online among more than 687 post offices throughout India.

The POSB has introduced on a pilot basis a smart card that contains an encrypted electronic computer chip. The smart card functions as a passbook, permitting transactions to be conducted from multiple post offices. As the modernization process gathers momentum, India Post plans to increase new facilities for its customers.

Marketing Products and Services

In order to maintain steady collections, POSB products and services are marketed using diverse strategies at different levels. Overall, the National Savings Organization (NSO) under the Ministry of Finance is responsible for promoting POSB business, and it does so using both electronic as well as print media (for details on the NSO's savings instruments and its operations, see chapter 8 and the Appendix that follows). Particular attention is being paid to target groups such as women and workers. At the State level, Small Savings Organizations have been established by the respective state governments and are responsible for marketing postal savings products. These organizations function under the guidance of State Level Advisory Boards, which have both official as well as non-official members.

At present the POSB provides a wide range of products and services including: POSB Ordinary Deposit Accounts, Time Deposits, Recurring Deposits, Monthly Income Plans, and National Savings Certificates. Some of these products and services target the requirements of specific groups such as women, farmers, and senior citizens. The POSB also disburses pensions to government employees as well as to the indigent aged under the social security programs of the government. A recent agreement with the Employees Provident Fund Organization provides for disbursement of pensions through twenty-six thousand post offices. Under this service agreement the monthly pension is credited to the beneficiary's Post Office Savings Bank account. The post office receives a per-transaction remuneration, which is a percentage of the total amount handled.

Recognizing the important role women play in influencing decisions relating to savings at the domestic level, the POSB has been paying special attention to their financial needs. In 1972 a Women's Local Area Savings Plan (Mahila Pradhan Kshetriya Bachat Yojana) was introduced with the objective of educating housewives about family budgeting, inculcating the habit of thrift, and utilizing their services in canvassing for investments in the Post Office Five-Year Recurring Deposit Account Plan. Under this plan, authorized individual women agents as well as women's organizations canvass and secure deposits from small investors and are in return paid a commission on the deposits mobilized by them. This plan has been successful not only in raising resources for financing public development projects but also in promoting thrift and savings among women, particularly those residing in rural areas of the country.

In 1993 a new Women's Empowerment Plan (Mahila Samridhi Yojana) was introduced by the government. Under this plan, women, particularly those residing in rural areas, are encouraged to open a special post office account in which deposits in multiples of Rs. 4 are made. An annual incentive of up to Rs. 75 (US$1.50) is paid for deposits not exceeding Rs. 300, (US$6.00). This plan has attracted the participation of more than 30 million women.

Similar efforts by the POSB to service other poor and dispersed sections of the population have achieved remarkable success in attracting the savings of the rural poor. Keeping in view the large population and land area of the country, the POSB has adopted an innovative plan called the Standardized Agency System. Under this system, individuals, cooperative societies, social service organizations, universities, and local institutions have been authorized by the government as agents to collect deposits on behalf of the POSB in return for a commission on the gross of their collections. The Standardized Agency System has been particularly successful in reaching marginalized populations that do not have ready access to banking or are not comfortable using them.

A program aimed at reaching poor laborers throughout India is the Pay Roll Savings Group Plan, under which an employee voluntarily authorizes his employer to deduct a fixed amount from his salary every month for deposit in one of the POSB's various savings plans. This plan has become an ideal source for mopping up small savings from salaried persons. The arrangement of Pay Roll Savings simplifies saving by making it easy for employees. The plan also helps the employer because a stable and satisfied staff is conducive to the efficient working of any establishment.

Most of the POSB plans are centered on the individual customer, have modest investment ceiling limits, and provide higher rates of interest than commercial banks. Income tax concessions are also available against deposits made in some of the plans. The primary objective of these plans is to serve the small saver; large investments are generally discouraged, and each plan normally prescribes a modest ceiling beyond which investments do not earn any interest. Of late, however, an effort is being made to level the playing field between the plans of the POSB and those of commercial banks. Making the most of the large postal network, all plans and accounts of the POSB are transferable from one part of the country to another. With the introduction of computers into its system, the POSB sees great potential in India for electronic and online banking.

Recent Expansion of Services

The Ministry of Finance of the Government of India appointed a specially constituted High-Powered Committee to make an in-depth analysis of the strengths and weaknesses of the POSB. It also solicited the views of the customers of the POSB as well as of the Chambers of Trade and Commerce in different cities. In its final report, the Committee recommended the introduction of the following new products and services, which the Department of Posts undertook, to diversify and expand the range of financial services provided. They are as follows:

Distribution of Mutual Funds

In February 2001 the department initiated a partnership to distribute a range of mutual funds through the post offices with IDBI (Industrial Development Bank of India)–Principal Asset Management Company. Subsequently, similar partnerships were extended to SBI (State Bank of India) Mutual Funds and ICICI (Industrial Credit and Investment Corporation of India) Prudential. Despite unfavorable market conditions, India Post has been able to sell mutual funds worth Rs. 12.5 million. The service is currently available through a network of two hundred post offices covering all the State and Union Territories' capitals. As market conditions improve, this service will be extended to other mutual funds as well in conjunction with the Association of Mutual Funds in India (AMFI), the chief industry forum.

International Money Transfer Service

In April 2001 the Department of Posts launched an international money transfer service in association with Western Union Financial Services International, a U.S.-based multinational company. This service was introduced in recognition of the long-felt need of the nonresident Indian (NRI) community abroad to send money to their loved ones at home quickly and reliably. With the help of Western Union's network, it is currently possible to swiftly remit money into India from as many as 185 countries worldwide. Within ten minutes recipients in India can collect money sent to them from any of 190 countries at nearly fourteen hundred post offices across the country. Since its introduction the service has delivered over US$15 million and made foreign exchange gains for the economy as well.

Alliances with Commercial Banks

In August 2001 the POSB signed a Memorandum of Understanding (MoU) with the United Trust Bank to explore the possibility of providing the following services to each other's customers:

- ATMs
- Cash management services
- Easy access to loans
- Use of Speed Post, Express Parcel Post, and other premium services of India Post

This alliance was initiated to build a mutually beneficial relationship with the banking industry in the field of cash management services. It has now been extended to other banks such as the Industrial Development Bank of India (IDBI), Housing Development Finance Corporation (HDFC Bank), and the Industrial Credit and Investment Corporation of India (ICICI Bank).

Memorandum of Understanding with MasterCard International

In September 2001 India Post signed an MoU with MasterCard International to explore the possibility of introducing card-based payment services. India Post is currently looking at the following options: prepaid cards and debit cards/smart cards (see proposed new services).

Prepaid cards—This plan would allow customers who do not have an account with the POSB to buy cards of desired value that can be immediately used to make payments at over sixteen thousand establishments in India that accept MasterCard. In addition, they can be used to withdraw cash from more than fifteen hundred ATMs countrywide. While credit and debit cards already exist in India, the post office will pioneer prepaid cards in the country. This product is for persons who are credit-averse and/or ineligible to receive credit cards.

Debit cards—Debit cards bearing the MasterCard logo will be issued to POSB account-holders, effectively giving them the free access available to MasterCard credit card holders at merchant establishments, ATMs, and various POSB branches that will be part of the network. In the future these services will available to customers for use outside of India as well.

Currency Exchange Facility for Tourists

India has a tremendous potential for developing its tourism sector. Similarly, the number of Indians traveling abroad is on the increase. Foreign currency exchange in this context is a business with immense potential. With post offices at virtually all transportation hubs (airports, railway stations, bus stands, etc.), and at major tourist spots as well, India Post can provide currency exchange facilities to both tourists and domestic outbound travelers like no other organization in the country. The post office is a universal institution that is trusted across the globe and likely to be the preferred point for currency exchange for international tourists unfamiliar with other organizations.

In 2002 India Post received a license from the Reserve Bank of India to provide money-changing services. Detailed operational plans are being formulated for introduction of this service in the near future.

Proposed New Services

Smart Cards and Debit Cards

The post office has a long-standing mandate of issuing identity cards. By virtue of its intrinsic knowledge of addresses, it is ideally positioned to provide and verify identities digitally. The POSB and MasterCard are developing a smart card program that can be used for integrating applications of private as well as public sector organizations (pension payments, driving license, ration cards, credit/debit cards, bank passbooks, etc.).

A debit card is essentially a direct payment instrument from the customer's bank account. A smart card on the other hand is a multifunctional instrument that uses a processor chip to conduct transactions, both financial and non-financial, in an offline or online mode.

Debit cards hold a huge potential in India. One of the key success factors for debit cards is the proliferation of ATMs and their wide acceptance at merchant outlets.

The POSB can serve as an issuer of debit cards for its large customer base. As an issuing bank, the POSB would get a share of the processing fee charged to the merchant outlet. From a larger perspective the POSB can facilitate the inevitable transition of the Indian economy from cash-based to cashless systems by taking the plastic card to the greater population.

India Post can utilize its current assets of VSAT and reputation for trustworthiness to make smart cards a successful multifunctional tool for conducting financial transactions. The market potential in India is very high for smart cards since they are conducive to transactions being done in an offline mode. The use of smart cards has started in specific single-function modes in different industries in India. India Post can utilize its network and influence to help set the standard across industries, ensuring that different applications can reside on a single smart card.

Electronic Funds Transfer (EFT)

EFT is the transfer of funds across geographic locations through electronic messaging systems. Clearing and settlement functions can also be performed electronically. EFT would become a substitute for the paper-based process, thereby increasing the speed and reliability of transfers, improving information processing, and providing customers with an increased certainty of payment by an exact date. EFT would also reduce costs for transfer of funds per transaction.

EFT could generate a significant amount of revenue from the overall float and transactional fees. After an initial investment, operating costs for EFT are negligible. EFT could become a highly lucrative business and a key complement to other proposed products like mutual funds, charitable funds, and the like.

The POSB's existing VSAT network provides it with a ready capability to provide this service. In the foreseeable future, after establishing connections with the payment gateway, the post office would also be able to effect interbank fund transfers.

Electronic Banking

As the largest retail bank in the country, the POSB is ideally positioned to take anytime, anyplace banking to the masses. This will involve establishing interbranch connectivity, card-based access to accounts, establishment of ATMs, and point-of-sale terminals. Reduced transactional costs, enhanced customer service, and integrated accounting systems could result from electronic banking. The Department of Posts has already made substantial investments in computerizing its branch operations, and the next logical step would be for it to introduce electronic banking.

Direct Debit of Utility and Tax Payments by Consumers

The average Indian wastes a great many man-hours year after year queuing up to pay utility bills (telephone, electricity, etc.) and to deposit taxes (local, state, and central). With the VSAT network and the postal service's door-to-door reach, India Post is well positioned to collect such payments and pass them on to the recipient organizations. The POSB can also provide direct debit facilities for this purpose to its savings account holders.

Distribution of Social Security Benefits

The post office with its large network is ideally suited to collect contributions to pension plans and then later disburse them. Disbursal of pension fund payments will also give the POSB access to a larger customer base that can be utilized for cross-selling other services.

Distribution of Government Securities

The post office can also utilize its network and large customer base to effectively distribute government securities, including those of the Reserve Bank of India.

Insurance and the Retail Distribution of Financial Products

The network of post offices, with its capability to collect and remit cash, can also be utilized to retail financial services provided by public as well as private sector organizations. The insurance sector, which has recently been deregulated, as well as privately managed pension systems, provide two immediate opportunities. Once again, this will give the post office an enlarged customer base and the possibility of cross-selling its own products.

Charitable Funds

This service would involve collecting funds from donors and pooling them into designated accounts and/or disbursing funds for the designated beneficiaries. This service can utilize India Post's large branch network and efficient delivery channels.

This product has the potential of tapping a new market for the POSB, that is, charitable funds/NGOs (non-governmental organizations). More specifically, the target for this would be internationally supported charities and multilateral institution-funded programs, and it would rely on the POSB's reputation of good service.

Electronic Business

The Internet is revolutionizing the way business is being conducted. Companies around the world are finding new ways of doing business over the Internet. The number of companies using business-to-consumer (B-2-C) e-commerce payments is on the increase. India Post would be able to deliver both physical and electronic payments in most transactions. It can also facilitate e-business in India by breaking down barriers relating to the safety of credit card transactions and the reliability of delivery service. In particular, India Post can provide the delivery of low-volume, low-weight packages as well as make payment to the supplier directly through customers' POSB accounts. It can also facilitate payment and delivery services between large corporations' dealers and suppliers.

Employee Training and Investor Education Program

Realizing the need for both upgrading the skills of its employees to enable them to transact these new financial services and to familiarize customers with the new market-based financial products and services, India Post has initiated a partnership with industry. A private organization called the Invest India Economic Foundation will draw corporate support to train post office employees and educate investors about the different financial services offered by the POSB. This will be done at no cost to the government and is an excellent example of government–corporate sector partnership.

Conclusion

This is a brief overview of the Post Office Savings Bank of India's strategy to draw upon its extensive "bricks and mortar" branch network while moving that network into the information technology age. While the POSB continues to serve as a vehicle for savings, it is also increasingly becoming a provider of diversified financial services to the greater population of India.

10
Postal Savings in Sri Lanka
Eastman Narangoda

The Establishment of the National Savings Bank and Its Relation to Postal Savings

Government-owned savings banking in Sri Lanka is over 170 years old, dating back to 1832 when the Ceylon Savings Bank was established under a Government Gazette Notification by the then British governor of Ceylon. The Ceylon Post Office Savings Bank (POSB) was established in 1885 by the colonial legislative council for the purpose of serving the general public through the post office system. A total of 2,195 accounts amounting to Rupees (Rs.) 30,300 were opened within a short time. In September 1938 the POSB achieved a milestone in its history with the inauguration of the Savings Certificates section of the Post Master General's (PMG) Department. In 1941 the management of the Post Office Savings Bank was reconstituted to include the Permanent Secretary to the Minister of Posts, the Deputy Secretary to the Treasury, and the Post Master General.

The year 1942 witnessed the birth of the Ceylon War Savings Movement (CWSM), whose mission was to meet the increasing financial costs the Second World War was exerting on Great Britain and its allies. The CWSM was formed to collect savings contributions for this effort from the then British colony of Ceylon, and it served both a propaganda and a sales function by marketing National Savings Certificates. In the postwar period the CWSM was renamed the National Savings Movement and continued to sell savings certificate instruments.

After Sri Lanka gained Independence in 1948, the Ceylon Savings Bank (CSB), the Post Office Savings Bank (POSB), the Savings Certificate section of the PMG Department, and the National Savings Certificate Movement (NSCM) all remained separate government-owned entities and carried on as before with their respective strategic purposes and organizational cultures up to 1971, when they were amalgamated to form a new institution, the National Savings Bank (NSB). It is pertinent to mention that these four institutions together accounted for an unimpressive savings rate of 8 to 9 percent of the GDP at the time of the NSB's formation, the NSCM being the least significant in the savings deposit market among the four. Instead, Sri Lankan families have traditionally kept their savings in-kind in the form of gold jewelry and land holdings.

At the time of the NSB's formation, apart from the above-mentioned savings organizations, two state-owned commercial banks, the Bank of Ceylon and the People's Bank, played a dominant role in the market. The Bank of Ceylon and the People's Bank provided the primary financing for the vast state-owned manufacturing and services sectors. There were also a few other financial services organizations whose role in the market was marginal.

It was against this backdrop that the need became clear for a dynamic single organization to mobilize funds at the grassroots level and boost the country's domestic rate of savings, thereby significantly increasing funds going toward national development. The assets and liabilities of the four savings organizations were placed with the new NSB, and the postal network became the exclusive legal business agent of the NSB for postal banking activities, although it remained under the aegis of the Ministry of Posts and Telecommunications.

The NSB was established as a public policy–based state-owned bank to invest as well as mobilize savings. Its Act of Incorporation permits it to invest in the following areas:

(a) Government Bonds and Securities;
(b) Housing finance lending (corporate and individual);
(c) Financial instruments issued or guaranteed by financial institutions and publicly listed companies approved by the NSB Board;
(d) Refinance facilities to licensed commercial banks and licensed specialized banks, for the purpose of medium and long-term project lending;
(e) Equity capital of licensed commercial banks, licensed specialized banks, or the subsidiaries of any licensed commercial or licensed specialized banks, and in any publicly listed company or those seeking a listing in a licensed stock exchange;
(f) Subsidiary companies formed with the written approval of the Monetary Board;
(g) Pawnbroking businesses;
(h) Foreign remittances from expatriates and their conversion into Sri Lankan rupee deposits.

As may be seen, loans and investments have grown steadily in the 1990s (Figure 10.1: Loans and Investments Portfolio) as have total deposits (Figure 10.2: Total Deposits).

The control, general supervision, and administration of the affairs of the NSB

Figure 10.1 **Loans and Investments Portfolio**

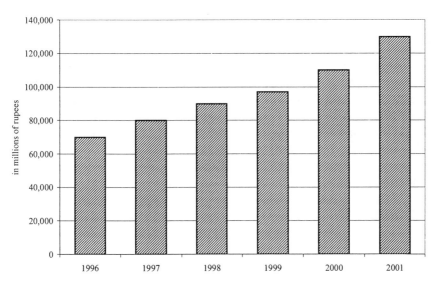

Figure 10.2 **Total Deposits**

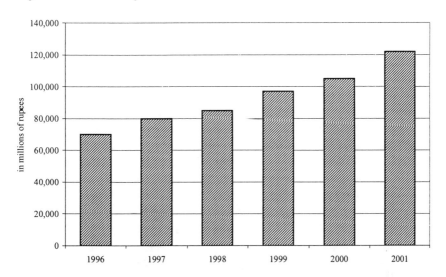

are vested with the Board of Directors, four of whose seven members are appointed by the Ministry of Finance. Included ex officio on the Board are the Post Master General and the Secretary of the Treasury (or their nominees). The Board in turn has delegated its authority to the rank-and-file officers of the NSB to carry out the day-to-day functions of providing services to the bank's customers.

The NSB and Postal Sector Agency Relationship

As stated previously, the Post Master General and the Secretary of the Treasury (or their nominees) are two ex officio Directors of the Bank. A liaison officer from the Postal Department's permanent cadre functions at the middle management level, with the head office of the bank attending to the routine day-to-day operations between the NSB and the Postal Department. The NSB pays the Postal Department an annual fee for its agency services. This fee is calculated on the basis of the volume of total annual transactions and the cost of living index. The volume of postal savings and amount of agency fees paid are shown in Table 10.1: NSB's Postal Savings Transactions and Agency Fee Payments. In addition, the bank provides all of the necessary forms and documents to the Postal Department for NSB postal savings activities. The Postal Department, however, has no ownership stake in the NSB and has at present an exclusive agency relationship with the NSB and is not associated with any other financial services organization.

A formula is used to compute service charges due the Postal Department, namely:

$$\frac{\text{Rs. 7,000,000} \times \text{Average Cost of Living Index for the Current Year}}{474.2}$$

In the formula, the year 1983 is taken as the base year. The average cost of living for that year was 474.2 while the service charge paid for the year was Rs. 7 million.

As the agency fee formula for computation of agency fees indicates, there is no relationship between either the volume or value of transactions serviced at the post offices and the agency fees paid to the Postal Department. Despite a 6.2-fold increase in net postal deposits as well as a 1.5-fold increase in the number of postal service transactions in the five-year period from 1997 to 2001, as indicated by Table 10.1, the relative level of agency fee remuneration to the Postal Department has stayed fixed at the 1983 level of compensation, adjusted only for the current cost of living index times the 1983 base fee of Rs. 7 million. The cost of living index, an indicator of the rate of inflation, rose less than 1.4-fold in the 1997–2001 period.

Although the NSB's rate of mobilization of savings through the Postal Department has increased, it lags significantly behind the rate of savings mobilized through the NSB's branch network. The postal sector contributes only some 9 percent of the NSB's deposits. Although the reasons for the relatively unequal performance of the two networks are complex and will be explored

Table 10.1

NSB's Postal Savings Transactions and Agency Fee Payments

Year	Net Transaction Value (deposits minus withdrawals) Rs.	Transaction Volume (no. of deposits plus withdrawals)	Annual Average Cost of Living Index (points)	Annual Service Charge Paid to Postal Department Rs.
1997	89,105,084.00	1,157,746	2,089.09	30,838,675.67
1998	22,296,450.46	1,114,386	2,284.89	33,729,017.30
1999	108,008,471.38	1,099,501	2,397.09	35,311,471.96
2000	385,327,500.94	1,762,120	2,539.83	37,492,218.48
2001	552,680,125.81	1,741,195	2,899.42	42,800,084.35

later in this chapter, suffice it to say at this point that it may reflect in large part the economic inequalities between the rural population, where the postal network is primarily based, and the relatively higher-income urban population, which is the core constituency of the NSB's separate branch-banking network.

Underperformance of the Postal Sector and the Market Share of Savings Mobilization

At the inception of the NSB, the postal network accounted for 66 percent of the total deposits of the bank. However, with the expansion of the NSB branch network there has been greater NSB deposit mobilization and market penetration. The performance of the postal sector's mobilization has gradually declined in relation to the NSB's branch-banking. As of 31 July 2002, the NSB's total deposits stood at an impressive Rs. 124 billion, whereas the postal sector contribution was Rs. 8 billion. In terms of market share, the NSB enjoys 25.7 percent of the rupee deposit market while the postal sector's share is 1.9 percent.

The sales outlets of the NSB consist of 104 branches, eight savings shops (NSB minisatellite branches that operate outside of traditional banking hours), and seven postal banking branches. Although the number of post offices presently stands at 4,047, the contribution of the postal sector to the NSB's total deposit mobilization is only 8 percent.

The products/instruments offered at the post offices are as follows:

1. Post Office Passbook Savings Accounts, the most popular product
2. Fixed Deposits
3. Premium Savings Certificates
4. National Savings Certificates (interest paid up front)

Marketing Strategies Adapted for Better Performance of the Postal Sector

The NSB and the Postal Department are two different entities and come under two different government ministries. The focus of the NSB's marketing effort is mainly on its own branch network. The Postal Department is expected to do its own marketing. Nevertheless, the NSB also conducts marketing campaigns aimed at the postal sector, but their impact has been negligible. The NSB is not in a position to conduct nationwide postal sector savings campaigns because of the vastness of the postal network, both in terms of numbers of locations and geographical scope. In addition, the postal sector is not a market-oriented, bottom line–driven entity. Providing conventional postal and telecommunications services constitutes its core business, with NSB transactions considered a peripheral activity.

The NSB's fast-expanding branch-banking network has adversely impacted the postal savings sector, with customers switching to the branch network. However, over the past twenty-five years some marketing efforts were made by the NSB, such as media advertising support, mobile banking programs in support of post office banking, house-to-house campaigns in strategic postal areas, and opening school banking units linked to the post office.

Sometimes the marketing efforts were deemed unsuccessful after only a brief trial. For example, the payment of an enhanced interest rate on postal savings accounts (1.5 percent more than the savings accounts in the branch-banking sector) was discontinued after only a one-year trial in 1998 after it appeared ineffective. Tax concessions on postal savings accounts had little effect as post office passbook accounts typically carry very small balances. Speedy authorization through fax facilities for withdrawals from postal savings accounts above the preset withdrawal limits at post offices was introduced; however, it is available at less than 4 percent of the post offices. A relationship-building approach involving the payment of emoluments to Divisional Superintendents proved to be not productive and was discontinued. Providing incentives to postal employees at lower levels was seen as too costly.

Decentralization of Postal Banking Activities

In order to improve services, the NSB took a major step in 1991 to decentralize its postal banking activities which, up to then, had been centralized at the Head Office. Under the decentralization process, the NSB has set up seven Decentralized Postal Banking Branches in district capitals. All postal banking functions can now be handled in the provincial capitals, providing the same level of customer service available at the Head Office.

Accordingly, the operations of 1,762 post offices out of a total of 4,047 now come under the purview of the decentralized postal banking branch network. The remaining 2,285 post offices are still under the Postal Banking Division at the Head Office.

Arrangements are being made to attach the remaining 2,285 offices to the decentralized postal banking branches in the future. This step has brought positive results in enhancing customer convenience. The bank has fully computerized its two most important operations, interest calculation and the processing of transactions by both the decentralized postal banking branches and the Postal Banking Division at the NSB's Head Office.

Strengths and Weaknesses of the Postal Sector and Savings Mobilization

The postal sector has shown only minimal performance improvement despite the meaningful and innovative steps taken by the NSB over a period of time as noted above. The slight growth in savings mobilization in the postal sector can be attributed mainly to the interest accrued on the existing deposit base. Sri Lanka has a population of 18.8 million, of which 72.2 percent live in rural areas and 21.5 percent live in urban areas. The remainder of the population, 6.3 percent, live in the plantation areas (tea, rubber, and coconut plantations). Assuming an average family size is five, there are 3.7 million families in Sri Lanka. The postal sector boasts a 4.2-million-strong customer base, however 45 percent are presently dormant account-holders. Therefore, if the NSB could motivate these account-holders to reactivate their dormant accounts, it would likely be that every Sri Lankan family would possess a Post Office Savings Account. This is a very desirable goal as well as a challenge for the postal sector. No Sri Lankan institution, public or private, other than the Postal Department has the benefit of such a huge network of service delivery points. Post offices are found in every nook and corner of the country.

The more than 30 banks in Sri Lanka are mostly concentrated within city limits. The more than 4,000 post offices, mostly in rural areas, all provide postal savings services. They far outnumber the combined total of 1,096 commercial bank branches and 1,418 cooperative rural Bank branches (see Table 10.2: Bank Branch Network). The density of bank branches by district has also been highly uneven (see Table 10.3: Banking Density by Districts, pp. 192–193). It is therefore a distinct advantage that one can open an ordinary postal savings account with a minimum sum of Rs. 5 and thereafter make deposits and withdrawals to the account at any post office. The NSB believes there is an enormous untapped savings potential in the rural areas that can be flushed out by popularizing the savings habit among the rural population

Table 10.2

Bank Branch Network

Item	1978	1992	1993	1994	1995	1996	1997	1998	1999[a]
Commercial Banks[b]	768	814	848	883	913	943	987	1,028	1,044
Domestic Banks	760	785	815	847	876	906	949	988	1,006
Bank of Ceylon	512	330	333	336	339	339	341	343	341
People's Bank	216	319	323	326	330	331	339	341	342
Commercial Bank of Ceylon	9	28	31	34	36	41	49	62	70
Hatton National Bank	23	48	53	56	64	75	94	105	111
Sampath Bank	–	16	18	21	24	27	30	33	35
Seylan Bank	–	44	57	74	81	87	87	88	89
Other	–	–	–	–	2	6	9	16	18
Foreign Banks	8	29	33	36	37	37	38	40	38
Regional Rural/Regional Development Banks	–	156	163	169	171	175	176	176	176
National Savings Bank	27	84	85	90	96	99	101	102	104
Cooperative Rural Banks	558	1,152	1,175	1,216	1,251	1,293	1,329	1,351	1,418
Total Bank Branches	1,353	2,206	2,271	2,358	2,431	2,510	2,593	2,657	2,742
Population per Bank Branch	10,488	7,899	7,770	7,587	7,460	7,305	7,155	7,066	6,945
Banking Branches per 100,000 Persons	9.5	12.7	12.9	13.2	13.4	13.7	14.0	14.2	14.4
No. of Commercial Banks	11	23	23	23	26	26	26	26	25
Domestic Banks	4	6	6	6	8	8	8	8	9
Foreign Banks	7	17	17	17	18	18	18	18	16

[a]Provisional; [b]Includes main branches and other banking offices except pawning centers and student savings units.

and encouraging them to come to formal savings institutions with their savings. The NSB therefore expects the postal sector to make a concerted effort to achieve better overall performance in savings mobilization.

Customer-Oriented Service: Shortcomings in the Postal Sector

There are, however, obstacles to overcome in the postal sector service, including:

(a) Inadequate facilities at post offices;
(b) Postal employees unmotivated to promote savings;
(c) Cumbersome manual bookkeeping systems and bureaucratic paperwork;
(d) Lack of savings-linked credit facilities to post office–based NSB accounts;
(e) NSB-imposed restrictions on withdrawals (Rs. 3,500 at sub-post offices and Rs. 10,000 at post offices);
(f) Retention of passbooks for one week following withdrawal through the post office;
(g) Lack of synergy between the Postal Department and the NSB as the institutions are under the purview of different ministries;
(h) Competition from commercial banks, cooperative rural banks, regional development banks, and the NSB's own branch-banking sector;
(i) Lack of interest shown by postal counter service employees who perform the NSB's transactions.

The total absence at the post office of some of the key elements of the bank marketing-mix has resulted in account restrictions and a limited number of financial products and services being offered. In addition, poor physical facilities and lackluster customer service have left postal savings operations at a competitive disadvantage against the average Sri Lankan bank.

The Success and Failure of Strategies during the 1994–2000 Period

Owing to the NSB's concern that the postal savings system was not fulfilling its obligations, both the Postal Department and the NSB jointly searched for ways to incentivize postal employees. The bank pursued the following strategies in order to stimulate greater interest in the postal sector during the 1994–2000 period:

(a) Organized seminars with the participation of the postal sector hierarchy at the regional level;

Table 10.3

Banking Density by Districts, 1998

District	Main	Other	People's Bank	Hatton National Bank Ltd.	Commercial Bank of Ceylon Ltd.	Sampath Bank Ltd.	Seylan Bank Ltd.	Foreign Banks & Others (a)	National Savings Bank	Regional Rural/Regional Development Banks	Rural Bank	Total No. of Branches	Population '000	Population per Branch	Banking Density Index (b)
Colombo	49	19	67	35	24	15	27	49	23	0	105	413	2,199	5,324	18.8
Gampaha	18	4	26	15	9	5	15	1	15	5	179	292	1,621	5,551	18.0
Kalutara	14	2	15	2	2	1	6	0	5	16	75	138	1,008	7,304	13.7
Galle	16	1	17	8	4	0	8	0	3	12	95	154	1,030	6,688	15.0
Matara	11	1	13	1	2	3	1	1	10	13	81	137	852	6,219	16.1
Hanbantota	8	1	10	5	1	1	3	0	3	8	40	80	558	6,975	14.3
Monaragala	7	3	7	2	0	0	0	0	1	6	21	47	389	8,277	12.1
Badulla	12	5	17	4	1	0	3	0	3	13	81	139	780	5,612	17.8
Kandy	15	3	20	4	2	2	3	4	5	15	96	169	1,359	8,041	12.4
Matale	7	2	8	2	3	1	1	0	1	6	39	70	457	6,529	15.3

Nuwara Eliya	10	1	10	5	1	0	4	0	2	8	42	83	568	6,843	14.6
Kegalle	10	1	15	3	1	0	4	0	4	14	76	128	784	6,125	16.3
Ratnapura	12	4	17	4	2	1	4	0	3	8	79	134	1,017	7,590	13.2
Kurunegala	20	3	21	2	3	2	2	1	3	17	166	240	1,541	6,421	15.6
Putta'am	10	1	10	4	3	1	3	0	5	10	41	88	664	7,545	13.3
Trincomalee	5	1	6	3	0	0	0	0	1	0	6	22	349	15,864	6.3
Batticaloa	5	3	7	1	0	0	2	0	1	0	9	28	480	17,143	5.8
Ampar	9	1	12	3	0	0	1	0	2	7	8	43	550	12,791	7.8
Anuradhapura	19	3	16	3	1	1	2	0	4	11	39	99	793	8,010	12.5
Polonnaruwa	7	1	8	1	1	0	3	0	1	7	26	55	351	6,382	15.7
Jaffna	10	1	12	1	1	0	0	0	4	0	31	60	921	15,350	6.5
Killinochchi	1	0	2	0	0	0	0	0	1	0	2	6	120	20,000	5.0
Mullative	2	1	2	0	0	0	0	0	0	0	5	10	109	10,900	9.2
Mannar	1	1	2	1	0	0	0	0	1	0	6	12	146	12,167	8.2
Vavuniya	1	1	1	1	1	0	1	0	1	0	3	10	128	12,800	7.8
TOTAL	279	64	341	105	62	32	88	56	102	176	1,351	2,657	18,774	7,066	14.2

(a) Foreign Banks: ANZ Grindlays Bank plc.; Standard Chartered Bank; Hong Kong & Shanghai Banking Corporation, Ltd.; Indian Bank; Indian Overseas Bank; Overseas Trust Bank, Ltd.; Citibank N.A.; American Express Bank, Ltd.; ABN-AMRO Bank N.V.; Habib Bank, A.G. Zurich; Deutsche Bank A.G.; Public Bank Barhard; Mashreq Bank PSC, State Bank of India; Habib Bank, Ltd.; Muslim Commercial Bank; Korea Exchange Bank; and Société Génerale.

Other: Pan Asian Bank, Ltd.; Union Bank of Colombo, Ltd.

(b) Number. of bank branches per 100,000 persons.

(b) Organized campaigns among the general public at the provincial level with the involvement of the local postmasters;
(c) Organized campaigns in selected areas through the seven postal banking branches, which are under the direct administration and control of the NSB.

These programs made a positive impact in building awareness among postal employees about the products and services of the bank; however, no comparable increase was shown in the deposit base of the postal sector compared to the total deposits of the branch-banking sector of the NSB.

The NSB's dissatisfaction with its relationship with the Postal Department is based upon the following:

(a) The NSB continues to pay an annual agency fee to the Postal Department in return for services rendered to the bank, although the performance of the postal sector has not lived up to the bank's expectations during the past several years. This has become a matter of concern for the bank.
(b) Since 1994 a monthly incentive payment of Rs. 1,000 has been paid to all Divisional Superintendents of Posts (DSP). A growing discontent, however, has been observed among the lower-echelon rank and file of the postal sector workers to whom this emolument is not extended. Nevertheless, the bank has no intention of providing this incentive to anyone other than the DSP.
(c) In order to promote sales in the postal sector, the NSB introduced a 5 percent commission to postal employees who sell the "Ridee Rekha" Premium Savings Certificates. Those postal employees who were not given this sales opportunity complained, however, that they should also be granted commission opportunities. The net outcome was that the overall results were not productive. There are no other commissioned sales of NSB products through the postal network or plans to appoint commissioned agents.

The bank's view is that the successful implementation of its strategies and plan of action depends a great deal on both employees and the organizational culture of the Postal Department. There has been an ongoing dialogue between the NSB and the Postal Department, but as far as the bank is concerned, its corporate objective is to develop, motivate, and transform the staff to play a more active role in the progress of the bank. In this direction, the bank has offered and will continue to provide for personnel development of the bank's own staff to encourage teamwork in order to achieve superior performance. In this context, the Postal Department is expected to play an equally important and even greater role, together with the NSB, in order to achieve better performance and maintain its unmatched network in a competitive environment.

This plan of action calls for a dynamic approach and the determined effort of in-house resource development in order to transform the postal workforce into one with the positive attitude and confident outlook required for achieving its savings mobilization goals. Such a change requires a flexible organizational structure geared to meeting new targets and promoting greater efficiency, providing better service by utilizing modern technological advances to meet the challenges of the day, and adopting a market-oriented approach to improving teamwork and performance.

The NSB has enjoyed an exclusive relationship with the Postal Department over a long period of time. Although there is some speculation that the Postal Department may establish relationships with other financial institutions, it is premature to comment in the absence of any concrete proposals. The bank, however, is optimistic that the historic relationship between the NSB and the Postal Department will continue in the greater interest of the community.

The Marga Institute's Market Research Survey and Suggestions

The Marga Institute, one of the leading research institutes in Sri Lanka, which is also known as the Sri Lanka Centre for Development Studies, undertook a study at the request of the NSB on savings patterns and issued its final report in November 2000.

This research was based on a sample survey of 2,105 persons in 1,050 households. In the absence of a sampling protocol for selection of households, the methodology was designed to encompass as diverse a universe as possible. The Marga Institute adopted a direct interview technique, utilizing an *aide-mémoire* that contained several open-ended questions. It thus enabled a free expression of responses by the householders and ensured that both qualitative and quantitative data were obtained. The data include and reflect both the qualitative response to the interviewer and quantitative analysis of discretionary income by occupational and familial status.

The key data collected related to savings practices, that is, types of accounts held and reasons for selecting these accounts, among other things. Sources of information canvassed included all earners/savers in each household.

An extended inquiry was conducted with two segments of subpopulations, one according to earner types and the other according to occupational types across a broad geographic distribution.

Marga's Observations with Direct References to Post Office Savings Accounts

1. The Post Office Savings Account system has carved out for itself an unassailable position in the market over a long period and is fairly well entrenched in the savings culture of the country.
2. This arose partly from accounts having being passed on as a tradition from parents to children for over a generation or more, with a high proportion being long-time account holders, 60 percent of fifteen years or more, 31 percent over twenty-five years.
3. Over half (53 percent) of the customers subscribed to the conventional general savings, fixed deposits accounts, National Savings Certificates, and Post Office Savings Accounts, with 77 percent having accounts only in this last category. While 15 percent had other, more modern accounts as well, 8 percent had only modern accounts. Very few persons in the rural areas were aware of these new savings products.
4. The clients of Post Office Savings Accounts are predominantly from the rural sector, but a fair proportion, some 35 percent, are in urban locations. More women (40 percent of women compared with 25 percent of men) had Postal Savings Accounts among those surveyed. While these account-holders were predominantly in the lower income group of under Rs. 15,000, with respect to occupation they were mostly self-employed or in clerical and related occupations; however, nearly 16 percent of account-holders were found in administrative and managerial occupations.
5. Nearly half of the accounts were deemed to be dormant, in that no withdrawals were being made, but were being maintained as an inheritance or gift from parents.
6. Another 20 percent of accounts were maintained because of the close proximity of the post office to the residence of the account-holder.
7. A major reason given by the account-holders for their accounts was that small sums of money could be saved in the Post Office Savings Accounts, and many of these customers had no access to bank branches.
8. Twenty-five percent of post office account-holders said they maintained their accounts because they could easily draw money from any post office in Sri Lanka.

The Marga report suggested that the NSB should continue modernizing its facilities and practices. The report emphasized the importance of the NSB maintaining its historic role of accommodating the small saver while providing new services for larger financial transactions as well. The report also recommended incorporating the Post Office Savings Account system within the structure of the NSB, enhancing the capacity of the NSB network to provide services in remote rural areas and underserved locations, and building on strengths that the post office savings system has acquired in its long history.

Scope of Market and Future Developments for Savings

The NSB is the premier savings institution in Sri Lanka. With respect to assets, the NSB is the third largest Sri Lankan bank. All NSB deposits carry a government guarantee; therefore, the NSB enjoys enormous public confidence and goodwill. The same applies to the nationwide post office branch network, which is the exclusive franchise holder for NSB products and services. It is noteworthy to mention here that the financial crisis that hit the Asian economies in 1997 has had only a marginal impact on the Sri Lankan banking system.

There is intense competition among the large number of players in the deposit-taking market at present. They include the People's Bank, a state-owned mass market commercial bank with a strong nationwide branch network, and the rural banks, village-based stand-alone entities that mobilize savings and extend credit for cottage industries and small and medium-scale industries. All of these institutions offer stiff competition to the NSB. Therefore, all of the state-owned banks, including the NSB, are undergoing large-scale reforms to become reoriented to market competition and enhance the financial stability and viability of their institutions.

One of the weaknesses of the NSB's agency relationship with the postal banking system has been that the funds it mobilizes are transferred to the NSB Head Office for investment and hence are not available for local lending. There is no suitable mechanism to retain NSB funds in their rural base and lend them to the customers in the area. Some other banks and lending institutions capitalized on this situation and have introduced rural credit schemes over the years. However, in 2002 the NSB started limited lending operations for personal and housing loans through its Decentralized Postal Banking branches. At present the NSB does not have any plans to intermediate mobilized funds through local financial institutions.

As mentioned earlier, the following have been key factors in the NSB's success against competitors: the security of its government-guaranteed deposits, its higher rates of interest than commercial banks, its nationwide branch network and post office network, and most recently market-driven institutional reforms.

About 50 percent of NSB branches are now computerized, covering over 75 percent of its customer base and providing ATM facilities at selected branches. The Postal Department has not kept abreast of the far-reaching effects of these developments. The present trend is thus likely to continue whereby postal customers turn to NSB branches for better quality customer service.

Sri Lanka switched its development strategy to a more open and deregulated economy in 1977. Vast strides have been made in the expansion and development of a vibrant economy. In the transformation process the Postal Department lost some of the lucrative business areas it formerly held, such as parcel delivery, cash remittances, telecommunications, and the like, to its competitors. Reform of the Postal Department is now being contemplated.

The NSB looks forward to continuing the long-standing relationship between the two organizations to the mutual benefit of both institutions in a profitable manner and with an awareness of their social responsibility toward society.

11

Report on the Postal Savings System in the Republic of Kazakhstan

Serikzhan Mambetalin, with Arken Arystanov and Dauren Moldagaliyev

General Information on Kazpost and Postal Savings

Postal communications, which includes the postal system, telephone, and telegraph networks, is a major component in the infrastructure of any state because it carries out a very important mission—upholding the constitutional rights of citizens to the free flow of information. Until relatively recently, postal communications throughout the world functioned under direct state control. However, in the 1980s restructuring took place in many of the world's postal administrations in the form of corporatization. In so doing, however, the post did not lose its social obligations.

In the case of Kazakhstan, over seven decades of the Soviet period (1920–91), the financial operations of the post and other communications services had been based on a principle of residual financing, that is, cash revenues less expenses. By the accounting standards of the Soviet era, the postal communications network as a whole was profitable; however, most of the post's net revenues went toward the development of a telecommunications infrastructure. This lopsided pattern of investment resulted in a significant backlog of missed opportunities for the postal sector to meet the needs of its postal delivery clientele. Less than 5 percent of the total amount of capital investment was directed toward the development of postal delivery service, about one-fifth of the actual amount needed to fully develop postal capacity

---

This chapter is based on the report initially presented by Serikzhan Mambetalin, then Director of Financial Services and Deputy Chairman of Kazpost, at the Postal Savings for Development Conference held at Keio University in January 2000. Important updates and additional information were subsequently contributed by Arken Arystanov, Chairman of the Board, and Dauren Moldagaliyev, Deputy Chairman of Kazpost.

and maintain normal delivery. However, despite the inherent unprofitability of conventional mail delivery service, the postal services were sustained by their revenues from the delivery of pensions through the postal system's network and from the provision of telephone and telegraphic services. After the transfer of these most profitable services from the post, the government turned to transforming the postal network into a postal savings system to replace its lost revenues.

Over the past decade the Republic of Kazakhstan has been in a period of economic transition, affecting the postal system as well. The basic purpose for postal corporatization in Kazakhstan was to provide new services of higher quality and greater profitability and to use the available infrastructure to gain additional income to sustain the post's network. The changes experienced by the post also mirrored a general tendency toward the gradual transition from state control to general oversight by the state through legislative means.

In 1993 the posts and telecommunications were brought under the control of the Ministry of Communications and separated into two different enterprises, with the expectation that they would become self-financing without any state subsidies (decision of the government of the Republic of Kazakhstan, 5 April 1993). Telecommunications assets were transferred to the Joint Stock Company Kazakhtelecom, and the postal network's assets in November 1999 went to the newly created Republican State Enterprise of Post Services (RSEPS) under the Ministry of Transport, Communications, and Tourism.

In September 1996 a government decree "On delivery of pensions and other social payments" reduced RSEPS commission fees by two-thirds for the delivery and payment of pensions, from 1.8 percent to 0.6 percent of the value of the remittance. Furthermore, a substantial portion of the post's remittance services was transferred to the National Savings Bank of Kazakhstan, also known as Halyk (People's) Savings Bank, with RSEPS as its agent for remittance payments in rural locations where Halyk did not have branches. As a result of these changes, RSEPS's income from its pension delivery service dropped sharply from 37 percent to 5 percent of its overall revenues. With the transfer to other enterprises of telecommunications revenues, the post's other most profitable service, the post's income fell significantly, although post offices still provide rows of telephone booths for the public's use.

The government thus faced the need to seek new revenues to sustain the post and looked to expanding the use of the postal services network into a postal savings system. This fiscal necessity of this plan was recognized by the government, which included the modernization of postal services as a project in its Public Investment Program of 1999–2001.

In May 1999 the government recommended the introduction and implementation of postal savings to provide RSEPS with the fiscal resources needed to improve the quality of its mail and parcel delivery operations as well as to provide other services adapted to the principles governing a competitive market economy. It permitted RSEPS to offer a wide spectrum of financial services by utilizing the RSEPS's post office branch network, including postal savings in every post office and financial services as agents for banks, pension plans, and investment funds. In the government decree of 27 May 1999, "On measures for stabilization and financial recovery of the postal branch of the Republic of Kazakhstan," the structure of the RSEPS was reorganized, and the RSEPS was recommended for consideration by the National Bank of the Republic of Kazakhstan for a license to carry out certain forms of banking activities.

The postal savings system is a special form of financial institution and, therefore, required working out a separate procedure of regulation. It was necessary to amend laws regulating the financial and banking field: "On banks and banking activities," "On non-banking financial organizations," and so on. It was also necessary to improve existing acts and to issue new normative acts through the authorized agencies regulating issues of supervision and accounting: the National Bank, the Ministry of Finance, and the National Security Commission of the Republic of Kazakhstan. On 30 June 1999, RSEPS was licensed by the National Bank of the Republic of Kazakhstan to carry out deposit operations. In accordance with the decree of the government, postal savings deposits are to be placed only in State securities of the Republic of Kazakhstan.

In December 1999 the Ministry of Finance reorganized RSEPS into an open joint-stock company (OJSC) known as Kazpost, to be under the supervision of the Ministry of Transport and Communications. The Committee of State Property and Privatization of the Ministry of Finance has ownership rights and can dispose of its controlling block of shares of Kazpost (OJSC shares may be sold without the permission of other shareholders), while the Ministry of Transport and Communications has the rights of possession and use of the government's block of shares.

The government adopted its overall 2001–5 economic plan in which the main priorities were aimed at: economic and financial stabilization; improving the quality of the regional infrastructure while expanding the provision of services; and reestablishing commission fees for delivery of pension and social payments in rural areas. In it, in addition to establishing postal savings, Kazpost was also mandated to provide agency services, including the payment of employee salaries by agreement with employers, the automatic transfer payment of salaries to employees, and payments such as student scholarships into personal student postal savings accounts.

Kazpost also provides other intermediary services to state institutions and commercial organizations, including accepting payments for public utilities, receipt of tax payments, compulsory payments, and other payments to the state budget, and so on. In each case an agreement is signed between Kazpost and the state institution or commercial organization to provide specific intermediary services.

Postal savings also requires the development of special mechanisms for its regulation that meet the legal basis of the activities of the postal service. An October 2002 draft law "On the Posts," submitted for consideration by the Parliament, takes into account the economic and technical transformation of the postal service and the development of the postal savings in the context of a market economy.

Kazpost is responsible for its own fiscal management and receives no subsidies from the state. As the national post operator of the Republic of Kazakhstan, it provides internal and international postal communications services and has the authority to enter into operational agreements on international postal communications and postal financial operations with the national postal operators and financial institutions of other countries.

Organizational Structure

Kazpost's organizational structure consists of four basic levels:

(a) The first level is the Central Administration, which carries out the direct management of regional branches, the organization and coordination of postal services at the national level, and represents Kazakhstan post at the international level.

(b) The second level is comprised of: fourteen regional branches that organize the work of the postal enterprise at the regional level; the main post offices in Astana (the capital) and Almaty (Kazakhstan's largest city and former capital); the Special Communications Service of the Republic of Kazakhstan; specialized companies such as Pochtasnab, an affiliated enterprise under Kazpost that supplies the regional branch network's post offices with all relevant materials for their day-to-day needs; and the Division of Postal Transportation, which provides vehicles, including armored cars, for postal financial services use.

(c) The third level consists of the twenty urban area (UAPS) and 150 district area (DAPS) postal service administrations that are subordinate to the regional branches. Their offices oversee the receiving, processing, transportation, and delivery of all types of postal matter throughout their city

and district areas. UAPS and DAPS perform management functions, including coordinating and examining the activities of the urban and rural post offices of the regional branch network.
(d) The fourth level is Kazpost's network, consisting of 3,387 post offices, of which 614 are located in urban areas and 2,773 in rural areas. All post offices throughout Kazakhstan serve as postal savings collection points, and 2,444 post offices, approximately 72 percent as of February 2003, provide full postal savings services, far exceeding any bank's branch network. The main demand for savings deposit accounts comes from inhabitants of rural areas, pensioners, and others receiving remittances and allowance payments.

The Formation of the Postal Savings and Financial Services System

The postal savings system began with the establishment of a headquarters for financial services in the structure of RSEPS, including a deposit department, currency department, operational department, and department for the payment of salaries, pensions, and allowances.

Both traditional deposits and new forms of savings products were introduced with the inauguration of postal savings. Today, for the creation of products, we use various types of market research, using both quantitative and qualitative research methods. Our main methods of research are public opinion polling, using focus groups and interviews, designing research questionnaires, and analyzing the activities of our competitors.

When first launched, promotional advertising and informational campaigns were implemented to attract the population's savings funds. Kazpost has initiated large-scale advertising campaigns through newspapers, radio, and display advertising on public transportation, which inform the public about postal savings and other postal financial services.

Kazpost plans to create a unified informational base at its main office and is working on improving the logistics and technical equipment of the postal and savings system. It is computerizing its subdivisions and equipping post offices with computers. The introduction of modern technologies based on computers is the most important condition for the successful realization of the post's modernization program. The development of informational technologies is directed toward achieving the maximum automation of all business and account processes and procedures within Kazpost. Customized software has been put into operation at regional branches that allows for the recording, processing, and transmittal of account information to the Central Administration of Kazpost. This computer network will encompass all savings accounts maintained at the post offices, posting deposits and withdrawals and automatically crediting interest payments to accounts.

As a deposit-taking and payment-making institution, Kazpost provides agency services to state organizations for paying salaries, scholarships, allowances, and other social benefit payments.

In 2000, Kazpost began to provide foreign currency exchange services, increasing its revenues from exchange operations. Its purchases of foreign currency in 2001 totaled 1.6 billion tenge (US$12 million), and its sale of currency 1.9 billion tenge (US$14.3 million).

Kazpost continues to search for new sectors of the financial services market that have high profitability. This includes: providing agency services to pension funds, insurance companies, brokerage companies, banks, and other financial organizations, and providing services for the transfer and servicing of payments by individuals and legal entities for taxes and other obligatory payments.

Establishment of the Deposit Base for Postal Savings

The public's rate of savings in bank accounts is highly dependent on the economic situation as the rate of deposits reflects the economic cycle. For example, the growth of total savings deposits in Kazakhstan, which had been rising during the first half of 1998, showing a 16 percent increase, was halted in the third quarter, with an 8 percent decrease after the Russian ruble crisis came to a head. This change in the pattern of savings was due to the sharp fall in the Russian ruble rate of exchange. Since the economies of Russia and Kazakhstan are closely interconnected, the population became concerned about the security of Kazakhstan's banking system. Their fears about the safety of their deposits at the time had a negative impact on the local currency placement of Kazakh savings.

It was within this economic background that Kazpost contemplated the establishment of a postal savings system. It was hoped that in its first year of operations, postal savings would attract 10 percent of the personal savings market, some 3 billion of the 30 billion tenge (1998), giving a net income of 50 million tenge for Kazpost. This goal was only partially achieved owing to the drop in interest rates on State securities, which decreased the profitability of the main vehicle for Kazpost's investment in funds. Nevertheless, the public's trust in the safety of the postal savings system grew.

In general the public has responded very warily to changes in the banking industry because the risk of bankruptcy is increasing with privatization and the establishment of many joint-stock banks. Under these conditions the participation of a state enterprise that has significant experience plays an important role. It is most important that such an enterprise be a state organization, one committed to the normal process of savings formation and prudent investment of the public's savings.

At present, to successfully realize the tasks of attracting the savings funds of the population and of putting them to use in building the country, Kazpost is focusing its financial activities on building a portfolio of State securities purchased both as an investment for Kazpost itself and on behalf of private and corporate clients. As of 1 July 2002, Kazpost's investment portfolio of State securities reached 409.1 billion tenge.

Kazpost's strategic plan is to develop traditional forms of deposits for individual savers such as on-demand, fixed-period, fixed-period with additions, and children's savings deposits. At present, time deposit and on-demand postal savings accounts are available in either tenge, Kazakhstan's national currency, or in U.S. dollars. U.S. dollar savings accounts comprise some 45 percent of the total volume of deposits. The terms of deposit are similar, whether in tenge or dollar accounts.

Time deposits are taken for three-, six-, nine-, and twelve-month periods as well as two-, three-, and five-years. For accounts of one year or more, in addition to the monthly payment of accrued interest, it is possible to deposit additional funds into the account during the term. Upon completion of the period, the time deposit can be rolled over for additional periods on prior instruction, without the account-holder having to take further action.

Kazpost's credibility as a special type of institution for carrying out banking operations has earned both the trust of the government and the people in postal savings. The market for servicing pension payments and other allowances is constantly increasing. Nearly 86 percent of bank accounts of individuals, including postal savings accounts, are for special pension-payment deposits. These accounts are opened for transfer of the pension amounts and the allowances budgeted from state and local budgets. Further work in designing and introducing suitable and attractive products for savings deposits in the postal savings system will continue.

One of the factors that attracts deposits to saving accounts is the tax exemption on the interest paid to depositors. The Law of the Republic of Kazakhstan of 1 September 1999 "On taxes and other obligatory payments to the budget" states that any interest on deposits in banks and organizations that carry out forms of banking operations under license from the National Bank of the Republic of Kazakhstan are not subject to taxation. Therefore, interest payments to individuals received on deposits in postal savings accounts are not taxed; however, interest payments to legal entities are subject to a taxation rate of 15 percent. At present, 100 percent of Kazpost's savings account holders are individuals.

Before postal savings operations were begun in August 1999, the banking sector was represented by sixty-three deposit-taking banks. Among them were five foreign-owned banks and four banks partly owned by foreign capital. The large Kazakhstan banks that had branch networks were the Halyk (People's) Savings Bank of Kazakhstan, Kazkommertzbank, and TuranAlem Bank. During the first six months of 1999 the public's savings deposits increased by 30 percent, and by 1 October 1999 the volume of deposits in banks had increased by 66 percent. This was substantially due to an increase in the average level of salaries and the settlement of pension plan funds.

Of the total volume of deposits in mid-1999, approximately 67 percent was concentrated in the Halyk Bank and approximately 10 percent at TuranAlem, owing to their developed branch networks and many years of experience in taking private savings deposits. However, the rural population, which makes up about 40 percent of Kazakhstan's total population, had no access to banking services as it was not profitable to set up and maintain a bank branch network in rural areas.

In 2001 the state sold at auction its controlling block of shares in Halyk Bank, and it became a commercial bank; the word "Savings" was removed from its name. Prior to Halyk Bank's privatization, it had signed an agency agreement with Kazpost for the payment in rural areas of pensions and allowances from state and local budgets through Kazpost's branch network. Halyk Bank, which then closed its unprofitable rural branches, now has the second-largest branch network behind Kazpost. Halyk and Kazpost do not own shares in each other's company.

By 2002 the banking situation had changed, competition among the largest banks had intensified, and other banks had reduced Halyk's deposit base. Privatization and the creation of many new private sector banks have caused the population to respond very warily out of concern due to these institutions' increased risk of bankruptcy.

Meanwhile, the deposit base of Kazpost in 2001 saw a 74 percent increase over the previous year, more than doubled in 2002, and as of October 2002 was 728 billion tenge.

Kazpost's Intermediation of Government Borrowing

The government has determined that, to protect the security of postal savings services, depositors' funds must be invested in the State securities of the Republic of Kazakhstan. In addition, customers can buy government securities through Kazpost. Therefore, Kazpost was given a first category license issued by the National Security Commission of the Republic of Kazakhstan, granting it the right to broker for its client-investors solely in the market of State-issued securities.

Table 11.1

Average Amount Invested in State Securities

Years	Amount of Average Annual Volume of State Securities Portfolio (billion tenge)
2000	225.8
2001	183.1
2002	345.5 (as of September 30)

Emphasizing the strategic significance of the post and its intention to consistently further the ability of the postal network to market securities, the government of the Republic of Kazakhstan issued a decree on 17 June 1999, "On placing private persons' funds promoted by the Republic State Postal Services." RSEPS became a member of the Kazakhstan Stock Exchange Closed Joint-Stock Company (CJSC) in order to carry out its functions as a primary dealer in the obligations of the Ministry of Finance of the Republic of Kazakhstan. RSEPS was authorized to open a similar account at the National Bank of the Republic of Kazakhstan and was later authorized to act as a Primary Agent to place short-term notes of the National Bank as well with the CJSC Central Depository of Securities. Besides purchases of securities on behalf of customers, all the savings funds deposited with RSEPS were to be invested exclusively in State securities. See Table 11.1: Average Amount Invested in State Securities.

RSEPS's investment portfolio at the end of 1999 consisted of euro-denominated bonds of the Republic of Kazakhstan, short-term foreign currency denominated bonds, tenge bonds of the Ministry of Finance, notes of the National Bank, and municipal bonds. This portfolio is managed through the purchase and sale of securities and depends on the state of the securities market and foreign currency exchange rate to maximize income against RSEPS's liabilities with its foreign currency postal savings deposits and other transactions denominated in tenge, U.S. dollars, and so on. For the most part, however, the growth in Kazpost's customers' deposits has been in demand accounts where their salary and benefit payments have accumulated and which require a high amount of liquidity in investments.

Today the postal savings system continues to advance the use of its clients' deposits toward enhancing the state's financial and credit system, contributing to the financial stabilization and economic development of the country. Moreover, the development of the postal savings system has decreased the circulation of cash and fostered the productive movement of monetary capital through savings bank accounts. Electronic cash cards will be introduced for service in post offices throughout the country. Postal savings has restored the fiscal underpinnings of the postal network.

Thus, transformation of the post into a financial organization has provided the population in the most distant parts of the country with access to many types of banking services, and also has provided the state with a substantial method to mobilize the population's monetary savings.

Financial Transfers, Foreign Exchange, and Remittance Services

Upon enactment of the Government Decree of 28 September 1999, "On measures on improving the order of payment of salaries, scholarships, pensions, allowances and other monetary benefits at the expense of state budget," the RSEPS obtained an opportunity to reassume its role as the largest institution for the payment of pensions, salaries, and scholarships, which it had lost to Halyk Savings Bank in 1996.

In addition to accepting deposits, Kazpost can perform the following types of banking operations: opening and administering bank accounts of individuals and legal entities; cash operations; remittance operations; collection and transfer of banknotes, cash, and valuables; organization of foreign exchange operations and the buying and selling of foreign currency; leasing; and factoring operations. Kazpost carries out brokering operations in government securities. It is not, however, permitted to provide credit or loan services.

In 2000, Kazpost began transacting foreign currency exchange, purchasing 1.7 billion tenge, of which some 10 to 15 percent came from overseas remittances, and selling 2.3 billion tenge of foreign currency purchased by individuals, residents, and non-residents. Reasons why individuals buy foreign currencies include business trips, foreign remittance operations, and savings by the general public.

Kazpost created and uses its own retail payments system and, along with the other deposit- and payment-taking banks, is required by law to participate in the Funds Transfers Interbank System (FTIS). Transfer of payments through its retail payments system enables Kazpost to reduce its own transaction expenses. One of the money transfer systems Kazpost introduced in 2002 is called Urgent Transfer, which permits the sending of domestic money orders throughout the country in electronic form within one to two workdays.

Internationally, Kazpost cooperates with the postal administrations of eighteen countries on international postal money order transfers. Its remittance operation is making plans to replace the use of paper forms with electronic transmission for international postal remittance transactions.

Kazpost's Agency Services

In addition to conducting financial operations on its own behalf (listed above), Kazpost also provides many of the same services on an agency basis for government, business enterprises, and commercial banks and other financial institutions. Kazpost makes significant agency profits from remittance operations, the payment of pensions, and other social payments from the state budget, cash-handling transactions, payments of salaries, grants, and other social allowances to employees of the state and other organizations, and receiving of payments for public utilities and other services. At the present time, post offices provide the following financial and agency services:

- Payment of salaries, grants, and other social allowances to employees of the state and other organizations;
- Acceptance of payments for public utilities such as electric power, gas, water, sewage, telephone, and other services;
- Receipt of taxes and other compulsory payments to the state;
- Acceptance of payments as agent for international payment cards such as VisaCard, EuroCard/MasterCard, and Cirrus/Maestro;
- Agency services for clients' applications for pension funds, insurance companies, and other enterprises;
- Commissions from broker and dealer activities in the securities market for investment of funds by individuals in state securities.

Utilizing its branch network, Kazpost expects to expand by further developing its State securities brokerage and other fee-based financial services with individuals at post offices. In 2002, Kazpost sought a license from the National Bank of the Republic of Kazakhstan to provide securities transfer services to further utilize its motor pool of armored vehicles that is used to transport cash for remittance payments and currency transactions to post offices throughout the republic.

Human Resource Development

The development of personnel is considered one of the most important ways for Kazpost to actively improve its services. The main principles of Kazpost's personnel policy are: to provide a complete and coherent managerial system at all levels of postal network operations, and to encourage and develop personnel into doing high-performance work characterized by motivation, creative labor, and innovation. Kazpost's human resources management thus focuses on the following issues:

(a) determining the real demand for staff within the system by monitoring and testing their quality of work;
(b) training and retraining staff at training centers;
(c) providing incentives for career advancement by targeted staff placement;
(d) outsourcing of staff functions;
(e) development of employees' career plans.

The primary way to professionally develop postal personnel and improve their qualifications is education. Developing human resources requires effective training seminars for both managerial and operational personnel. In some post offices, postal and financial services are provided by separately trained personnel; however, in most post offices, postal counter staffers also handle financial services. Significant efforts are directed at developing the counter staff's understanding of customers' needs in postal savings services and the instilling of principles of social-ethical marketing of Kazpost's financial products.

Development of Branch Technologies

Kazpost plans to create its own automated information technology system, which will allow the integration of its services and enable the transfer of account and other information with a high degree of protection through a multilevel secure informational network. Installation of computers and peripheral equipment is the foundation for building a unified informational network. The plan for development of information technologies has the aim of providing the greatest degree of automation in all business processes and procedures in Kazpost.

Realization of the technology project will allow Kazpost to increase its quality of postal services, enabling each post office to provide a wide range of financial services—savings banking, pension, and investment products using the postal network's branch system.

The goals of the technology project are as follows:

(a) to equip each post office with software and hardware-equipped postal counter terminals;
(b) to set up telecommunications networks for communicating information at high speed and with accuracy;
(c) to computerize postal savings services and set up a multilevel protected information network;
(e) to set up a unified computer processing center;

(f) to organize the training of specialists to introduce new operational service technologies in software and hardware;
(g) to increase attention to the development of Kazpost's website;
(h) to improve transport and communications facilities.

At the post office level, the introduction of new technologies will give better service to the public, ultimately leading to the creation of a highly automated postal department in which clients can comfortably serve themselves or with the help of a department employee. The introduction of new electronic data communications through virtual networks will substantially expedite Kazpost operations. It will also allow the communication of voice/sound messages, electronic data files, and graphic images. Post offices will then have the additional role of mini–savings bank branches—oriented toward their usual clients—capable of providing a wide range of banking services. Such offices can also become centers for providing a wide range of informational services such as access to information databases for booking airplane tickets.

Currently, three new postal technologies are being emphasized: marketing of communications; financial operations for processing accounts and payments information, claims, and waybills; and unification of production and distribution of goods into one network. New information technologies will provide new opportunities. Kazpost, like many other postal administrations, is continually searching for new ways to carry out traditional postal tasks. Together with its clients, Kazpost expects to find new uses for its network to solve new tasks.

Taking into account the specific character of activity of the post's broad branch network and its nationwide representation, the postal savings system brings each citizen of Kazakhstan a wide range of financial and informational services, both in large cities and rural areas. It also provides the state with a practical way to accumulate and effectively use the monetary savings of the population.

12

Vietnam's Postal Savings Service

Cao Thi Hoai Duc

The Decision to Introduce a Postal Savings Service in Vietnam

Recent Changes in Vietnam's Economic Situation

Vietnam is a developing country with a very poor infrastructure. Since 1986, when the government's "renovation policy" (*doi moi*) began, Vietnam has been in the process of transforming from a centrally planned economy into a market economy. Despite a generally high rate of economic growth averaging 6 to 7 percent a year, the social and material infrastructure of industry, agriculture, transportation, science, technology, and other economic facilities still remains weak.

In Vietnam there are 4 state-owned commercial banks, 43 privately owned commercial banks, 4 commercial banks jointly owned by the state with foreign banks, and more than 25 different foreign-owned banks. Over the past several years the banking sector has been rather weak. Vietnam is currently restructuring and strengthening the organization and operation of the whole system. The many failures among privately owned banks have negatively impacted the public's confidence in the banking system quite strongly. As a consequence, when postal savings services were introduced in 1999, many depositors withdrew their money from banks and put their funds into postal savings accounts.

A shortage of capital is a major factor in the lack of development of infrastructure. Although Vietnam has managed to attract foreign direct investment (FDI) and has received official development assistance (ODA) from international organizations and some foreign countries, foreign investors on the whole are very reluctant to have their money channeled into infrastructure projects. ODA funds are limited and not enough for the many projects. It is estimated that for the period from 2002 to 2005, the total capital needed for socioeconomic development will be about US$60 billion, of which FDI and ODA funds will account for only 30 percent. Therefore the balance of the required capital must be raised from domestic financial resources. As in other developing countries, it is essential for Vietnam to mobilize capital from its own people to meet the development investment needs of the nation.

The Objectives of Providing Postal Savings Services in Vietnam

In 1999 the postal savings system was introduced with the purpose of mobilizing investment funds for building infrastructure and key economic facilities. The new postal savings system was intended to be a consistent and stable way to gather capital for the National Development Assistance Fund (NDAF, described later in more detail) in order to achieve policy targets in the industrialization and modernization of Vietnam. It was anticipated that capital mobilized from the postal savings system would contribute a substantial amount to the government's investment program, adding to the capital raised from the banking system and government bonds.

Postal savings systems in general also create a widespread savings network rooted in communities in order to promote savings, especially in rural areas where people do not have access to banks, and thereby help stabilize lives and guarantee the future.

Another important goal of the postal savings system is to give all people, regardless of location, access to a range of financial services, particularly in view of the fact that the private banking system gears its services to customers who are generally wealthier and located in cities and more developed provinces. As in many countries in Asia and throughout the world, the introduction of a postal savings service also enables the development of vital postal remittance services. Post offices have thus become enhanced public facilities where people can conduct payment transactions and utilize other postal financial services.

Finally, postal savings services provided at post offices increase the efficacy of the postal network. Vietnam's postal network is broad, but the postal infrastructure and the employees working in post offices are not utilized to their fullest capacity. The launch of postal savings in Vietnam was not only intended to diversify the services available, but also to make better use of the labor force, thus increasing income at little to no extra cost. Postal savings service is provided at post offices by the Posts and Telecommunications (P&T) staff. At most post offices the same counter personnel handle both savings operations and other postal services. Only at post offices with a very high volume of transactions, for example, the Hanoi Central Post Office, are the savings operations provided by specialized assigned P&T staff.

With the above-mentioned objectives, Vietnam Posts and Telecommunications (VNPT) submitted its proposal to the government to introduce the postal savings system as a new capital-mobilizing channel of the government. Following the November 1998 decision of the Office of the Prime Minister to permit the VNPT to establish the new service, the Vietnam Postal Savings Service Company (VPSC) was organized in May 1999 as a subsidiary of VNPT to manage postal savings. In August 1999 postal savings was inaugurated at 48 post offices in Hanoi and Ho Chi Minh City, and on 1 September 1999 initial phase services were extended to 202 post offices in sixty-one cities and provinces.

The size and scope of VNPT's operations have grown considerably in recent years, from 2,730 post offices in 1996 to 7,130 post offices in 2000, doubling the number of staff but tripling its reach in customers served. The purpose of this expansion was to serve more people and mobilize more funds. According to the VNPT's development plans, by the end of 2005 the total number of post offices will be increased to 12,435 so that each post office will serve 6,720 persons, in contrast to the present average of 8,885 persons. Much of the recent network expansion is due to the creation of "cultural post offices," which are small post offices that have been introduced primarily in rural areas and are staffed by personnel from outside the postal administration. These cultural post offices provide public telephones and include a community library with a reading area for newspapers and other periodicals, along with the customary postal services.

From 1999 to 2002 the savings service within the postal system has been continuously developing and expanding. In 1999, as noted above, service was provided in 202 post offices. By 2000 service was being provided in 234 post offices, and by 2001 the system was in 539 post offices located in sixty-one cities and provinces of the country. In the coming years VNPT will focus on agency post offices and cultural post offices. The VPSC is preparing a plan to provide postal savings and remittance services at some cultural post offices. Although it is still unavailable in most post offices (early 2004), it expects postal savings and other postal financial services will be provided throughout the VNPT's postal network by 2006. This includes the more than 3,500 administration-run post offices, the 500 agency post offices staffed by non-VNPT personnel, and many of the more than 5,000 cultural post offices.

An Introduction to the Vietnam Postal Savings Service Company

The Vietnam Postal Savings Service Company (VPSC) has the responsibility of managing the daily operation of the postal savings system, including supervision of all matters relating to postal savings at individual post offices. In addition, the VPSC manages funds transfers from the VNPT to the Ministry of Finance. The VPSC maintains its central account at the Vietnam Agricultural Bank and holds another sixty-one accounts at the provincial level.

Postal savings funds are mobilized from cash held by the public, that is, monies not deposited or invested with any institution. The funds are transferred to the National Development Assistance Fund (NDAF), a government organization, in the form of long-term loans with one-year, two-year, three-year, and five-year periods. The VPSC is not allowed to open accounts for enterprises, only for individuals, and it is not allowed to provide credit services.

Vietnam has sixty-one provinces and special districts. Each VPSC provincial office opens a "savings service" account for the district; at the end of each business day the postal savings funds from all post offices within the district are placed into the district's savings service account. Twice a month, on the fourth and nineteenth day, the VPSC withdraws the money from its provinces' accounts and then it makes the transfers to the NDAF on the tenth and twenty-fifth of the month. Each day the post offices calculate and keep back enough reserve funds for the next day's savings operations. The reserve usually represents at most 30 percent of the total value of the certificates due to mature the next day, and on average 26 percent of the deposits roll over into new CDs. In case of a shortfall of funds due to early withdrawals, the local post office can borrow money from other postal and telecom service units. The VPSC then transfers compensatory funds, within two days at most, upon receiving the request from the province's post office.

The Vietnam Postal Savings Service Company also conducts research to improve service quality and develop new financial products.

The VPSC's two main products are Time Savings and Collection Savings. The Time Savings plan allows customers to withdraw principal and interest only on an account's maturity date. Under the Collection Savings plan, customers are required to make fixed deposits every month to their plans, with the longest plan term being two years. Both of these plans are inflexible and thus not attractive to all depositors. In 2002 the VPSC introduced different kinds of Time Savings plans including withdrawal at maturity date, periodic interest withdrawal, and multiple withdrawals. Also, Collection Savings plan periods were extended to five-, ten-, and fifteen-year terms.

For each post office, the VPSC calculates a reserve level based upon the number of passbook accounts, the total value of the passbook accounts, and the average number of transactions made per day. In order to facilitate liability management of Ordinary Savings deposit accounts when they were introduced in September 2002, some restrictions were imposed on the ability of customers to make withdrawals from post offices other than where the original account resides. Withdrawals in those cases are limited to three per day, with an allowed daily maximum of 10 million Vietnamese dong (VND) (US$600).

The Ordinary Savings deposit account is one of the VPSC's new savings products. Funds deposited into this type of account will also be transferred to the NDAF, but the retained reserve must be kept higher than that for other services. In order to maintain the proper level of liquidity, it is estimated that the VPSC will transfer to the NDAF only 20 percent of the total funds on deposit in the Ordinary Savings accounts, and the remaining balance of 80 percent will be reserved in cash at post offices.

Until the introduction of postal savings, postal money orders were the only financial service available at post offices. Currently, Money Orders are a VNPT product managed by another subsidiary, the Vietnam Postal Services Company (VPS). However, it is expected that in the near future, responsibility for Money Order services will be transferred to the VPSC. At most post offices, money orders and savings services are already provided at the same counter. Both services may use the other's cash on hand, with final account balances fully reconciled for each at the end of the day.

In January 2002, individual payment account services were introduced whereby customers can make payments from their passbook accounts. By the end of 2002 the VPSC offered payment services through individual accounts for the payment of telephone bills, electricity, and other recurring utility bills.

Other financial services and products currently being developed include such modern postal financial services as ATM cards, IC card payment (integrated circuit, stored-value card), and Internet payment. The VPSC is responsible for the development of new plans for the expansion of Vietnam's postal savings service for the future. (See Development Plans section that follows.) The VPSC has the following organizational structure (see Figure 12.1: Organizational Structure).

The Vietnam Postal Savings Service Company has eight functional divisions and one branch in Ho Chi Minh City, with a staff numbering 101 employees in 2002. The purpose and function of the eight divisions and branch are as follows:

1. *Administration and Human Resources Division:* responsible for human resources, training, organizational structure, reception, and security.
2. *Investment Division:* responsible for preparing investment projects and products, researching and making proposals on business development strategies, carrying out international cooperation activities.

Figure 12.1 **Organizational Structure**

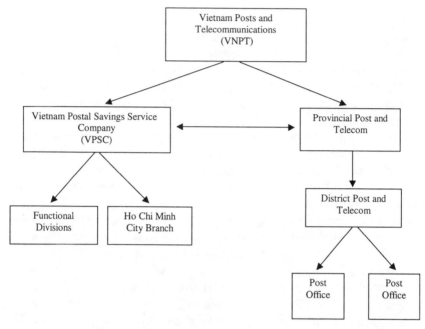

3. *Information Technology Division:* responsible for management and control of the nationwide computer network.
4. *Postal Savings Management Division:* responsible for management of the savings network, making plans to introduce new services, and preparing services procedures.
5. *Finance and Accounting Division:* responsible for supervision of income and expenditures of the company, management and control of cash flow for postal savings.
6. *Business Planning Division:* responsible for making short-term and long-term development plans and the marketing of services.
7. *Research and Development Division:* responsible for research on new technologies, and development of technology to introduce modern financial services.
8. *Inspection Division:* responsible for checking documents from post offices, verifying clearances, and ensuring the safeguards surrounding financial services.

Ho Chi Minh City Branch: manages the daily postal savings operations in post offices, the marketing of services in southern Vietnam, and manages and controls the VPSC computer center in Ho Chi Minh City.

Financial Management Operations

The VPSC is an internal attached-accounting unit of the VNPT. Its registered capital funded by VNPT is VND 50 billion (US$4 million).

The amount of funds to be lent by the VPSC to the NDAF is decided annually by the Ministry of Planning and Investment. The interest rate for loans is set by the Ministry of Finance, with the agreement of the VPSC and the NDAF based on the prevailing interest rate of government Treasury bonds with similar terms. Purchases of NDAF securities have increased fivefold between 2001 and the first quarter of 2002 (see Table 12.1: Mobilized Savings Transferred to the NDAF).

Starting in 2001, VPSC was also permitted to buy Government Bonds after fulfilling its predetermined commitments to the NDAF. These purchases provide the VPSC with extra liquidity and also serve as an investment reserve fund. If the VPSC should need cash, it can sell its holdings of Government Bonds in the securities market. Since the interest rate on Government Bonds is slightly higher than the negotiated interest rate paid by the NDAF, the purchase of Government Bonds provides the VPSC with a better return on its investment capital.

The VPSC has been restricted by the government to offer only interest rates for its products that are consistent with interest rates offered by banks and other financial institutions. At the same time, it is highly dependent on the interest it earns from its investment of funds in NDAF and Government Bonds. Therefore the interest the VPSC pays to its depositors is usually similar to interest rates offered by state-run commercial banks and somewhat lower than rates paid by non-bank financial institutions, such as rural credit cooperatives. For example, the People's Credit Cooperatives and Agricultural Bank take small savings deposits.

The government encourages financial institutions to set up payment service systems in order to reduce the amount of cash in circulation. In accord with this policy, the VPSC will provide payment services through an individual's postal savings accounts.

National Development Assistance Fund

The overwhelming majority of funds mobilized by the VPSC are deposited in the NDAF, a state financial institution chartered by the Prime Minister's Office for the medium- and long-term mobilization of funds. These funds are allocated in the form of development investment credits to implement state policy by the NDAF, which reports to the Ministry of Planning and Investment on projects it will fund. The credits are allocated to a wide

Table 12.1

Mobilized Savings Transferred to the NDAF
(in billion VND)

	1999	2000	2001	2002 (estimate)
Mobilized Funds (total):	634	2,561	3,802	5,600
Time Savings	627	2,523	3,736	
Collection Savings	7	38	66	
Transferred Funds (total):	475	1,205	1,500	1,700
1 Year	100	240	280	340
2 Years	200	240	380	340
3 Years	75	480	560	510
5 Years	100	245	280	510

range of economic development projects, including: infrastructure projects such as agricultural irrigation systems, highways, bridges, and airports; industrial projects such as food processing and forestry products, power plants, textile mills, ceramics, and woodworking; and short-term credits for promoting exports. Before supplying credits, the NDAF evaluates the economic and financial aspects of the proposed projects. Its major customers include both state-owned enterprises and small and medium-sized private enterprises that operate in agro-forestry-fishery processing, export goods production, transportation, and construction. The Ministry of Finance supervises the financial operations of the NDAF and receives credit guidance for the implementation of monetary policy from the State Bank of Vietnam.

The Growth of Postal Savings Operations

Service Implementation

When postal savings in Vietnam first began in August 1999, all bookkeeping tasks were processed manually at the post offices. The types of savings products offered and the level of service were frequently less attractive than competing services offered by commercial banks.

From 1999 to 2001 the postal savings system was limited to introducing only two basic products: Time Savings fixed-term deposits of three-, six-, twelve-, and twenty-four-month certificates, and Collection Savings monthly installment deposits of six-, twelve-, eighteen-, and twenty-four-month-term plans.

There are marked regional differences in the capacity to mobilize funds. The amount of funds mobilized from the northern provinces is much higher than that from the southern provinces and accounts for 81 percent of the total funds. This difference may be attributed to the fact that people in the northern provinces tend to be very thrift-conscious and prefer to put money into savings accounts in order to receive interest. People in the southern provinces tend to use their money more flexibly, for example, investing in projects, real estate, stocks, and the like. It is thought that savings services are better developed in the North and remittances services are better developed in the South. The task now for the VPSC is to diversify its services quickly in order to attract all types of people from both regions to use the postal savings system. This is being done by offering new products and increasing the customer's accessibility to his or her accounts through the computerization of the network.

At the end of 2001 the VPSC started to computerize post offices and prepare for the introduction of Ordinary Savings services. However, at that time the number of post offices equipped with computers was limited, and less than 100 of the 539 post offices offered computerized postal savings. As soon as the VPSC put the small-scale computer network into operation, it introduced Ordinary Savings (individual accounts) and remittance services through these branches (in 2002). Since these new services enable customers to access their accounts at different post offices to make deposits, withdrawals, and remittance payments, the new services are available only at those post offices equipped with the computerized system.

Although the State Bank of Vietnam audits the operations of the VPSC, including the new ordinary savings and remittance services, credit operations are not available pending a banking license, which the VPSC does not expect for at least another two years.

Assessment of Achievements and Limitations

Achievements

Although still in its first stages of development, based on the amount of funds transferred to the NDAF through the capital-mobilizing channels of the government, the postal savings system has proved to be highly effective (see Table 12.1: Mobilized Savings Transferred to the NDAF and Table 12.2: Business Results of the VPSC).

The savings services provided by the VPSC are highly appreciated by the government and its relevant ministries, including the Ministry of Finance, the Ministry of Planning and Investment, and the State Bank of Vietnam. The Vietnamese people have also demonstrated their trust and confidence in the

Table 12.2

Business Results of the VPSC (in billion VND)

Business Results	1999	2000	2001	First Quarter of 2002
Transferred to the NDAF	475.0	1,205.0	1,500.0	480.0
Government Bonds	0	0	12.0	20.0
Revenue	8.7	73.9	160.9	45.3
Expenses	9.8	66.3	154.2	43.4
Profit	−1.1	7.6	6.7	1.9

VPSC and postal savings services, with a sharp increase in the number of people opening postal savings accounts each year:

1999:	49,424
2000:	171,525
2001:	262,880
January–June 2002:	178,450

The above-mentioned results have mainly been achieved through two factors—the trust of the people in the service, and the convenience of postal savings. Postal savings services are provided with the objective of supporting the government's investment program, and the government guarantees all deposits in the system. This guarantee underlies public confidence in the postal savings service, making it a very successful enterprise in Vietnam.

Convenience of the service, for consumers, is based on the extensive postal savings network, which is wider than the branch networks of commercial banks. Postal savings post offices are located in all provinces of the country and are very well known and familiar to the public. Working hours at post offices are longer than those at bank branches: from 7 A.M. to 5 P.M., even to 7 P.M. at some post offices, compared to 7:30 A.M. to 4 P.M. at banks.

Limitations

Among the chief limitations of the postal savings system is that of the more than 3,500 post offices (7,130 if including all agency and cultural post offices), only 539 accepted savings deposits as of 2002. Expansion of the postal savings network is therefore essential and planned.

As of 31 December 2001, after two years of operations, postal savings accounted for approximately 5 percent of the total individual savings market. This represents more than 400,000 people saving their money in the system. The four state-owned commercial banks account for nearly 75 percent of individual savings accounts, and other banks and people's credit cooperatives account for the remaining 20 percent of savings accounts. Overall, the total number of savings accounts in Vietnam is still quite small, only some 10 percent of the country's 80 million people have one. The VPSC expects that the number of its depositors will more than double, to 813,000, by 2005. Other savings institutions in Vietnam, such as the People's Credit Cooperatives, have proven less successful in increasing their base of depositors.

As of 31 December 2001 the total mobilized funds were nearly VND 7,000 billion (US$570 million), while available money in people's pockets was estimated at around VND 50,000 billion (US$4 billion). This leaves a huge amount still to be mobilized. Surplus funds are also often held in U.S. dollars and competing in-kind savings, including gold. The VPSC plans to introduce U.S. dollar–denominated savings accounts as soon as the NDAF is allowed by the government to receive U.S. dollar funds for investment.

Other significant limitations, as mentioned earlier, include the manual operations of the system and the limited types of products offered. These tend to make postal savings facilities and products less attractive than those of commercial banks in urban areas.

Problems of a New Postal Savings Start-Up

After more than four years in operation, the Vietnam Postal Savings Service Company has encountered many difficulties. Among them, the VPSC has not been allowed to provide many banking services, particularly credit services. This is because the VPSC operates under a special decree issued by the Prime Minister's Office. As its activities are different from those of commercial banks, it cannot operate under the Law of Credit Organizations. A banking license is not expected in the near future.

The VPSC has also experienced some operational difficulties. The Ministry of Planning and Investment (MPI) decides the amount of funds to be transferred, and the Ministry of Finance decides the lending interest rates. As Vietnam is a developing country, it needs a huge amount of investment capital. The MPI is continually requesting the VPSC to transfer more money to the NDAF. As the postal savings funds are meant for investment in government-sponsored development projects, the Ministry of Finance wants the lending interest rate paid to the VPSC to be as low as possible. In practice, this approach creates difficulties for the VPSC. Although the interest rate the VPSC provides to its depositors is not the primary factor in encouraging savings, the VPSC must maintain an adequate spread between the rates it offers and the returns on its investments in order to sustain the profitability of its operations.

One of the aims of the VPSC in introducing postal savings services in Vietnam is to provide service in remote areas where bank branches are not available. After several years of operation this goal still has not been reached.

Although manual service is satisfactory for rural people, the VPSC wants to computerize the entire network. The postal savings network is currently just in provincial cities and towns and in districts (Vietnam has 10,538 districts with populations of at least 1,000 people). Postal savings is not yet available in remote areas due to its newness and a shortage of investment capital.

Another difficulty is the quality of service provided by VNPT staff, which is often very inexperienced. Particularly in remote areas, VNPT personnel still have a very poor knowledge of financial service procedures and need further training. To remedy this, VPSC training courses are being conducted and will continue whenever new products and services are introduced. Further investment is also required in equipment and facilities. An additional problem for the VPSC is its need to not only provide services in new areas but also to increase the level of security for post offices as well as its customers.

Development Plans

To maintain its achievements and address its problems, it is necessary for the VPSC to build a long-term master plan.

In the period between 2001–3 the VNPT invested about 75 billion VND (about US$6 million) to set up a small-scale postal savings computer network. The first stage, with VND 26 billion (nearly US$2 million) invested, includes two network computer processing centers in Hanoi and Ho Chi Minh City and one hundred post offices equipped with PC terminals, printers, and PIN pads that will enable customers to have direct access to their accounts. Relying on its own efforts, the VPSC computer network started operations at the end of 2002.

In the second stage, about VND 50 billion (nearly US$4 million) of the investment will be used to extend the network. Six hundred post offices throughout the country will be connected to VPSC computer centers. With the introduction of this network, in addition to savings plans, the VPSC will offer many other services, such as Ordinary Deposit accounts, payments, and remittance services.

By 2006 the VPSC is planning to replace its small-scale computer network with an online postal savings network and to transfer the small-scale equipment to remote areas. The limitations of the small-scale computer network restrict the VPSC from being able to provide services of many kinds, including point-of-sale VPSC debit cards, withdrawals at ATMs, receipts of electronic transfers, and agency services for payment of utility bills and paying out of social insurance from Ordinary Savings accounts as well as VPSC agency services on behalf of other financial institutions such as credit card companies.

With a more extensive online postal network, the VPSC would have the capability of introducing a greater variety of services and products, including integrated circuit cards ("stored-value cards") for non-cash payments at shops, supermarkets, restaurants, pay phones, and so on. It could also offer a broad range of electronic banking services through Internet banking, e-commerce, and telephone banking facilities. These added capabilities would also allow the designing and offering of a wider range of savings products with new features, such as automatic rollovers on maturity of Time Savings, scheduled withdrawal of interest income, partial withdrawal of interest and principal, extending the periods for Collection Savings accounts to five and fifteen years, and adding special-purpose Collection Savings accounts dedicated to education expenses and family housing construction.

With a more extensive online postal network, the VPSC forecasts that it will be able to increase its market share of savings and increase the number of its accounts to 2.8 million in 2006, and by 2010 to some 7 million accounts.

Conclusion

The introduction of a postal savings service in Vietnam is proving to be a sound decision by the government. Postal savings has mobilized a sizable sum for the government, which is very significant for a country like Vietnam that needs much capital investment. The service has been strongly encouraged by the people and has created the potential for all people to save money and by such means help stabilize their lives.

The postal savings service with its many good features will be further developed and made much stronger in Vietnam.

Concerning the Future

There will be some changes in the VNPT's organization in the near future when a Posts, Telecom, and Internet Ministry will be formed. The VNPT was designated by the government in 1992 as a "first economic group," charged with developing its own "powerful financial sources" in a variety of businesses with diversified subsidiaries within a holding company structure. Posts and Telecom will be split into two separate businesses under the new ministry, with postal savings remaining as a subsidiary unit of the posts. The VPSC expects to continue its role as a supplier of development funds to the NDAF.

13

The Philippine Postal Savings Bank, A Thrift Bank

Evangeline Felix-Racelis

Historical Origins

The Postal Savings Bank (PSB) was established on 24 May 1906, principally to provide facilities for the safe investment of savings, especially in the rural areas, and has operated profitably from its inception. At that time the Postal Savings Bank was a division of the Bureau of Posts. All post offices were, in fact, branches of the PSB in order to bring banking services to the rural areas.

The Japanese occupation in 1942–44 caused severe inflation and crippled the operations of the Postal Savings Bank; however, the ravages of war did not prevent the bank from regaining its growth and profitability. On 6 May 1946, the PSB resumed service in Manila with 15,737 savings accounts representing a total value of 4.1 million peso (P). Soon the PSB deposits grew to P14.4 million in 1947, to P25.0 million in 1948, and to P33.0 million in 1949. The PSB paved the way for more demand for banking services and opened up opportunities for the expansion of banking facilities.

The Postal Savings Bank offered the following services: (a) general savings deposit accounts including personal guardianship, parental, and society accounts; (b) special deposit accounts including firearm licensing guaranty deposits; (c) thrift stamps; and (d) home savings boxes. Deposits and withdrawals from general savings accounts and special deposit accounts were accepted at all Postal Savings Bank branches regardless of the bank of origin. The types of withdrawals were: (a) withdrawal by mail; (b) by telegraph; (c) by mail-telegraph; (d) by telegraph-mail; and (e) special withdrawal. The various options for withdrawal, including telecommunications-based processing, affords the Postal Savings Bank's clients the convenience of withdrawing from their own accounts from other branches. This option was not adopted by the private banking institutions until the advent of electronic money transfers, which essentially operate using the same principle. It can therefore be seen that the PSB had operational systems that offered better services to its clientele than private banks.

The operations of the Postal Savings Bank were under the supervision and guidance of the Director of Posts through a Superintendent of the Bank. A Chief Teller who furnished the bank's accounting records to the PSB's Accounting Officer and its Auditor assisted the Superintendent. On the other hand, all Postmasters managed the bank operations of their respective post offices. However, when the Central Bank introduced new requirements to "professionalize" and upgrade the qualifications of the people handling highly technical and specialized fields of banking services, it defined post office personnel as less qualified to handle banking matters under the new standards.

Operations of the PSB proved profitable until the proliferation of banks under market liberalization policies in the 1960s and 1970s, which brought the PSB into competition with the private banks. The sudden growth of an aggressive private banking sector, especially in provincial areas, led many clients to transfer to privately owned banks, which at first offered much higher interest rates. The bigger privatized banks were better capitalized and had higher-yielding investment outlets than smaller ones. As a result of this competition, the financial condition of the PSB and the physical condition of the post offices deteriorated due to the reduced revenues and deposits. The poor physical condition of the post offices following wartime destruction could not be redressed. Then President Ferdinand Marcos, by Presidential Decree, ordered the complete discontinuance of operations of the PSB in January 1973, effective within three years. The PSB had deposits of P111.9 million when it was finally phased out in 1976.

Creation and Functions of Philpost

On 3 April 1992 the Philippines' national postal system was transformed from a regular government bureau, dependent on budgetary allocations from the national government, into an income-generating and self-reliant Government-Owned and Controlled Corporation (GOCC)—the Philippine Postal Corporation or Philpost. The corporation, which is capitalized at P10.0 billion, is attached to the Department of Transportation and Communications for purposes of policy coordination.

As a GOCC wholly owned by the government, Philpost was mandated as follows:

1. To operate a nationwide postal system with a network that extends at least ordinary mail service to every settlement in the country;
2. To provide for the collection, handling, transportation, delivery, for-

warding, returning, and holding of mails, parcels, and like materials throughout the Philippines and to and from foreign countries.

Its corporatization gave the national postal service the much-needed financial and management flexibility to immediately address problems inherent in a bureau-type organization. However, it no longer receives budgetary allocations or subsidies from the national government and has had to generate enough revenue or outsource funds to finance its operations.

The Philippine Postal Corporation is a profitably operating corporation, professionally managed and run by a corps of committed personnel, providing the highest quality and widest range of postal services to meet customers' needs in all areas of the country and throughout the world. Philpost is governed by its Board of Directors. The total manpower complement of the corporation is 17,102.

Among its objectives are:

1. To enable the economical and speedy transfer of mail and other postal matters.
2. To provide a wide range of postal services to different users and meet their changing needs, including the transfer of monies and the like.
3. To ensure that sufficient revenues are generated by Philpost to finance the overall cost of providing the varied range of postal and delivery services and for the expansion and continuous upgrading of service standards.

Philpost and the PostalBank

In 1992, when the Philippine Postal Corporation (Philpost) was created by Republic Act 7354, the act provided in its creation the mandate to reopen the Postal Savings Bank. The law specifically provided Philpost the power to "offer services such as the postal savings bank" (Section 6) and "in the event that the corporation decides to reactivate or reopen the Postal Savings Bank after ascertaining its financial viability and in response to the public clamor, it shall reopen such services without, as much as practicable, unduly competing with rural, commercial or universal banks" (Section 32).

On 21 July 1994 the Philippine Postal Savings Bank, Inc. (PostalBank) was born. The bank was opened in response to popular demand to provide banking services, to promote entrepreneurship, and to widen economic opportunities in the countryside. Its vision is to offer substantial contributions to nation-building through savings mobilization, and to support entrepreneurship in the countryside by extending credit facilities in those marginalized areas of the economy.

The PostalBank was reopened with P1.0 billion of capital, and was authorized to issue 1 million shares of common stock with a par value of P100.00 per share. Subscribed shares now amount to P500 million, of which P300 million was paid by Philpost while P200 million remains receivable from Philpost.

The bank is mandated by its Articles of Incorporation and bylaws to borrow funds for its operational requirements. Being a government entity, the PostalBank may request the financial assistance of the Congress of the Philippines to strengthen its operations by way of legislation or fund allocation.

The PostalBank mission statement says it shall:

1. Be a strong, dynamic national institution that will mobilize savings and promote entrepreneurship to widen economic opportunities.
2. Provide the Filipino people with a full range of professional banking and financial services accessible in all areas of the country, and promote the values of thrift, industry, and prudence, especially among youth.

Objectives and Constraints

The following are the objectives of the bank:

1. Provide the best possible rate of return to the Filipino saver.
2. Raise domestic savings to new levels and enable the country to lessen its dependence on foreign borrowings.
3. Be the vehicle for the efficient delivery of countryside credit and provide financial investment to widen economic opportunities.
4. Enhance the level of awareness among youth about the benefits of thrift and industry as crucial elements to national self-reliance and independence.

In accordance with the national policy to "develop the rural financial sector to ensure adequate supply of credit to the countryside," the PostalBank aims primarily to deliver banking services to all Filipinos, particularly those in the countryside. The goal of the PostalBank is to reach out to even the most remote rural areas where there are no banks and provide them with the necessary services.

An obvious way to provide such services is through the postal network. Philpost has a total of 2,917 post offices nationwide, broken down as follows:

Post Offices	1,898
Postal Stations	29
Barangay (hamlet) Post Offices	932
Private Mailing Centers	58

However, the Central Bank, the Bangko Sentral ng Pilipinas (BSP), had prohibited the PostalBank from using the postal network, including its post offices and counter personnel. The BSP's grounds are stated in Circular No. 268, Series of 2000: "Sec. 2.1 No bank or any director, officer, employee, or agent thereof shall outsource inherent banking functions (nor) shall refer to any contract between the bank and a service provider for the latter supplies, the manpower to service the deposit transactions of the former."

Not being able to utilize the existing postal network has been a severe handicap for the PostalBank in expanding small savings. At the moment its bank branches are restricted to fourteen regional branches, separate from the post office buildings and unable to currently access the postal network's post offices in far-flung rural areas.

The Head Office of the PostalBank is located in Manila, and its fourteen branches/servicing units are strategically located around the country (see Figure 13.1: Geographical Distribution of PPSB Branches). Of the fourteen PostalBank branches, nine branches and the Head Office in Manila are located on their own exclusive premises. This includes the Naga, Baguio, Dagupan, Malolos, Tuguegarao, Cagayan de Oro, Tacloban, Asingan, and Legazpi branches.

In this situation, the PostalBank is working to reach outside its branch locations via correspondent banking arrangements with rural banks, since it is still prohibited by Central Bank regulations from utilizing the post office network. Should the use of the postal network be approved, the PostalBank would implement a "hub and spokes" arrangement whereby its urban centers will be the "hub" to serve as control centers with the rural post offices and rural banks as the "spokes" or outlets to service the rural networks via a correspondent banking arrangement.

Operating and Marketing Strategies

As a bank that encourages small savers who would not likely be served by the big banks, the PostalBank has offered special rates to small saver clients. For example, while other private banks gave only 2 percent interest rate per annum on savings deposits, the PostalBank offered 4 percent to its private depositors. the PostalBank could offer the higher rate because it is also a government depository bank, and mandatory government deposits receive lower rates than

Figure 13.1   **Geographical Distribution of PPSB Branches, PPC Post Offices, and Rural Banks**

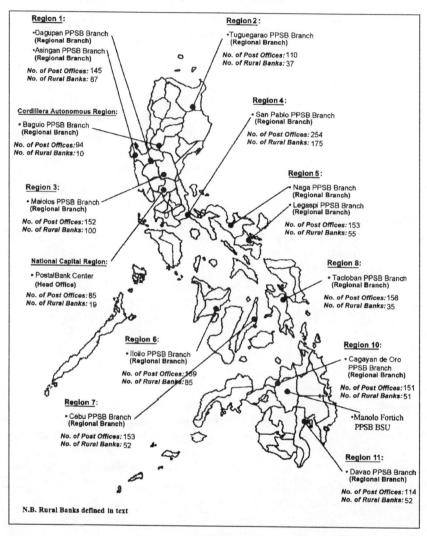

N.B. Rural Banks defined in text

private deposits. Since 80 percent of the bank's total deposits are low-cost government accounts, the spread (the difference between interest income and expense) that the bank derives enables it to give better rates of return to private savers—the small savers. In addition, the bank's accreditation as a Government Securities dealer allows the PostalBank reasonable investment returns while at the same time it can offer its clients interest rates on some types of accounts that are much higher than the 4 percent regular savings rates.

In order to realize its objective to raise domestic savings and minimize the nation's dependence on foreign borrowing, the PostalBank diligently encourages all its branches, through a program of targeted goals, to promote deposits. With more deposits, the bank has greater opportunity to invest in loans and in government securities.

As an efficient vehicle for countryside credit, 75 percent of the funds (less reserves) generated by PostalBank from its regional branches are invested in the same region as a means to develop that region. Loans are extended to local government units (LGUs) to finance revenue-generating projects that will be beneficial to the local populace (e.g., public markets, sports complexes, equipment, etc.). Such financial investments in the form of projects or programs for the constituents widen the economic opportunities of the region. This benefits investing in the region by enabling loan beneficiaries to earn income from the projects while at the same time these projects become vehicles for economic development in the local area.

The PostalBank also supports campaigns among schoolchildren to promote the values of thrift and industry. It introduced the "thrift stamps savings account" program whereby the bank, in coordination with the Department of Education, Culture, and Sports, makes visits to various elementary and secondary schools to introduce the product and encourage schoolchildren, with the assistance of teachers, to save a portion of their allowance money. For every P5.00, the children can buy one thrift stamp at the nearest post office or any authorized dealer. The stamp is pasted in a Thrift Stampbook. When one hundred stamps have been collected, the children then bring the stampbook to the nearest PostalBank office for deposit. With this method, children are taught the value of thrift and the rewards of saving for the future. The bank has also sponsored "piggy bank" contests whereby the artistic talents of schoolchildren in making various designs of savings containers are harnessed, and the artistically made piggy banks increase their interest in saving.

The Competitive Environment

The PostalBank, as a depository bank, does not compete directly with commercial banks and their subsidiaries. However, the PostalBank's rates are within savings bank market rates, and at one time the rates offered by the savings subsidiaries of big commercial banks were higher due to the greater diversified (and riskier) investment activities of these banks. Since the last quarter of 2001, however, both deposit and lending rates have gone down enormously. Although the PostalBank was constrained to reduce its interest rates twice, nonetheless, the present 2.5 percent interest rate on *regular deposits* of the PostalBank is still higher than the prevailing 1.0 to 2.0 percent rate of commercial and other

Table 13.1

Philippine Bank Rate Structure (as of September 2002)

	PPSB	Other Thrift Banks	Commercial Banks
Regular Savings Deposits			
Private	2.5%	1% to 2%	1% to 2%
Government	1.5%	—	1% to 2%
Lending Rates			
Prime	12%	11% to 17%	6% to 9%
Non-prime	14%	11% to 21%	9% to 13%

thrift banks. Table 13.1: Philippine Bank Rate Structure, illustrates the prevailing Philippine bank rate structure as of September 2002.

While smaller banks embark on limited forms of investments due to lower capitalization and scope of authority, bigger banks like the commercial banks and universal banks can diversify investments in trust activities, foreign exchange dealing, big volume trading, and money market activities, equities, credit card business, and so on.

The safety of deposits, however, is an important factor in the public's confidence in the PostalBank. The Philippine Deposit Insurance Corporation guarantees all bank deposits per depositor up to P100,000. Even so, when the year 2000 witnessed bank mergers and scandals that implicated some big banks, the PostalBank experienced an inflow of deposits coming from accounts formerly held at commercial banks. At the height of the impeachment controversy involving the then president of the republic, deposits poured in, not because of the interest rate offered by the PostalBank, but because of the public confidence in the security afforded deposits at the Postalbank, especially with the high reserve requirements that the PostalBank must maintain in government securities as a government depository bank. Both political and socioeconomic factors greatly affect the shifting or movement of deposits. The primary concern of depositors is the safety of their deposits. In times of economic difficulties, ordinary banks experience a huge outflow of deposits whereas the PostalBank shows an inflow.

Organizational Structure of PostalBank

Organizational Setup

As noted above, the PostalBank is established and operated as a wholly owned subsidiary of Philpost. The bank is an Authorized Depository of the Republic of the Philippines, and it is autonomously managed and governed by its own Board of Directors. The management of its operations rests with it own officers, a President and a Chief Executive Officer. Three Vice Presidents as well as Department and Branch Managers assist the President.

The bank has its own Corporate Treasurer, Assistant Corporate Treasurer, Corporate Secretary, Assistant Corporate Secretary, Internal Auditor, Legal Counsel, and Comptroller. The Internal Auditor likewise serves as the Compliance Officer, who is primarily responsible for the oversight function of the organization. It has a total manpower complement of 186 officers and rank and file nationwide.

Although the PostalBank and the Philpost maintain separate infrastructures, they both work hand in hand to complement each other's services, utilizing the post office network to the extent permissible, particularly in remittance services. However, as of 2004, post offices are still prohibited from performing any banking function such as deposit-taking and withdrawals.

Financial Highlights

As of the end of 1994 (six months after opening), total resources of the PostalBank stood at P332.2 million. By 2000, total resources had soared to P1,845.9 billion, a 456 percent increase.

By the end of 2000, the PostalBank had generated deposits of P1,047.7 billion. Government deposits of P808.8 million accounted for 77 percent of the total deposits, with the P238.9 million balance coming from private depositors. Continuing its support of countryside development, the bank has extended P553.5 million in loans.

At the end of the year, outstanding investment in bonds and other debt instruments (IBODI), consisting mainly of treasury bills and fixed-rate treasury notes and interbank placements, stood at P475.5 million.

Total revenues of the bank registered P199.2 million in 2000, with the major source being the interest on loans of P115.7 million. Interest paid to depositors amounted to P52.3 million, with a weighted average rate of interest on deposits of 4.992 percent. Net income before taxes was P48.8 million.

Products and Services

Effective marketing strategies are indispensable tools in Philippine banking culture, considering the stiff competition in the industry. Promoting deposits and generating loans are dependent, to a large extent, on the individual bank's marketing strategies. Interest rates on deposits, loans, and terms are factors that attract customers. Although there are no restrictions as to maximum account sizes, minimum deposits are required for each type of account to be opened (income on deposits and investments are subject to a 20 percent withholding tax).

Among the products and services of the PostalBank are the following:

Time Deposits: Deposits of specific amounts for a fixed term given at a predetermined competitive rate. The minimum amount accepted for placement is P1,000 with a flexible payment term from 30 to 360 days. Although the deposit remains with the bank for the chosen term, interest earnings are computed according to the terms and conditions of payment, either monthly, quarterly, semiannually, annually, or upon maturity. A documentary stamp tax fee of P0.30 for every P200 is charged for time deposits.

Premium Savings Accounts: A minimum deposit placement of P100,000 earns slightly higher rates that are free of the documentary stamp tax. It also offers flexible placement terms from 30 to 360 days and can earn a higher interest rate depending on the amount of placement.

Savings Deposits: The bank accepts a minimum deposit of P100 from private depositors to open an account; a minimum balance of P500 earns interest of 2.5 percent per annum, which is, as already noted, higher than other banks, and is posted quarterly. For government depositors, a P1,000 initial deposit and minimum balance is required, which pays an interest rate of 1.5 percent per annum, computed quarterly.

Demand/Current Accounts: Offered in addition to regular checking or on-demand accounts, which are non–interest bearing. An initial deposit and minimum balance of P5,000 is required of private depositors; P15,000 is required from government entities.

Interest-Bearing Current Accounts: Special checking or demand accounts that earn a specified interest rate depending on the volume of deposits.

Automatic Transfer Accounts: A combined savings and current account. Deposits are maintained under the savings account, which is interest-bearing. Once the depositor issues a check, the corresponding amount is automatically transferred from the savings account of the depositor to a non-interest-bearing current account and is paid out. Interest income to the depositor is maximized since only the exact amount of check issuance is transferred to the current account. Initial deposit and minimum balances is P5,000 for private account-holders, and P15,000 for government-held accounts, both with interest posted quarterly.

Thrift Stamp Savings Accounts: As noted above, the Thrift Stamp Program is a national savings awareness program aimed to promote thrift and encourage savings consciousness among youth. Students, mostly those in elementary and high school, can buy thrift stamps at the nearest post offices or from authorized sellers of Philpost. Thrift stamps in five-peso denominations may be purchased and pasted in Thrift Stampbooks. A collection of one hundred stamps, valued at P500, can then be credited to the holder's account at the PostalBank.

Special Remittance Services (S-PRES): This is a special remittance service involving the payment of remittances to a specific payee or beneficiary residing in the Philippines or in a foreign country with which the PostalBank has a correspondent banking relationship. This service provides for the issuance and fast delivery of S-PRES checks or via electronic fund transfers. These checks can be cashed at any post office nearest the beneficiary, and at any PostalBank branch, or other banks' branches as well (see Figure 13.2 for schematic flowchart of its operations).

Safe Deposit Facilities: Safe deposit boxes are available at the Head Office of the PostalBank in Manila at a minimum rental of P200 per annum plus a refundable deposit of P650.

Collecting Agent of Social Security System (SSS): the PostalBank is the collecting agent of the Pensioner's Bank Remittance Program's monthly contributions of premiums and loan amortizations.

Collecting Agent of Philippine Health Insurance Corporation (Philhealth): Collecting medical care premiums of both private and government sector employees and workers.

Payroll Servicing Program: This service is available at any office or agency.

Loans to Small and Medium Enterprises (LSME): Extended to any business activity or enterprise engaged in industry, business, and/or service, whether individual, sole proprietorship, cooperative, partnership, or corporation; loans to be used for acquisition of fixed assets, passenger trucks, and other fixed assets, credit lines, trading operations, building improvement/ expansion, construction of plant activities, or for permanent working capital. Some 14.5 percent of loans in the bank's net loan portfolio (P470.6 million, 31 December 2000) was to small enterprises, and another 10 percent went to medium-size enterprises.

Large-Scale Enterprises Loans (LSEL): Available to any business activity or enterprise engaged in land development, building, housing, construction, industrial, manufacturing, and/or service, whether individual, sole proprietorship, cooperative, partnership, or corporation.

Financial Assistance to Government and Private Employees (FAGPE): Financing program designed to provide credit to government and registered private institutions, for example, educational, medical, and so on.

Government Securities Dealership: The bank buys and sells to the public marketable securities such as treasury bills, treasury notes, and treasury bonds as instruments for providing alternative investment outlets to clients in addition to traditional deposits. The Bureau of Treasury auctions these government securities every week with terms of 91, 182, and 364 days. Rates are determined through the bids tendered at auction by accredited banks and are influenced to a large extent by prevailing market forces.

238 ASIAN COUNTRY CASE STUDIES

Figure 13.2 **PPSB IRS (International Remittance Service) Flowchart**

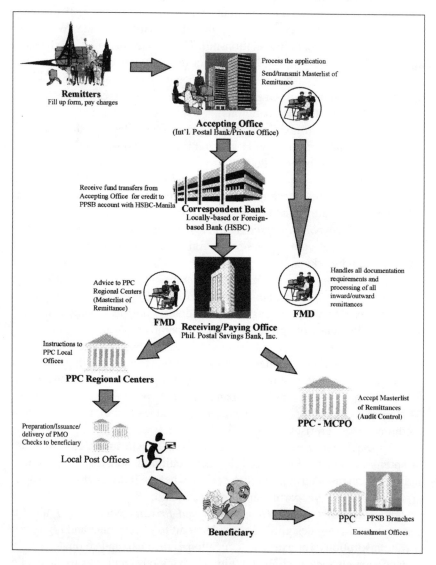

Discontinued products:

Super Savings Plan: Double Your Money Account: For a minimum of a P10,000 deposit, the amount doubled to P20,000 in five years, tax-free, if continuously maintained. Effectively, the Super Savings Plan cost 20 percent per annum to the bank. This product was a good source of long-term deposits to close the maturity gap between deposits and liabilities. It has been a very popular product offered by most banks. Nevertheless, with the downward trend in interest rates lately, banks have stopped offering this high-cost product. The PostalBank ceased offering this product in 1999.

Services for Overseas Filipino Workers

Overseas Filipino Workers (OFWs) are a good source of fee-based income from international remittances. As much as possible, the bank anticipates having an association with international organizations, such as the UPU remittance system, in order to improve its fee-based revenues and to provide high quality and efficient service to OFWs (see again Figure 13.2).

OFW Family Club: The PostalBank and the Overseas Filipino Workers (OFW) Family Club have planned to cobrand a PostalCash Card that will function as an ATM card and provide support for the banking and financial service needs of OFWs.

Electronic Postal Money Orders (ePMO): offered by the PostalBank and affiliated countryside banks, these are also expected to facilitate the inward and outward remittance of funds, especially from OFWs. The PostalBank's 14 regional branches and 2,000 post offices and postal stations, along with more than 1,900 Rural Bank branches, plan to utilize a state-of-the-art secured Internet and electronic card system network. Recipients will have multiple options for receiving cash—through points of sale (POS), Postal Money Orders, S-PRES Remittance checks, or via affiliated Rural Banks.

In 2002 a Memorandum of Agreement (MoA) was signed with a Canadian-based payment system, Ciphercom Network Corporation, to provide international money remittance businesses in the United States and Canada facilities for funds transfer to the Philippines through the PostalCash Card to be issued by the PostalBank. In 2002, the PostalBank had agreements for inbound/outbound remittances with Caixa Economica Postal De Macau, Singapore Post, and Chew Eu Hock Holdings Ltd. (CEH), a private company in Singapore. There were also preliminary negotiations with the Greek Post Office Savings Bank, Global Money Transfers, and Western Union.

As with the other remittance service providers, the PostalBank aims for an efficient and fast delivery of money to its local beneficiaries. The PostalBank lacks a nationwide online computer ATM system. Therefore, in remote areas where there are no PostalBank branches, there is a special arrangement with Philpost for the delivery of S-PRES checks (special remittance checks) using the Express Mail Service. (The MoA with international remittance service foreign counterparts is a tripartite agreement between the PostalBank, Philpost, and the foreign counterpart.)

As the preceding has involved peso payments, the PostalBank has sought the authority to operate a Foreign Currency Deposit Unit (FCDU). It is the intention that with the activation of its FCDU operations, the PostalBank would be able to trade (buy and sell) U.S. dollars, and invest as well as accept U.S. dollar deposits. The bank has requested FCDU status in anticipation of the forthcoming signing of MoAs with international remittance services. However, all Thrift Banks have been hit by an increased capitalization requirement of P650 million to qualify for FCDU operations.

Therefore, inbound foreign currency remittances are presently deposited by the PostalBank with correspondent banks. For example, HSBC is a correspondent bank with the PostalBank whose primary role is limited to receipt of incoming dollars (U.S. and Singapore dollars) for credit to the account of the PostalBank. Should the Postalbank need to unload its dollar deposits, HSBC facilitates the transfer of funds through its Hexagon software. HSBC also assists the PostalBank in providing letters of credit to valued Postalbank clients, since the bank does not have this product yet.

Proposed New Products and Services

For better efficiency and a wider product base that will serve those who are without a big bank's services, the PostalBank envisions offering the following products and services in the future:

Individual Housing Loans (IHL): To be available to employed or self-employed individuals for the purchase of a lot, construction of a residential unit or a home, or expansion and/or renovation.

Home Savings Boxes Programs: The issuance or sale at all post offices of metal savings boxes wherein coins and notes are held until the accumulated amount is deposited in the box-holder's savings account.

The POSTeller: In order to revolutionize countryside banking, the PostalBank intends to introduce its own ATM card, POSTeller, to boost customer service and bring "big bank" convenience to small depositors nationwide. POSTeller is to be used for payment and withdrawal of ordinary deposits, acceptance of salary, pensions, payments, fund transfers, automatic payment of public utility charges, and credit card payments. In addition to ordinary deposit-backed accounts, POSTeller will be linked to time deposit accounts as collateral for providing cash overdraft facilities.

Tax Collecting Agent: To be authorized by the Bureau of Internal Revenue.

Trust and Underwriting Operations: The PostalBank is seeking to undertake in all of its regional banking centers (RBCs) and branch servicing units (BSUs) the following securities operations:

Trustee: for individuals or corporations.

Underwriting Bonds: as financial advisers for bond flotation of qualified corporations as well as local government units.

Underwriting IPOs of Selected Corporations: as a participating financial institution (PFI) of selected corporations and to engage in selective blue-chip trading in the Philippine Stock Exchange.

Letters of Credit: to generate service income, the PostalBank plans to issue domestic letters of credit. It is also seeking to enter into agreements with selected commercial banks that will guarantee and process import letters of credit.

Collecting Agent Services for Private Companies: such as water and electric utilities, credit card companies, and so on.

Human Resource Development

To ensure the efficiency of its personnel, training programs for different levels are being conducted. Topics include: management, negotiable instruments, loans, credit, and treasury operations. Qualified personnel are likewise allowed by the PostalBank to attend seminars, workshops, and training programs conducted by other banking institutions and regulatory bodies.

Management of Assets and Liabilities

Deposit Liabilities and Reserves

All deposits generated by the PostalBank from both the government and the private sector are managed by the Head Office through its Treasury Department. After compliance with all the required reserves prescribed by the Bangko Sentral ng Pilipinas, the bank's funds are invested in government securities or the interbank market, or loaned out to qualified borrowers.

Strict compliance with reserve requirements on deposits assures that funds will be available as needed. The bank manages its funds to strike a balance between liquidity and income. At no instance should liquidity suffer in exchange for yield. Investments and loans are the main sources of the bank's income. Investments in government securities require the approval of authorized signatories as specified in its Codified Approving and Signing Authorities (CASA).

The types of reserves, liquidity requirements, and loan policies mandated by the BSP are as follows:

Legal Reserves: 10 percent of total deposit liabilities must be set aside as reserve compliance in the form of short-term government securities (Circular 10), cash-in-vault, and deposits with the Bank's Demand Deposit Account with the Bangko Sentral ng Pilipinas.

Trust Reserve: comes in the form of (a) deposits for the faithful performance of trust and other fiduciary business, and (b) reserves of 10 percent for common trust funds.

Liquidity Floor: requires thrift banks to maintain 50 percent of total government deposits in the form of short-term government securities.

The funds of PostalBank are deposited in its Demand Deposit Account (DDA) maintained with the Bangko Sentral ng Pilipinas from where check disbursements are charged. All transactions in interbank and sale/purchase of government securities are carried out through automatic debits/credits from this account. Interbank transactions are done through computer terminals using the Multi-transaction Interbank Payment System (MIPS), an online system that links all accredited banks with the Central Bank (BSP) and the clearinghouse (PCHC).

Loan Policy Mandates

Loan-to-Deposit Ratio: requires that 75 percent of total net deposits (less the required reserves) that are sourced from outside the National Capital Region be invested in the same region as a means to develop that region.

Magna Carta for Small Business: requires that 10 percent of net lending funds be loans to small businesses. Small business is defined as an enterprise with capitalization of less than P10 million (after deducting the value of the real estate assets).

Agri-Agra: 25 percent of lending funds must be allocated for agricultural credit, with at least 10 percent of those loan funds available for agrarian credit. Agrarian borrowers are small-scale farmers who have tilled and occupied the lands that they farm for a very long time. This qualifies them to be beneficiaries of agrarian reform, which entitles them to the portion of the farm lot that they are tilling.

Investment and Loan Portfolio Disbursements

As of 31 December 2000, P38,122,994 (US$719,302) of Agrarian Reform Loans (Agri-Agra) had been disbursed. Agricultural credit refers to loans intended to finance activities relating to agriculture and the processing, marketing, storage, and distribution of agricultural products. In the absence of qualified borrowers, the amount set aside may be invested temporarily in acceptable government securities. The PostalBank's portfolio of financial investments as of 31 December 2000 was:

Government Securities	P362,451,759	76%
InterBank Call Loans	P113,000,000	24%

Table 13.2

Schedule of Loan Portfolio (as of 31 December 2000)

As to Type of Borrowers	Amount	Percentage
I. Government		
• City, Provincial, and Municipal	12,544,000	2
• Central Bank of the Philippines	113,000,000	15
• Philpost Leasing & Financing Corp.	20,074,000	3
II. Private Residents of the Philippines		
• Individuals	423,616,000	58
• Companies/Groups	158,053,000	22
Total	727,287,000	100
As to Economic Activity		
Agriculture, Hunting, and Forestry	60,662,000	8.34
Fishing	215,000	0.03
Manufacturing	9,779,000	1.34
Electricity, Gas, and Water	280,000	0.04
Construction	20,317,000	2.79
Wholesale and Retail Trade, Repair of Motor Vehicles, Motorcycles, and Personal and Household Goods	40,018,000	5.50
Transport, Storage, and Communications	1,085,000	0.015
Financial Intermediation	133,414,000	18.34
Real Estate, Renting, and Business Activities	100,976,000	13.88
Education	50,000	0.01
Other Community, Social, and Personal Service Activities	302,084,000	41.54
Private Households with Employed Persons	58,407,000	8.03
Total	727,287,000	100

The PostalBank also maintains a diversified loan portfolio as to type and activity of borrowers (see Table 13.2: Schedule of Loan Portfolio).

Governance Procedures for Loans

The PostalBank's credit facilities are managed through its loan department. Loan funds of the bank are lent to qualified borrowers in various ways such as consumption loans, agricultural loans, real estate loans, or loans to small and medium-size enterprises (SMEs) in support of rural development.

Loan approval is required as follows:

Up to P50,000, by a Manager
Up to P500,000, by Vice president of Operations Group
Up to P5,000,000, by the President
Over P5,000,000, by the Board of Directors

The bank employs the following procedures in qualifying loans.

The bank appraiser must prepare an inspection and appraisal report that includes a physical inspection of the real estate and chattel offered as collateral, a measurement survey of the premises, a description of the land and neighborhood, market survey data, and a valuation summary providing appraisal and loan values of the property.

The loan value should be no more than 60 percent of the appraised value. The bank reviews comparative appraisals presented by other banks, together with supporting documents, for cross-verification of the appraised value or the written statement of the official who furnished the data. If the bank makes the loan, the collateral, including real estate and chattel, must be insured in favor of the PPSB. The maximum loan amounts (principal plus interest) relative to the collateral are:

1. Peso deposits—100 percent;
2. Actively traded government securities—90 percent of market value;
3. Mortgage on real estate situated in prime locations—70 percent of appraised value;
4. Listed and actively traded equity securities (except speculative stocks)—50 percent of market value;
5. Chattel mortgage on machinery/equipment/inventory or assignment of receivables—50 percent of cost, if brand-new, and from 30–40 percent of cost for secondhand.

The PostalBank in the Philippine Banking System

Physical Composition

The PostalBank, a thrift bank, functions within the Philippines' sizable banking system, which encompasses the following categories of banking institutions (see Table 13.3: The Philippine Banking System).

1. *Commercial Banks*
1.1. Expanded Commercial Banks

Table 13.3

The Philippine Banking System (as of 31 December 2001)

Type of Banks	Total Offices	Head Office	Other Offices
Total	7,585	929	6,656
1. Commercial Banks	4,320	44	4,276
Expanded Commercial Banks	3,575	15	3,560
Non-expanded Commercial Banks	538	11	527
Government Expanded	418	3	415
Foreign Banks	207	18	189
2. Thrift Banks	1,351	104	1,247
3. Rural Banks	1,914	781	1,133

1.1a. Domestic Banks
1.1b. Branches of Foreign-Owned Banks
1.2. Non-expanded Commercial Banks
1.2a. Domestic Banks
1.2b. Subsidiaries of Foreign-Owned Banks
1.2c. Branches of Foreign-Owned Banks

2. Thrift Banks
The term Thrift Bank encompasses the PostalBank as well as savings and mortgage banks, mutual savings and loan associations, and private development banks. A Thrift Bank is authorized to engage in any or all of the following transactions: (1) granting loans, whether secured or unsecured; (2) investing in readily marketable bonds and other debt securities, including commercial paper, accounts receivable, and other notes arising out of commercial transactions; (3) issuing domestic letters of credit; (4) extending credit facilities to private and government employees; (5) extending credit against the security of jewelry, precious stones, and articles of similar nature; (6) accepting savings and time deposits; (7) rediscounting paper of government-owned or -controlled corporations; (8) accepting foreign currency deposits; (9) acting as correspondent for other financial institutions; (10) purchasing, holding, and conveying real estate under the same conditions as commercial banks.

With prior approval of the Monetary Board, Thrift Banks may also perform the following services: (1) open checking and NOW accounts; (2) engage in trust, quasi-banking functions, and money market operations; (3) act as collection agent for government entities, including the Bureau of Internal Revenue, Social Security system, and Bureau of Customs; (4) act as official depository of national agencies and of municipal, city, or provincial funds in the municipality, city, or province where the Thrift Bank is located; (5) issue

Table 13.4

Regional Distribution of Banking System with Balance Sheet Accounts (as of 31 December 1999) (in million pesos)

Region No.	Name	Commercial Banks			Thrift Banks			Rural Banks		
		Resources	Loans	Deposits	Resources	Loans	Deposits	Resources	Loans	Deposits
	NCR-Metro Manila	1,462.86	635.35	641.32	411.87	182.89	170.31	55.35	16.45	19.06
I	Ilocos	191.92	52.51	182.91	73.60	37.15	48.40	28.03	11.92	12.93
II	Cagayan Valley	194.49	79.41	160.95	59.18	19.09	51.27	27.49	13.35	10.13
III	Central Luzon	218.10	68.90	186.33	82.14	37.86	56.85	34.68	15.18	16.41
IV	Southern Tagalog	205.28	54.83	178.06	69.45	19.41	51.18	37.58	16.87	19.56
V	Bicol	185.63	64.07	156.19	57.93	23.38	43.76	33.82	13.53	15.01
VI	Western Visayas	207.50	72.32	176.93	69.31	34.43	43.37	25.18	8.45	9.07
VII	Central Visayas	370.46	162.47	287.21	170.31	46.24	132.35	31.35	12.03	15.56

	Region									
VIII	Eastern Visayas	172.31	54.10	148.90	89.25	17.25	80.88	19.31	6.84	5.67
IX	Western Mindanao	223.32	58.53	196.10	57.38	9.38	52.38	33.21	13.50	8.88
X	Northern Mindanao	256.72	145.25	170.41	100.54	43.72	32.18	34.99	13.68	10.41
XI	Southern Mindanao	239.48	114.88	164.20	111.59	61.48	56.00	23.15	8.99	10.52
XII	Central Mindanao	180.95	79.58	147.03	82.50	24.00	65.00	28.55	11.14	10.03
XIII	CAR	252.63	34.94	245.19	142.20	22.40	122.70	28.39	7.44	11.75
XIV	ARMM	162.89	38.97	148.11	126.00	0.50	122.50	13.33	(0.33)	0.67
XV	CARAGA	176.58	74.83	152.20	73.56	40.89	35.11	17.71	7.92	7.35
	Highest	1,462.86	635.35	641.32	411.87	182.89	170.31	55.35	16.45	19.06
	Lowest	162.89	34.94	147.03	57.38	0.50	32.18	13.33	(0.33)	0.67
	National Average (excluding Metro Manila)	231.30	82.50	192.90	97.50	31.20	71.00	29.80	11.50	11.70

mortgage and chattel mortgage certificates and deal in them on behalf its own account or on behalf of others, and receive them in payment for loans; (6) invest in the equity of allied undertakings.

3. Rural Banks

Rural Banks are organized essentially to extend loans and advances primarily for the purpose of meeting the normal credit needs of farmers, fishermen of farm families, cooperatives, merchants, and private and public employees. Like any other bank, a Rural Bank can establish savings, time, and NOW accounts. It can also accept current or checking accounts provided that it has net assets of at least P5 million. What distinguishes Rural Banks from Thrift Banks are the lower capitalization requirements, which are P32 million in Metro Manila for Rural Banks as compared to P400 million required of Thrift Banks and range as low as P3.2 million to P8 million for Rural Banks in smaller municipalities and large cities as compared to the P64 million required of Thrift Banks outside the Metro Manila area. See Table 13.4: Regional Distribution of Banking System with Balance Sheet Accounts, and Table 13.5: Savings and Mortgage Banks' Selected Indicators.

Competition between Private and Public Sectors

Generally speaking, the private sector has a wide array of banks to choose from. However, the public sector is allowed to deposit its funds or working capital in only four government banks duly accredited by the Department of Finance: Landbank of the Philippines, Development Bank of the Philippines, Philippine National Bank, and the PostalBank. As an accredited government depository bank, the bulk of the PostalBank's deposits are public funds.

The role of the PostalBank in the banking system is not to compete with established big banks but rather to complement and provide service to underserved sectors, particularly small savers and borrowers. Nationally, by the end of March 2000 there were 21 offices for savings and mortgage banks and 83 offices for commercial banks. At present, the PostalBank's network consists of 15 branch offices all over the country, including its Head Office in Manila. If the PostalBank, however, were able to utilize the Philpost network, it would then be able to reach even the remotest rural areas in the country.

As to operations, while the PostalBank caters to the needs of the small saver and offers for the most part regular bank products and services, commercial banks have the capability, technical facilities, and extensive networks to offer a wider range of banking services. But because of their size, commercial banks are slanted toward serving larger clients in the banking industry. Small depositors and entrepreneurs are left to banks like the PostalBank.

Table 13.5

Savings and Mortgage Banks' (SMB) Selected Indicators (as of 30 June 2000)

	Total	Average	Postal Bank Rank	Share of Total in %
No. of Authorized SMBs	29.00			
No. of Branches	725.00	25.00	12	2.07
Assets	130.56	4.50	16	0.91
Loans	68.22	2.35	19	0.63
Liabilities	105.08	3.62	12	1.02
Deposits	95.18	3.28	10	0.98
Capital	24.88	0.86	27	0.67

	Industry Average	PPSB Actual
ROA (as of March 2000)	0.7%	1.01%
ROE (as of March 2000)	2.9%	4.43%

Source: Chamber of Thrift Banks

Both market forces and the government have encouraged a sizable number of Philippine commercial banks to merge. Mergers are expected to broaden the range of financial services that banks can offer their customers and strengthen their capital base. The recent merger wave in the Philippine banking system was instigated primarily by: (a) the need to maintain competitiveness, and (b) to comply with increasing capitalization requirements imposed by the Bangko Sentral ng Pilipinas (BSP), which also affects the thrift banks (see Table 13.6: Minimum Capital Requirements).

In the context of financial market liberalization and the onset of globalization, the rules of competition have changed in a way that requires the PostalBank to expand its range of bank products offered domestically and internationally as a strategy to ensure its survival. To further improve the operations of both the PostalBank and Philpost, both organizations are looking at modernization of their services for better efficiency. This may be possible through a number of options such as mobilization of internally generated funds, or strategic partnerships and privatization.

In Conclusion

Strengths and Weaknesses of the PostalBank

Since 2000, the PostalBank has consistently been operating profitably. However, the growth of the bank also has been constrained by an inadequate

Table 13.6

Minimum Capital Requirements (in billions of pesos)

Type of Bank	12/24/98	12/31/99	12/31/2000
Expanded Commercial Banks	4.50 b	4.95 b	5.40 b
Commercial Banks	2.00 b	2.40 b	2.80 b
Thrift Banks: (in millions of pesos)			
With Head Office in Metro Manila	250 m	325 m	400 m
With Head Office Outside Metro Manila	—	52 m	64 m

electronic banking system, a limited number of international remittance service partners, and its inability to fully use the Philpost network due to legal restrictions.

The PostalBank's strong points include its role as an accredited government depository bank and the future potential use of the Philpost network. As a government depository bank, the PostalBank is assured of a ready clientele; with the Philpost network, it would be able to reach rural areas where no big commercial banks find it profitable to go.

The PostalBank hopes to tap the existing postal facilities and establish Branch Servicing Units (BSUs) in post offices. This would give the bank the potential of becoming more cost effective compared to other banks, which need greater capital outlays to establish new branches. The PostalBank has received a favorable response from the Central Bank (the BSP) concerning the opening of three BSUs and now awaits its final approval from the Monetary Board. The bank's plan, subject to approval, further envisions a wider network of 98 BSUs in selected areas by 2005.

The PostalBank would then have a strategic advantage in establishing a banking presence in areas deemed unprofitable by other banks, by its potential of utilizing the 2,917 post offices throughout the country. Today, more than seven hundred small-sized municipalities have no banking facilities and consequently lack the availability of credit facilities for enterprise activities in many areas. The PostalBank will thus become a welcome service to the non-banking poor in economically depressed areas.

Authors' Biographical Notes

Mark J. Scher initiated and led the Postal Savings for Development Project on behalf of the United Nations Department of Economic and Social Affairs (UN-DESA), where he was Economic Affairs Officer in the Finance and Development Branch. He is now the Director of Postal Financial Services Development, (scher@postalsavings.org) and works with savings institutions and postal administrations to promote savings and international remittances through the postal infrastructure.

Previously, Dr. Scher was in the International Economic Relations Branch of the Development Policy Analysis Division of UN-DESA where he was responsible for monitoring and analyzing economic, trade, and financial developments in Japan, and was Senior Research Fellow and New York liaison with the U.S. financial community for the Institute for Financial Affairs of Japan (Kinzai), a non-profit educational and research organization supported by the Japanese financial community. He is also the former publisher of *Japan Financial Market Report*, a weekly publication of analysis of Japanese economic and financial developments.

He was Visiting Professor at Keio University, and a former Professor of International Business and Management at New York University Stern School of Business. He has also taught international business, international trade and financial management at Baruch College of CUNY, University of Bridgeport MBA and Pace University MBA programs.

Dr. Scher has over 35 years' professional and business experience in Asia. He is the author of *Japanese Interfirm Networks and Their Main Banks* (London and New York: Macmillan Press/St. Martin's Press, 1997), *Mainbank shinwa no hokai* (Collapse of the Main Bank Myth) (Tokyo: Toyo Keizai Shinposha,1998), and is the author of numerous articles and chapters in books. He received his PhD from the Manchester School of Business and Management, University of Manchester (U.K.).

Naoyuki Yoshino is Professor of Economics at Keio University. He is Director of the Financial Research and Training Center of the Financial Services Agency and serves on several senior government councils, including the Foreign Exchange Council and the Fiscal Council, Ministry of Finance; the Postal Council, Ministry of General Affairs; and the Prime Minister's Cabinet Office Committee on the Privatization of Postal Savings.

Professor Yoshino received his doctorate from Johns Hopkins University in 1979, an honorary doctorate from Gothenburg University, Sweden in 2004, an M.A. and B.A. in Economics from Tohoku University. He was a Visiting Scholar at the Institute of Fiscal Research, Ministry of Finance, as well as at the Institute of Monetary and Economic Studies of the Bank of Japan, and is a former Fulbright Scholar.

Biographical Notes
Country Case Study Authors

Anil Bhattacharya is Head of the National Savings Organisation of India, having worked at the national level in the field of resource mobilization for 20 years. He has published and presented numerous papers on such topics as "Mobilisation of Savings," "Payment Systems," and "Micro Finance" in different national and international conferences and workshops. He did his post-graduate studies in Administrative Management at Jamnalal Bajaj Institute of Management, Mumbai (India) and also received a M.Sc. in Finance from Strathclyde Business School, Glasgow, U.K.

Cao Thi Hoai Duc is Deputy Director of the Vietnam Postal Savings Service Company (VPSC). She joined the Vietnam Post and Telecommunication Corporation in 1994 and has worked for the VPSC since its inception in 1999. Mrs. Duc continues to manage many postal savings projects, as well as supervise the implementation of investment projects, and design and manage postal savings products. She is a graduate of Vietnam's Foreign Language College and Vietnam Economic University.

Serikzhan Mambetalin at the time of the writing of this book was Director of the Operational Department and Deputy Director General of Kazpost. He received his M.D. degree from Aktobe State Medical Institute, and after two years of scientific work at the Research Institute in Almaty, he enrolled in the first MBA program at the Kazakhstan Institute of Management. After receiving his MBA, he worked as economic adviser to the Trade Representative of Kazakhstan in France. He then joined the World Bank Resident Mission in Kazakhstan as an economist, supervising agricultural, environmental, and medical projects. He then was asked to serve as Director of the Operational Department and Deputy Director General to implement financial services at the State Post Organization known as "Kazpost." Currently Dr. Mambetalin works in London for an international company.

Chan Ki Nam is Dean of the School of Business at the Information and Communications University, Daejon, Korea. He worked at the Korea Information Society and Development Institute from 1988 to 2000, where he was engaged in research related to strategic management of post and telecommunications. Professor Nam received his B.S. degree in management from Seoul National University, Seoul, Korea in 1978, and a Ph.D. degree in business administration (finance) from Georgia State University, Atlanta, Georgia in 1988.

Eastman Narangoda is the General Manager/CEO of the National Savings Bank of Sri Lanka. He joined the National Savings Bank in 1975 as an executive officer and has held many positions including assistant general manager for postal banking and Deputy General Manager for Operations and Marketing. His academic credentials include a Bachelor of Arts Special Degree in Economics (Banking and Currency), University of Ceylon, Peradeniya; Diploma in Business Management, UK; Diploma in Advanced Bank Management, Stockholm; a Fellowship of the Institute of Management Specialists, UK; and a Fellowship of the Sri Lanka Institute of Training and Development. He is a member of the Board of Governors of the Institute of Bankers of Sri Lanka; Vice President of the Association of Professional Bankers of Sri Lanka; a Director of the NSB, Fund Management Company; Director and Vice Chairman of Financial Ombudsman (Sri Lanka) Ltd.

Jaeseog Park has been a research member with the Korea Information Society and Development Institute since 1985. His current research areas include electronic banking and strategic management in post and telecommunications. Dr. Park received a B.S. degree in management from Yeoungnam University, Daegu, Korea in 1981, and a MBA in business administration (finance) from Pusan National University, Pusan in 1985.

Peng Min'an served as director of the International Business Department of the Postal Savings and Remittance Bureau, State Post Bureau, P.R. China. Dr. Peng obtained a master's degree of laws at Beijing University in 1994 and a doctoral degree in economics in the graduate department of the China Academy of Social Science in 1999. He has worked as teacher at the senior high school in He'nan Province and as an economist at Zhengzhou Trade House of Future Goods.

Evangeline Felix-Racelis at the time of the writing of this book was Manager of the Treasury Department and concurrently Assistant Corporate Treasurer of the PostalBank (1995-2003), and represented PostalBank in several international venues. Prior to her present position as Chief of Investment at the Treasury Department of Philippine Health Insurance Corporation, which she has held since January 2003, she has worked in various other positions at the Bureau of the Treasury (1981–1995). Her academic credentials include a master's in management in public administration and a Ph.D. in development administration. She is a part-time professor at the Philippine Christian University teaching Managerial Accounting, Financial Management, Public Fiscal Administration, Local Fiscal Administration and Theories and Practice in Public Administration.

Ashok Pal Singh, at the writing of this book, was the Director of the Post Office Savings Bank (1999-2003) and was responsible for the diversification of financial services. He has also worked as Private Secretary to the Minister of Communications of Government of India, where he was associated with deregulation and liberalization of the Indian Telecommunications Sector, and with the Ministry of Social Justice and Empowerment of the Government of India, where he initiated the National Child Helpline Project, the National Policy for Older Persons, and the Government's privately managed pension program. Mr. Singh is currently working as a Director in the Ministry of Health and Family Welfare of Government of India.

Dhirendra Swarup is the permanent Secretary of the Department of Expenditure and Budget, Ministry of Finance, Government of India. He has extensive varied experience of more than 35 years, primarily in public finance, budgeting, accounting and finance expenditure management. Mr. Swarup reports to the Finance Minister and is responsible for the policy regarding public expenditure. This covers such matters such as market borrowing, accounting standards, small savings, and the preparation of the Union Budget. He is the Chairman of the Public Investment Board of the Government of India and the Government nominee on the Boards of the largest mutual fund of India, the Unit Trust of India, the Capital Markets Regulator, and the Securities and Exchange Board of India.

Index

A

Africa, 23, 25, 28, 44, 55
Agency relationships with posts, 5, 6, 9, 12, 16–17, 42, 62–64, 71; China, 80; Rep. Korea 106, 117–20; Japan, 144; India, 157–58, 167–68, 176–77; Sri Lanka, 186–95; Kazakhstan, 201–2, 204, 209; Vietnam 224; Philippines, 237, 241
Agricultural Bank of China, 88
Agricultural credit, 41, 43, 69, 71, 88, 96, 219, 242–43
Alliance & Leicester (giro, U.K.), 46
Aloqabank (Uzbekistan), 31
Asian financial crisis 1997 & postal savings, 10, 82, 100, 123
Austria, 22, 23, 32, 42
  model postal savings & giro, 56
Automatic teller machine (ATM), 19, 27, 44, 65, 88, 91, 132, 134, 176–79, 197, 217, 224, 239–40
  See also technology

B

Banamex (Mexico), 27
Banco Santander (Spain), 27
Bangko Sentral ng Pilipinas (Central Bank, Philippines), 228, 231, 241–42, 249–50
Bangladesh, 8, 55, 57, 62, 72
Bank of Agricultural Credit (Rep. Korea), 70, 93
Bank of Japan (central), 33, 65, 131
Bank of Mongolia (central), 70

Banks and commercial banking strategy, 4, 5, 16, 41–44, 47, 50–53, 56, 60–62, 64–66, 71–72; China, 76, 82; Rep. Korea, 96, 109–15; Japan, 121, 130–35, 142–43; Sri Lanka 187–89, 197–98; Kazakhstan, 204, 205–6; Vietnam, 213; Philippines, 233–34, 244–49
Banking system crisis
  Czech Republic, 49–50
  Finland, 43
  Indonesia, 14, 50
  Japan 11, 33, 64–66, 121, 130–31
  Kazakhstan, 204
  Rep. of Korea, 50, 100, 109–15
  Philippines, 14, 50, 234
  Sri Lanka, 197
  Thailand, 14
  Vietnam, 13, 50, 213
BAWAG (bank, Austira), 42
BBVA (bank, Spain), 27
Belgium, 6, 51
Bital, Grupo Financiero, (Mexico) 27
Brazil, 23, 28

C

Cash cards, 19, 88, 178, 225
  See also technology
Chaebol (Korean conglomerates), 109
China, 6, 7, 8, 10, 19, 28, 32, 56, 57, 59, 70, 72–73, 76, 123
  "big four" State-owned banks, 10, 59, 92
  See also country case study, 79–92
    history & development, 79–84

255

256 INDEX

China
  See also country case study *(continued)*
  organizational structure & operations, 84–8
  deposit base & institutional capacity, 88–92
China Post
  revenues 7
  reestablishment of postal savings 10, 56, 59
China Postal Savings & Remittance Bureau, 10, 59, 70
Citibank, 27, 50
Credit facilities & postal savings, 3–4, 16, 17–18, 59, 69–71
  postbanks, 41
  Philippines, 14, 242–44
  See also agricultural credit; micro-credit
Central banks, 6, 71, 73
  See also by countries and names of banks
Československá Obchodní Banka (Czech), 49
Commonwealth of Independent State (CIS), 18, 23, 31, 56, 57, 59–60
  See also transition economies
Cross-subsidization, private sector cross-selling. See subsidization
Czech Republic, 49–50

D

DBS Bank (Singapore), 61–62
Deregulation. See market liberalization
Deutsche Post A.G., 28–9, 34, 35, 51–53, 62
Deutsche Postbank, 32, 51–53, 62
Deutsche Telecom, 30
Developing economies
  financial markets, 9, 75
  market liberalization, 8, 20, 31, 50, 57
    loss of postal savings, 8, 16, 19–20, 228
  overseas worker remittances, 8, 19, 57, 71–73
  savings, 3–4, 23, 36, 40, 57, 73
    financial technology, 66–69
  See also transition economies
Development banks, 6, 10, 33, 73, 126–27
  See also by countries and name

DHL Courier Service, 34
Dinero Seguro (Safe Money), 27

E

Economic and social development
  goals, 73–5, 96
  infrastructure, 6, 10, 18, 73, 95–96, 123, 213–14, 219–20
  policy reforms, 14–19, 28
  & postal savings, 73–75, 95–96, 219
  self-sufficiency, 3, 20, 214
  Japan, 4, 10, 123–30
    inflation fighting, 74, 124–25
    pump-priming, 74, 124–25
    stabilizing financial markets, 74–75, 124–25
Electronic money orders. See Money Orders & transfers
Erste Bank (Austria), 50
Eurogiro, 28
European Bank for Reconstruction & Development (EBRD), 31
European Commission, 29, 32
European Union, 29–30, 35
Express Mail Service (EMS), 35, 239

F

Federal Express, 34–35
Financial exclusion, 8, 16, 20
  loss of services in developed countries, Finland & Sweden 42–46; Japan 122, 134; Singapore, 61–62; United Kingdom, 46–49
  developing economies, China, 84; India 175; Vietnam 223; Philippines 250
Financial markets
  developing economies, 9, 75
Financial Services Authority (U.K.), 47
Finca microfinance (Mexico), 18
Finnish Bankers Association, 45
Finland, 36, 43–46, 53, 65, 136
Fiscal Investment and Loan Program (FILP, Japan), 11, 74–75, 126–30
  & financial markets, 75

France, 6, 29, 34, 52, 123
  colonial model postal savings, giro, 8, 22, 55
France Telecom, 30
Foreign currency exchange, 5, 13, 72–73, 177, 208, 240
Fortis (financial group Belgium-Netherlands), 51

G

Geopost (France, et al.) 34
Germany, 6, 23, 28–29, 32, 39, 41, 51–53
Giro accounts and postal checking, 5, 19, 22–23, 25, 28, 46–47, 52
  history 21–22
  survey, 36, 38
  technology, 68–69
  universal postal giro proposed, 19
Governance of posts, 15–17, 36–41, 228–29
  models, 15, 39–41
Government bonds
  investment, 5, 33, 46, 73–75, 95, 128–30, 242–43
Great Britain. *See* United Kingdom

H

Halyk Bank (Kazakhstan), 56, 60, 200, 206
Hapsburg empire. *See* Austria
Hashimoto Ryuichi, 135, 144
Hellenic Post, 35
Hokkaido Takushoku Bank (Japan), 33
Hong Kong (S.A.R. China), 6, 72
Household Finance International, 27
Households, 4, 65, 97, 121–22, 125–26, 148–49
Housing
  sponsored, 95
  mortgages, 6, 41, 71, 75, 248–49
HSBC (bank), 27
Hungary, 24, 50

I

India, 6, 8, 70, 75
  National Sample Survey Organization, 150, 153
  National Savings Organization, 11–12, 55, 57, 58, 62, 64, 147–65
  sales agents, 11, 58, 150–52
  Post Office Savings Bank, 12, 55, 58, 62, 64, 156, 167–81
  State governments, 11, 58
  See also India country case study
    chapters and appendix, 147–62, 163–65, 167–81
  NSO's origins & the demographics of household savings, 147–49
  savings plan design, promotion & sales agent outreach, 149–156
  utilization of the postal network, 156–59
  management of savings assets & liabilities, 159–60
  sales agents training program, 160–61
  public sector savings vs. private sector banks, 160–62
  savings plans offered through POSB, 163–65
  origins & organization of POSB, 167–68
  scale and scope of postal savings operations, 168–72
  technology & marketing of savings products, 172–75
  expansion of postal financial services, 175–81
Indonesia, 6, 50, 56, 71
Industrial development, 4, 6, 10, 16, 18, 123, 213, 219–20
ING Barings Bank, 39, 51
ING Postbank, 52
Interest rates, 3, 18, 59, 60; China 87–88; Japan, 141; Rep. Korea, 99, 102; India, 73, 156, 159, 161–65, 169, 175; Kazakhstan, 60, 204, Vietnam, 219, 223; Philippines 231–34

International donor assistance, 16, 213
International Financial Systems, 68
International giro, remittances. *See*
  Overseas remittances
International Monetary Fund, 50, 109–10, 114
International Money Orders. *See* Money Orders
Internet & postal banking, 44, 48, 225
  See also technology
Investční a Postovní Banka (Czech), 49
Investment, postal saving funds:
  consumer credit, 75
  government bonds, 5, 34, 46, 73–75, 129–31, 206–7, 242–43
  financial market risk, 73–75, 114–17
  Japan, 74–75, 139–41
  management 114–17, 137–41, 158–59, 206–7, 215–16, 241–44
  publics funds, 5, 10, 73, 95
  policy-based financial institutions, 5, 10, 33 73, 95, 102–3, 126–28, 242
  See also Asian country case study chapters; development banks, national development funds
Iran, 9, 58
Iraq, 57
Italy, 34

J

Japan, 4, 6, 10–11, 25, 28, 33, 57, 71–72, 76
  banking crisis, 11, 24, 33, 64–66, 123, 127–28, 130–31
  culture of savings, 123–24, 141–42
  colonial model postal savings, 8, 23, 56
  main bank system & household savings, 66, 125, 132–33
  military, 123
  policy-based financial institutions, 126–27
  postal savings & economic policy, 11, 56, 74–75, 121–22
  savings deposits, big-six banks, 65
  taxation, 124, 131

Japan *(continued)*
  See also Japan country case study, 121–45
  origins & development of postal savings, 121–24
  intermediating savings for development, 124–30
  commercial banks vs. postal savings, 130–35
  postal reform & investment policy, 135–41
  depositors' confidence & politics of privatization, 141–44
Japan Development Bank, 126–27

K

Kazakhstan, 6, 7, 8, 12–13, 31, 36, 50, 55, 59–60, 71
  linkage of remittance and payments to savings, 8–9, 57, 60, 72–73, 201–6, 208
  financial technology, 68, 203–4, 210–11
  See also Kazakhstan country case study, 199–211
  origins & organization of Kazpost, 199–203
  establishment of postal savings & payments, 203–6
  intermediation of postal savings, 206–8
  foreign exchange, brokerage & agency services, 208–9
  human resource development, 209–10
  technology development, 210–11

Kazpost, 59–60, 72–73, 199–211
KBC (bank, Belgium), 50
Keio University workshops, 3, 9, 20, 57
Koizumi Junichiro, 121, 135–38, 144
Korea, Republic of, 6, 7, 8, 10, 19, 28, 31, 50, 57, 70–72
  establishment of postal savings, 10
  1997 financial crisis, 10, 24, 109–20
  market liberalization, 10
Korean Postal Service, 70

INDEX 259

Korea, Republic of *(continued)*
See also Korea country case study chapters, 93–107, 109–20
role & structure of postal savings system, 93–98
postal savings accounts & products, 98–102
investment & regulation of funds, 102–5
human resource & technology development 105–6
financial crisis & role of postal banking, 109–117
developing postal savings in the post-crisis era, 117–20
KPN (Netherlands), 30
Kreditanstalt fur Wiederaufbau (KfW), 33, 39

L

La Poste (France), 52
Landesbanks (Germany), 32–33
Lebanon, 57
Leonia Bank (Finland), 44
Long-Term Credit Bank (Japan), 33
Latin America & Carribean, 23, 26
Low-income populations, 4–5, 15, 16, 43–49, 62, 122

M

Maeshima Hisoka, 122, 143
Malaysia, 6, 9, 24, 55, 57, 60–63, 75
Market liberalization, globalization & deregulation services, 28–36, 92, 161, 249
loss of services, financial exclusion, 8, 15, 16, 20, 28, 41–49, 65
mail & parcel delivery, 34–35, 51–52, 198
policy reform, 14–19, 30, 41, 103–5, 109–15, 117–119, 122, 198
postal savings, 7–8, 19, 57, 104
closure in Indonesia, 50, Rep. Korea, 7, 93, Philippines, 14, 228
establishment Kazakhstan, Vietnam, 7, 12, 13, 200, 203–4

Market liberalization, globalization & deregulation services
postal savings *(continued)*
governance, 8
re-establishment postal savings Rep. Korea, Philippines, 7, 14, 93, 229–30, 249
transition economies, 8, 13, 49–50, 56
Matsukata Masayoshi, 124
Mediterranean Partnership Agreement (European Union), 34
Merita Bank (Finland), 45
Mexico, 18, 26, 27–28, 72
Microcredit, microfinance 4, 18, 71
See also credit
Ministries of agriculture, 71
Ministries of commerce, 71
Ministries of finance, 6, 71; Rep. Korea, 103–6; Japan, 124, 126, 128–30; India, 148, 150, 167–68, 173, 175; Kazakhstan 201, 207; Vietnam, 219–21, 223
See also by countries
Ministries of Housing, 71
Ministry of Information & Communication (Rep. Korea), 70, 93, 103–6
Ministry of Planning and Investment (Vietnam), 219, 221, 223
Money Orders & transfers, 26, 52, 68–69, 90, 133, 217
See also remittances, postal money orders
Moneygram, 26, 68
Mongolia, 6
State Posts, 70
Empire, 21
Morocco, 6, 18, 67
Mortgage lending. See housing

N

National Bank of Kazakhstan (central), 201, 207
National Savings Agency (U.K.), 46–47
National savings banks, institutions, 6, 18, 55, 57, 60–64

National savings banks, institutions (*continued*)
  Germany, 32–34
  Japan, 33–34
  Kazakhstan, 13, 60, 200, 206
  Malaysia, 60–61, 75
  postal savings model, 9, 12, 62–64
  Sri Lanka, 12, 57, 60–64, 75, 183–98
  United Kingdom, 46
National Development Assistance Fund (Vietnam), 13, 216, 219–22, 225
National development funds, 10, 73, 95
National Savings Organization (Institute, India), 58, 62, 64, 76, 147–65
National savings organization model, 8, 9, 11–12, 18, 55, 57
Nehru, Pandit Jawaharlal, 147
Netherlands, 6, 24, 29, 34, 39, 52
  colonies, 22, 55–56
Netherlands Middenstandsbank, 52
Netherlands Post, 51–53
New Zealand, 29, 36
Niger, 24
Nippon Credit Bank (Japan), 33
Nomura Investment Bank (Japan), 50
Norway, 36
Non-performing loans. *See* banking crisis
Nordbanken (Sweden), 45
Nordea Bank, 26, 45

O

OKOBank (Finland), 45–46
Ottoman Empire, 56, 123
Overseas migrant workers, 7, 19, 25–28, 71–73
  Philippines, 14, 72–73, 239–40
Overseas remittances, 4–5, 6, 7, 18, 19, 22, 25–28, 57, 68–69, 176, 184, 208
  Philpost, 14, 237–40
  economic development, 25–26, 71–73
  reducing costs, 8

P

Parcel delivery services, 34–35
  See also individual carrier companies by name

Parcelforce (U.K.), 46
Pakistan, 71
Payments
  pension & social benefits, 5, 45–47, 51–53
  CIS countries, 18, 51–52, 57
  Kazakhstan, 13, 57, 60, 200–1, 205–6, 208–9
  & savings, 18, 48, 57, 59–60, 65–66, 72–3, 174, 208
  taxes & fees, 5, 47
  utilities, 5, 66, 217, 224
  See also giro, money orders, postal checking, overseas remittances
People's Bank of China (central), 56, 59, 71, 74
People's Committees (China), 70
Philippines, 6, 7, 9, 13–14, 24, 50, 57, 71
  Postalbank 8, 14, 58
  See also Philippine country case study, 227–250
    origins of Philippine Postal Savings Bank, 227–28
    creation of Philpost & PostalBank, 228–31
    marketing & competitive environment, 231–34
    PostalBank's organizational structure, 234–35
    products & services, 235–39
    Overseas Filipino Workers services, 239–40
    proposed new products & services, 240–41
    management of assets & liabilities, 241–44
    PostalBank & Philippine banking system, 244–50
Portugal, 55
Posbank (Indonesia), 50
POSBank (Singapore), 61–62
Post and Kreditbanken (Sweden), 45
PostalBank (Philippines), 8, 14, 58, 227–50
Postbank (Hungary), 50
Postbank model of postal savings, 9, 13, 16, 17, 24, 41–46, 57

INDEX   261

Postbank model of postal savings
    (*continued*)
  Asia, 57–58
  China, proposed, 74, 91
  credit, 41, 45
  franchise fees, 42–45, 53, 64
  governance, 74
  Japan, proposed, 137
  ownership, 41–43, 52–53
  postal network, 42–44, 52–53
  Philippines, 227–50
  privatization, 42, 49–53
  strategy, 43
  regulatory environment 16, 41, 74
Postipankki (Finland) 43–46
Postsparkasse (Austria), 32, 42
Policy objectives & proposals, 4–5, 14–19, 30, 34, 39–41, 45–46, 53, 73–74, 95–96, 109–20
Post Office Savings Bank model, 9, 55, 60
  India, 11–12, 58, 64, 157–60, 167–81
Post Office Counters (U.K.), 46
Post offices, 6
  China, 59
  cultural post offices (Vietnam), 13, 214–15
  Czech Republic, 49
  Finland & Sweden, 42–45, 62, 136
  Hungary, 50
  India, 58, 64, 157–58
  Japan, 65, 122–23, 134–35
  Kazakhstan, 59–60, 202–3
  Malaysia, 61–63
  Singapore, 61–62
  Sri Lanka, 61–64
  U.K. 46–8
  Vietnam, 214–5, 222
  See also Asian country case study chapters
Postal checking. *See* giro systems
Postal life insurance, 5, 51, 65, 132–3
Postal Life Insurance Welfare corporation (Japan), 75

Posts
  agency agreements with financial institutions, 5, 6, 9, 12, 16–7, 42, 62–64, 71; China, 80; Rep. Korea 106, 117–20; Japan, 144; India, 157–58, 167–68, 176–77; Sri Lanka, 186–95; Kazakhstan, 201–2 204, 209; Vietnam 224; Philippines, 237, 241
  economic viability, 6, 7, 15–17, 35–36, 39–40, 47–48, 199–200
  fiscal analysis, 15–17, 39–40
  governance models, 15, 36–41
    government department, 39
    government-owned corporation, 16, 39–40, 121, 135, 228–29
  history, 21–22, 55
    privatized, 16–17, 21, 28–36, 40–41, 47, 121–22
  letter & parcel delivery, 7, 35–36, 135–36, 201
  market liberalization, 8, 19–20
  monopoly status, 8, 28–29, 35, 136–37
  network, 5, 6, 12, 15, 21–22, 28, 35–36, 41–42, 47–53, 58, 60–64; China 82; Rep. Korea, 106, 119; Japan, 122–23, 132; India, 150, 157–58, 167–69; Sri Lanka, 187–89; Kazakhstan, 202–3; Vietnam, 214–15; Philippines, 230–31
  India Post, 12
  Vietnam cultural post offices, 13, 214–15
  policy reforms, 14–19, 39–41, 121–22, 135–37
  postbank ownership, 16–17, 41–46, 49–53, 62, 91, 229–30
  privatization, 7, 16–17, 20, 40–41, 46–47, 52, 121–22, 135–37
    and cross-border acquisitions, 8, 19–20, 28–29, 34–35
  politics, 143–44
  rates, postal, 16, 36, 39–40, 136
  regulatory framework, 40–41, 199–202
  revenues & finances, 6, 7, 8, 15–16, 35–36, 39–40, 41–43, 63–64, 88, 200

262   INDEX

Posts *(continued)*
  socio-economic asset, 16, 40, 41–42, 121–22
  social mandate, 5, 6, 16, 40, 122, 199
  subsidies, 6, 8, 15–16, 28–29, 36, 40
  universal service obligation, 5, 8, 132, 136, 228–29
  See also under individual countries; Asian country case study chapters
Postal savings
  Asian models, 57–62
  & banks (commercial) 4, 25, 41, 46–47, 58, 59, 69, 106, 109–15, 121, 130–35, 161, 169–72, 195, 205–6, 213, 228, 231–4
  community works & savings, 73, 233
  confidence, 24–25, 65–66, 73–74, 88, 141–42, 149, 221–22, 234
  & credit services, 17–18, 41, 57, 69–71, 171
  economic development, 10, 20, 73–74, 122–30, 219–20
  foreign acquisition, 57
  foreign currency accounts, 60, 73, 205, 223
  funds investment & development 5, 8, 10, 34, 57, 58, 73–75; Rep. Korea, 95–96; Japan, 124–30, 137–41; India, 159–60, 168; Sri Lanka, 184–85; Kazakhstan, 206–8; Vietnam, 219–20
  governance, 14, 158–59
  history, 21, 55–57
  in-kind savers, 69, 122, 184, 223
  interest rates, 59, 60; China 87; Japan, 141; Rep. Korea, 99, 102; India, 73, 156, 159, 161–65, 169, 175; Kazakhstan, 60, 204, Vietnam, 219, 223; Philippines 231–34
  management, 52–53, 57–64, 215–19
  marketing 17, 57, 62–64, 69–71, 173–75
  microcredits, 69–71
  online systems, 67–68, 225, 239, 249–50
  & private sector 4, 8, 10, 16–17, 25, 28, 31, 47–53, 57, 62, 64–66, 69, 71; Rep. Korea, 105–6, 119–20; Japan 121–22, 130–37, 142–43

Postal savings
  & private sector *(continued)*
    Philippines, 14, 57, 228–29
    See also postbanks, privatization
  partnerships, 57, 62–64, 69–71, 106, 119–20
  & postbanks, 41–53, 57, 62, 64
  product & services development 57, 58, 65–66, 69–71, 155–57, 163–65, 173–75, 187–88, 235–41
    agricultural businesses, 69
    civil servants, 69
    households, 69, 99, 101
    in-kind savers, 69, 84
    industrial workers, 69, 99, 163–64
    overseas workers, 69, 72–73, 164, 239–40
    professionals, 69, 163–64
    religious laws (Shari'a), 69
    repurchase agreements (RPs), 98, 101–2
    salaried workers, 69, 99
    savings thrift stamps, 66, 124, 227, 233, 236
    small businesses, 69, 163–4
    small-scale farmers, 69–71, 149, 154, 164–65, 174
    tax-exempt, 69, 76, 133, 155–56, 162–65, 175, 205, 238
    women, 69, 150–51, 174; *See also* postal financial services
    youths and students, 69, 152, 208
  public ownership 4, 15, 16–17, 62–66
    households and individuals 4, 65–66, 97, 106, 121–24
  religious laws (Shari'a), 69
  revenues, 59, 222
  rural areas, 57, 58, 59, 62–3, 65, 69–71, China, 83–84; Rep. Korea, 96–97, 120; Japan, 122–23, 134–35; India, 150, 152–53 169–72; Sri Lanka, 189; Kazakhstan; 201, Vietnam, 224; Philippines, 233
    credit cooperatives, 59, 70–71, 219, 223
  safety, 8, 65–66, 222

Postal savings *(continued)*
　savings promotion, 17, 57, 58, 62–64,
　　69–71; China, 80, 88–89; India,
　　122–23, 124, 152, 173–5; Sri
　　Lanka 188–95; Kazakhstan, 203,
　　Vietnam, 220–21; Philippines 233
　social mandate, 6, 16–17, 69
　survey, worldwide 36–38
　technology, utilization; *See also*
　　technology
　youth & students, 69, 99, 188, 201, 208,
　　233
　See also Asian country case study
　　chapters
Postal savings bureau model, 8, 9, 10, 57
Postal Financial Services
　defined 4–5
　fiscal analysis, 15–16
　foreign currency exchange, 177, 208
　giro and postal checking 5, 19, 46–47,
　　133, 142
　life insurance, 142, 180
　low-income populations, 4–5, 15, 17,
　　20, 28, 46–49
　market analysis, 9, 69
　management & scope of operations,
　　6–7, 8, 168–72
　pension plans, 140–41, 164
　private sector opportunities, 50–52, 176
　payments & savings, 18, 48, 57, 59–60,
　　65–66, 72–73, 174, 208
　　CIS countries, 18, 72
　　synergies, 19
　product development, 8, 9, 11, 65–68,
　　176–81
　policy proposals 4–5, 6, 14–19, 75,
　　117–20
　postal network, 133–35; *See also* postal
　　savings
　synergies, 42–43, 52–53, 69–71, 132
　research on, 6
　remittances 4–5, 6, 7, 8, 21, 68–69,
　　71–73, 176–79, 208–9, 237
　rural populations, 4–5, 11–12, 13,
　　15–16, 17–18, 20, 41–42, 47–48,
　　65, 69–71, 142, 150–53; *See also*
　　postal savings

Postal Financial Services *(continued)*
　social development, 4–5, 16
　survey, 36–38
　technology. *See* Technology
　training centers & programs, 6, 105,
　　160, 180–81, 209–10, 224
　women, 4–5, 11, 15, 17, 20, 69,
　　150–51, 174
　See Asian country case study chapters;
　　See also postal savings, postal
　　insurance, giro, payments,
　　overseas remittances
Privatization
　communications, 29–32, 199–200
　development assistance, 31
　governance model, 40–41
　public bailouts of private sector, 8, 16,
　　33, 49–50, 52
　public services, 7, 16, 20
　policy reforms, 14–20, 40–41, 53,
　　121–22
　postal services, 8, 28–36, 40–41
　　politics in Japan, 135–37, 143–44
　　regulation, 40
　technology, 29–30
　World Bank loans, 31

R

Regulatory environment, 16, 17, 30,
　40–41, 71; Rep. Korea 103–5,
　119; Japan, 133, 135–36, 139;
　Sri Lanka, 184; Kazakhstan,
　200–1; Vietnam, 220–23;
　Philippines, 229–31, 241–42,
　245, 248–50
postbanks, 41
See also market liberalization
Remittances. *See* overseas remittances;
　payments
Reserve Bank of India (central), 158, 161,
　177, 179
Royal Mail Letters (U.K.), 46
Rural development, 6, 18
Rural Credit Cooperatives (China), 89
Russia, 56
Russo-Japanese War, 123–24

S

Sales agents, NSO India 11, 58, 150–52
  training programs, 160
Savers values, 3–4, 17–18, 47, 122–24, 141–42, 220–21, 233
Savings
  access, 3–4
  Africa, 25
  Asia, 4, 55
  & credit services, 41
  in developing countries, 3–4, 55, 122–24
  in developed countries, 4
  economic development, 3–4, 124–30, 214–15
  farmers, 4–5
  government sponsored (*See also* postal savings, national savings banks), 4, 32–34
  history 23, 55
    see also individual countries and case studies
  households and individuals, 4, 10, 65–66, 148, 196
  informal, cash economy, 19
  in-kind, 3, 84, 122, 184, 223
  interest rate, 3; *See also* interest rates; & postal savings
  investment, 3, 66
  market liberalization, 7
  mobilization, 41, 55, 76
  small businesses, 3, 18
  products, 3, 133–34
  safety & risk, 3, 7–8, 11
  tax incentives. *See* Tax incentives on savings
  See postal savings; *See also* Asian country case study chapters
Savings banks, 23, 32–34, 125–26, 245–48
  See individual countries; *See also* Asian country case study chapters
Scher, Mark J., 6, 9, 17, 56, 66, 125, 132
  field research, 6, 20
Scotland, 23
Singapore, 6, 9, 24, 29, 57, 60–62

Spain, 27, 55
Sparkassen (Germany), 23, 32–33, 53
Sberbank (Russia), 23, 56
Sri Lanka, 6, 9, 55, 57, 60–64, 68, 72
  Marga Institute for Development Studies, 12, 195–77
  National Savings Bank (NSB), 12, 55, 61–64, 75, 183–98
  See also Sri Lanka country case study, 183–98
    origin & organization of NSB, 183–185
    NSB & postal savings, 186–89
    scope & performance postal network, 189–94
    Marga report on postal savings & savings culture, 195–97
    scope of market & development of savings, 197–98
Small-savings mobilization, 4, 9, 17–18, 20
  See also savings, postal savings
Small Savings Organization (Indian States), 58, 152, 174
Small- & medium-sized enterprises (SMEs), 15, 18
  loans, 6, 18, 34, 41, 127–28, 131, 237, 242–43, 248
Smith, Adam, 31
Sonera (Finland), 30
South Africa, 44
State Bank of Russia (central), 56
State Bank of Vietnam (central), 220–21
State Development Bank (China), 88
Sweden, 26, 36, 45, 65, 136
Switzerland, 6, 23
Subsidization
  cross-subsidies, 8, 28–29, 32–34, 39–40, 45, 131–32, 161
  and acquisitions, 29
  cross-selling, 40, 47, 132–33, 180
  policies, 15–16, 40, 229
Syria, 57

T

Taft, William Howard, 57
Taiwan Province of China, 56

INDEX   265

Tanzania, 67
Tax incentives on savings, 9, 12, 69, 76, 133, 155–56, 162–65, 175, 205, 238
Technical assistance programs, 34, 67–68
Technology, 8, 9, 15, 19, 20, 29–30, 44, 48, 57, 66–69; China, 81, 90–91; Rep. Korea, 100, 105; India, 157, 160, 172–73, 175; Sri Lanka, 188–89, 197; Kazakhstan, 203–4, 207–8, 210–11;Vietnam, 217, 224–25
 low-tech vs. high-tech, 66–69
 vendors & consultants, 67–69
Teigaku chokin, 133, 144
Telecomunicaciones de México, 27
Telecommunications
 effects on postal revenues, 7, 12–13, 15, 31, 35, 56, 70, 198, 199–200, 225
 privatization, 29–31
Telefonica (Spain), 30
Thailand, 6, 31, 71, 72
Thurn und Taxis, 40–41
TNT Post Grope (Netherlands), 34, 51
Togo, 24
Tokyo Stock Exchange, 66, 75
Transition economies, 8, 9, 25, 33, 36
 market liberalization, 8, 12, 49–50
 financial markets, 208
 overseas worker remittances, 208
 payments system, 201, 204–6, 208–9
 savings
  financial technology, 203, 211
Treasury Loans & Investment Special Accounts (TLISA, Rep. Korea), 10, 97–98, 102–3, 106
Turkey, 57
 See also Ottoman Empire

U

Unbanked. *See* financial exclusion
United Kingdom, 6, 44, 46–49, 53, 62, 123
 British & colonial model postal savings, 8, 22, 41, 55, 58, 122

United Nations, 9
United Nations Postal Savings for Development Survey, 17, 36–38, 41, 45
United Parcel Service (UPS), 29, 34–35
United States, 24, 27, 35, 57, 72, 123
U.S. Postal Service, 27
Universal Postal Union (UPU), 19
Universal service obligation (posts), 5, 8, 21
Uzbekistan, 6, 31

V

Vietnam, 6, 7, 8, 12, 31, 36, 50, 56, 57, 71–72, 75
 See also Vietnam country case study, 213–25
 development objectives & establishing postal savings, 214–15
 Vietnam's economic situation, 213–14
 fiscal management & organization of VPSC, 215–18
 investment in development, 219–20
 growth of postal savings market, 220–22
 start-up problems & limitations, 222–24
 future development plans, 224–25

W

Western Union, 26, 68, 90, 176, 239
Women, 4–5, 11, 15, 20
 See also postal financial services
World Trade Organization (WTO), 30, 92
World Bank, 31

Y–Z

Yoshino Naoyuki, 9
Yubin chokin (*Yu-cho*). *See* Japan, postal savings

Zaito-system. *See* Fiscal Investment and Loan Program; *See also* Japan